40 MORE WOODWORKING PLANS & PROJECTS

W9-BFT-742

First Published in 1986 by Guild of Master Craftsman Publications Ltd, 166 High Street, Lewes, East Sussex BN7 1XU. Tel: 0273 478449

Reprinted 1991, 1994

ISBN 0 946819 10 6

Editor: Bernard C Cooper

Technical Advisers: Parkin Loy, A R Wells

Art Director: Ian Hunt

Designed by Guild Graphic Services Ltd

Typeset by Eager Typesetting Company

Printed by The Alden Press Ltd, Oxford

AN OCCASIONAL TABLE

This table is a relatively straightforward project, but demands a high level of accuracy if it is to be structurally sound as well as visually satisfying.

DESIGN SPONSORSHIP BY

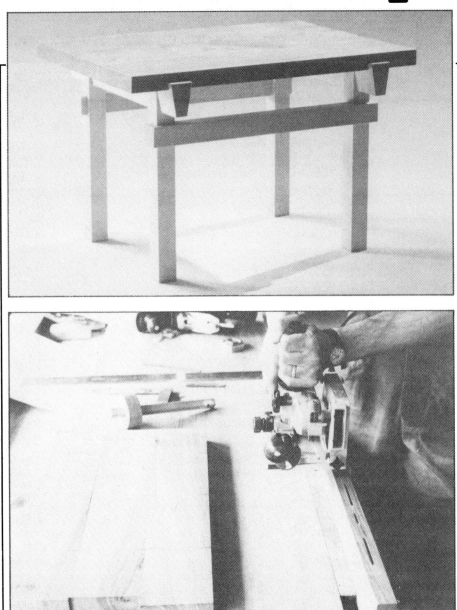

1. Biscuit jointing the top, showing the top boards in sequence, shot straight and marked out for biscuiting.

2. Cramping up the top, checking for flatness across the width.

The choice of timber for the top is largely a matter of personal taste and subject to what is available. However I would recommend a relatively neutral timber for the underframe. A cherry top with a sycamore underframe would make a pleasing combination.

THE TOP

First the top can be made. The widths of the board are determined by the type of wood used: I have shown it made from 4 x 500 x 95 x 25 (finished sizes). These should be prepared and the joints shot straight and square. I have used a biscuit jointer partly to reinforce the butt joint, but mainly as a speedy and effective way of locating the boards in one plane when cramping up. Once the top is assembled it can be left to settle prior to further work being done.

THE UNDERFRAME

Next prepare the underframe stuff to the sizes given in the cutting list. The first joints to be cut are the stopped bridle joints on what will eventually be the tapered battens. These joints are cut while the stock is still square.

The bridle joint is divided into three in the thickness of the leg. First mark out the batten: vertical shoulders 45mm in from the ends. Use the prepared legs themselves *(number them so they don't get mixed up)* set tight against the first shoulder and mark the width of the bridle with a sharp marking knife. Gauge in the top shoulder, 10mm down from the top edge, that is the depth to which the tapered batten is dove-tailed into the top. Lastly set a mortise gauge to mark out the thickness of the bridle centrally on the bottom edge of the batten, the pins set at 10mm (⅓ the thickness of the leg). The pin setting remains the same, of course, for marking out this joint on the leg, but

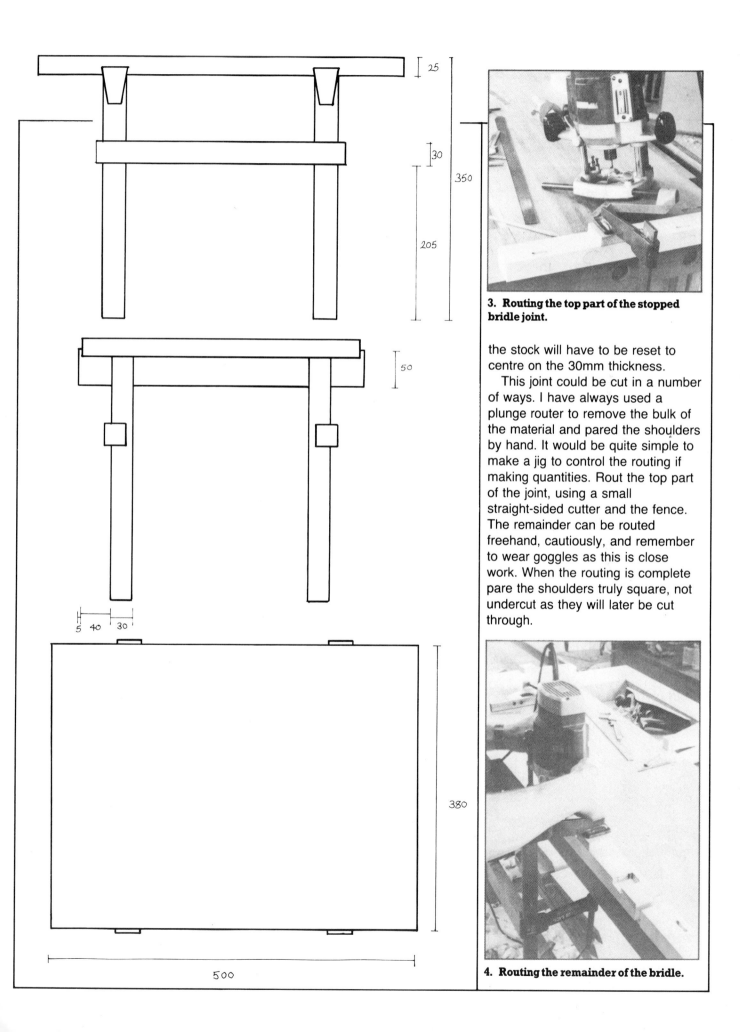

25

30

350

205

50

5 40 30

380

500

3. Routing the top part of the stopped bridle joint.

the stock will have to be reset to centre on the 30mm thickness.

This joint could be cut in a number of ways. I have always used a plunge router to remove the bulk of the material and pared the shoulders by hand. It would be quite simple to make a jig to control the routing if making quantities. Rout the top part of the joint, using a small straight-sided cutter and the fence. The remainder can be routed freehand, cautiously, and remember to wear goggles as this is close work. When the routing is complete pare the shoulders truly square, not undercut as they will later be cut through.

4. Routing the remainder of the bridle.

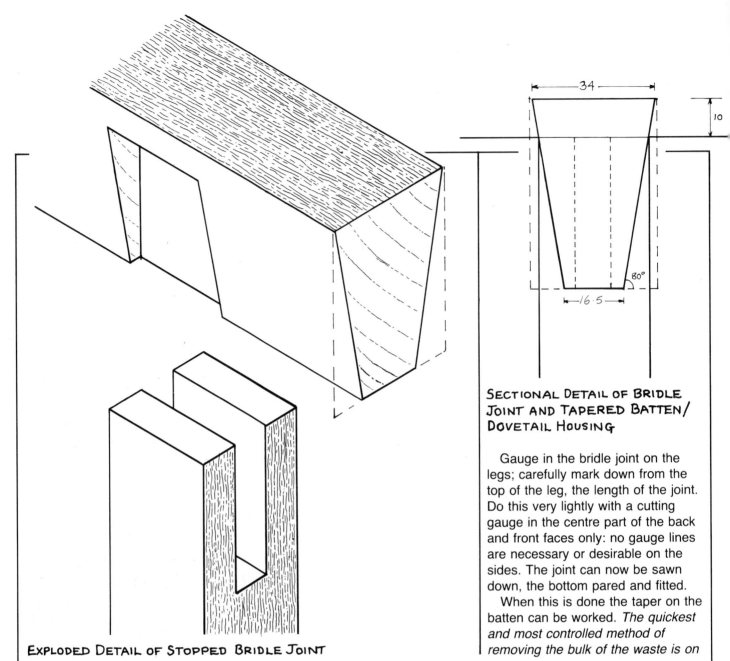

SECTIONAL DETAIL OF BRIDLE JOINT AND TAPERED BATTEN/ DOVETAIL HOUSING

EXPLODED DETAIL OF STOPPED BRIDLE JOINT

Gauge in the bridle joint on the legs; carefully mark down from the top of the leg, the length of the joint. Do this very lightly with a cutting gauge in the centre part of the back and front faces only: no gauge lines are necessary or desirable on the sides. The joint can now be sawn down, the bottom pared and fitted.

When this is done the taper on the batten can be worked. *The quickest and most controlled method of removing the bulk of the waste is on*

5. **Bridle joints pared and assembled dry.**   6. **Sawing the taper.**

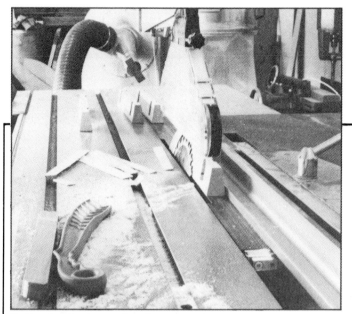

7. Sawing the taper, showing saw set up.

8. End frame cramped up dry, showing tapered batten and halving joint cut on the face of the legs.

9. Routing the dovetail housing against a straight edge.

10. Dovetail housing complete.

the circular saw. First mark the exact angle of the dovetail cutter to be used in the table top housings on the ends of the battens. Gauge along the bottom edge. Tilt the saw to the required angle and set the fence appropriately, leaving a small flat on the sawn face which will be used against the fence to saw the opposite side of the taper. *It is essential to use push sticks in this operation.*

Finish by hand planing to exact angle; use a protractor square or sliding bevel to check this in the length of the batten. The joints can now be knocked together and checked and any final fitting done, before the halvings are cut.

In a sense these are not true

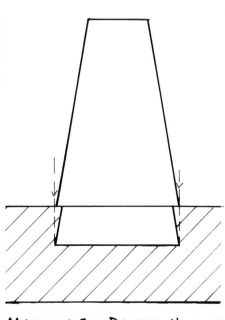

MARKING OUT DOVETAIL HOUSING

halvings as only a third of the thickness is removed, thus the rails stand proud of the legs. Nevertheless halvings need to be tight to be effective and particularly in blonde timber will look unsightly if sloppy.

The top shoulder line on the legs and 'outside' shoulder line on the rails should be knifed or cutting-gauged in on the front and back edges respectively. The width of the joint should be marked using the leg or rail as a template rather than relying solely on measurement. Gauge in the depth of the joints. Again, number each joint.

The joints can be cut by hand or using the radial arm saw. If the latter is used, it is helpful to set up stops

11. Tapered batten fitted.

12. End frame assembled, prior to entry into dovetailed housing.

13. Assembled table, view from below.

14. Completed table.

to work against. This saves time 'eyeballing' each cut. Finally, pare shoulders and check fit.

The underframe is now complete but for sanding and final assembly, and should be knocked together dry. We now return to the top which should be planed flat and dimensioned all round.

THE TOP

Mark out on the underside for the dovetail slots, using the underframe as a guide. Be careful to mark the slope correctly, squaring down then using the protractor square to mark the position of the housing in the thickness of the top. (See Diagram.) Square across with a knife, mark in depth of slot with gauge and knife-in

bevels to help prevent break out when routing. Rout bulk of waste with straight-sided cutter, using a fence cramped across the top. Take extreme care to be accurate when routing the bevels. Err on the side of caution and make these battens a very tight fit. It is better to have to ease the tapered battens with a shaving or two, than to have to deal with a sloppy fit, which totally defeats the object.

The table can now be sanded prior to gluing up. Be careful not to affect the fit of the halvings or the dovetail housings with over enthusiastic sanding.

Glue up the side frames first, i.e. the legs to the tapered battens, checking for squareness and winding. Then knock these into the housings, glue and G cramp the halved cross rails onto the legs.

Finally clean up and polish.

CUTTING LIST						
PART	DESCRIPTION	L	W	T	MATERIAL	QTY
1	Legs	325	30	30	Sycamore	4
2	Rails	340	30	30	Sycamore	2
3	Battens	390	50	34	Sycamore	2
4	Top	500	95	25	Cherry	4
NOTE: All measurements refer to finished sizes.						

CARVING A RED SQUIRREL

A step by step project in carving in the round

the paper. If you have any doubt, take the drawing to the window, place flat against this and the lines will be clear on the reverse side. Go over these lines.

Once the outline is drawn on both sides of the wood, turn to the drawing with the numbered stages of progression.

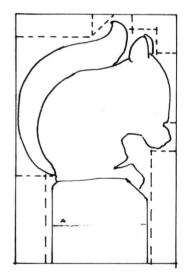

Stage One
Broken-lines indicate the position of saw-cuts square through the block to depth shown. Line A shows the actual base, but leave the rest on for holding, see text

There are two types of squirrel in Britain, the native Red Squirrel and the 19th Century importation, the Grey Squirrel.

The native *Sciurus Vulgaris*, once abundant throughout the country, is now rare. Its remaining strongholds, if such they can be called, are the Lake District, parts of East Anglia and Scotland.

The import *Sciurus Carolineusis*, on the other hand, has thrived. Indeed so successfully has it adapted itself that it is now a pest, causing quite a lot of damage to trees in woodland and forest.

MATERIAL

Brazilian Mahogany is now available and is a pleasant wood to work in. The colour also is suitable for the subject of this project.

Size 6″ (153mm) high plus 2″ (50mm) at the base to hold the wood in the vice whilst working on it.

The base can be squared off to the base line on completion. Width 4¾″ (120mm), thickness 3″ (77mm) would be a comfortable amount. Do not use less than 2½″ (65mm); take this as a minimum thickness.

Use the wood with the grain running vertically up the subject.

PROCEDURE

It is advisable with a subject such as this to draw the main profile and its contents on each side of the block of wood. Draw the design on tracing paper and transfer it to the wood with carbon paper or carbon film. By squaring lines from various points on the outline, across the width and squaring these across the thickness and then across the other side of the wood, we can locate the position for the drawing by measuring in from the block edges at these points.

With tracing paper you can reverse the design and see the lines through

Stage One shows the amounts which can be removed by handsaw. Do not profile the entire work on a band-saw; the object of the exercise is to gain experience in "roughing out" with fairly large size gouges. This experience will not be gained if the procedure is not followed as written. In addition there is the pleasure you will find in the actual physical effort involved and in seeing the chippings fly. Use a No. 6 or No. 7 gouge ⅝″ or ¾″ wide.

Stage Two is shown in the next drawing; using either of the above

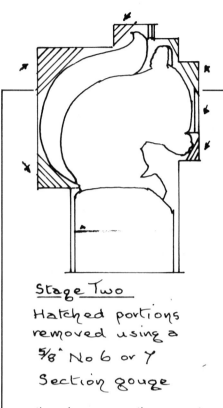

Stage Two
Hatched portions
removed using a
⅝" No 6 or 7
Section gouge

mentioned gouges or the nearest you have, provided these are not too small in width. Work in the directions indicated by the arrows and remove the shaded amounts.

If the grain objects, reverse the direction of the cuts or if necessary

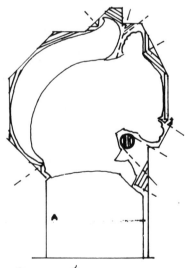

Stage Three
Shows outline
progression and a

drilled hole with
saw-cuts into this
and at various other
positions

use a diagonal cut. The wood will tell you, so heed its advice and *cut* do not *tear* the wood.

Stage Three This shows additional saw-cuts.

At places on an outline where the shape tends to be trapped it is often a good thing to drill a hole. This drawing shows such a hole drilled squarely right through the thickness of the block.

The diameter should not be less than ½", about 12mm. If you are able to make a ⅝" (15mm) diameter hole comfortably, that will be better still.

By making two saw-cuts as shown into this hole, quite an awkward piece of wood will be removed comparatively easily.

Use a No. 3 or No. 4 gouge ⅝" or ¾" wide, work as before around the curve of the tail and into the latest series of saw-cuts shown on the drawing. You are removing less timber now and the shallower gouges will be easier to work with.

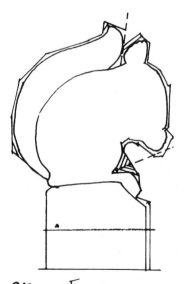

Stage Four
Outline progression
nearing completion
saw-cut between
end of tail & back
of ears cut

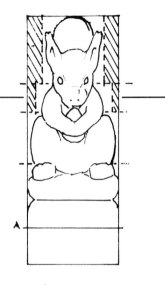

Stage Five
Shows saw-cuts
for removal of areas
shaded.

Stage Four is the completion of the main profile of the subject. Take this as near as you can whilst still leaving the outline clearly showing. Now run a centre-line right around the front, top rear and even underneath the profile work. This latter may be needed as a point of reference when the others have disappeared in the course of carving.

Attention must now be turned to arriving at a similar stage with the front elevation of the subject.

Stage Five shows the position of saw-cuts, again square through the block so that some of the excess wood is removed altogether.

Stage Six indicates further saw-cuts, some cut on an angle. Then working with Nos. 3 or 4 in section in the directions shown, the work can be carried forward until the front view is arrived at and the main outlines established.

The working of these stages gives a rather abstract looking block, profiled as a Squirrel on the two larger sides but with very little to see when viewed from front or rear.

DEVELOPMENT OF FORM

Our next task is to begin an exploration into this block to find the forms and the planes to define those necessary to reveal the squirrel.

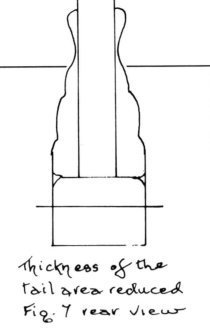

1. A very important line to begin with is the one giving the separation between the back and the tail lying against it.

The best tool to use for this line is a Parting-Tool. This has a vee-section. One not too large in size, say ¼″ wide 60° section.

Make sure that the tool is sharp, I have written elsewhere on sharpening. Treat a parting tool as two flat chisels joined to form the vee-section when sharpening. Use a natural slip-stone of appropriate section to deal with dressing the inside faces of the tool prior to stropping.

Do *not* apply levels to the inside of this or any other carving tool.

With this tool cut in the line of the curve of the back, the lower portion of the rear foot will require 'setting in'. This means selecting the gouge with section curve to match the line to be set in, placing it on the curved line and tapping with a mallet.

Always hold the gouge to give a slight slope, a buttress effect away

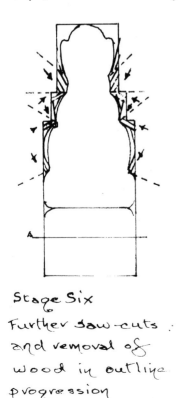

Stage Six
Further saw-cuts
and removal of
wood in outline
progression

Thickness of the
tail area reduced
Fig. 7 rear view

from the higher towards the lower level required. Avoid undercutting at this stage.

2. Remove a small amount of wood from the tail surface to remind you that the body is fatter than the tail. Eventually quite a lot will have to be removed, but take a little only away now at both sides of the profiled block.

3. The next important line is that around the haunch of the rear leg. This is a tighter curve which the vee-tool would find hard to negotiate without tearing. Find the appropriate gouges and set these lines in on both sides of the block.

Then deal with actual ground-line; the line under the hind leg where it rests up on the ground of the base. This is a slow curve until the toes are reached and a parting-tool will cut this as far as the toes. Set in the remainder but do not attempt any details of the foot yet.

Remove a small amount of wood around the top above the haunches, inclining the cuts into the set in line. This again is a reminder, in this instance, that the haunches are the higher and fuller part in that area.

4. At this stage it is advisable to return to the back of the animal. Deepen the lines defining the back, then remove more wood from each side of the tail surfaces. Continue this until the tail width is about 1¼″

(30mm), i.e. ⅝″ (15mm) on each side of the centre-line. After this reclarify the line of the back with the parting tool. See Fig. 7.

5. The back is a soft rounded shape and work can now be started to achieve this. With a shallow gouge, No. 4 in section, begin when the work is securely fastened in a vice. Take off wood in small amounts only, until you can see the effect produced. The aim is to make the back the shape as stated above.

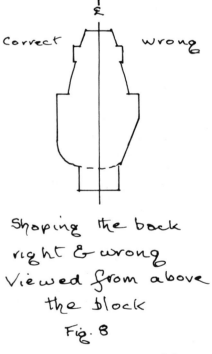

Correct   wrong

Shaping the back
right & wrong
viewed from above
the block
Fig. 8

It is better when carving a full rounded shape as now, to be conscious of the fullness and to work for this quite deliberately. If this is not done there is all too often a tendency to produce an inclined plane which is rather flattish and to arrive at the shape shown to the right of the centre-line when viewed from above as in Fig. 8.

View the result, looking down at it, a sort of "bird's eye view" and make sure that the curve round from side to side flows as a continuation with the tail mass planted centrally upon this curve. The broken line on Fig. 8 shows this. This illustration shows the part of the animal forward of the hind legs becoming narrower towards the front of the head and this is the next stage to deal with.

6. The ears of the subject are large and lines at the front and rear of these must be set in. These will provide a stop for tools being used and allow the necessary amount to stand proud of the general narrowing of this area mentioned above.

7. Set in the lines of the forelegs at the elbow and take a little wood from the rear of this and follow into that surface above the crest of the haunches already started.

8. The main lines to the top of the forelegs can now be set in; the almost vertical short line opposite the elbow position, gently. The remainder of the line deeper.

The sides of the forelegs are inclined towards the paws and wood can be removed to begin this effect. Not too much at a time, setting in the deeper line before each layer of outer surface is removed.

Remember that the paws hold an acorn so do not diminish too much at this point. The width across the paws

Lines surrounding the ear position set in & the upper line of the front leg Fig. 9

when viewed from the front should not be less than 1½″ (40mm) now. The finished width will be less and will be reached later.

9. The Head: carve to the profile lines first should any excess wood be remaining at this position. The front view of the design shows the difference in width across the head to that at the shoulders. These in turn are less wide than the haunches.

10. The lines to the front and back of the ears have already been set in, but in order to have enough wood at this position to give the slight outward tilt to the ear tips etc., the remainder of the ear position should be set in. See Fig. 9 which also shows the upper line of the foreleg dealt with in this manner.

Remove a little material from around and up to the set in line of the ears, isolating the latter on both sides of the head.

11. The muzzle, the narrowest part of the head, can now be slimmed down at each side. Remember to leave the fullness of the cheek pouches above the muzzle. Also bring the sides of the head nearer to the shape required but leaving the ears alone for now.

12. Some wood can however be taken from between the ears, not too much but the flow of line from the back of the head to the brow should be made apparent.

You can at this point work between the ears to obtain the slight outward tilt. Deal with inner sides first but some work has still to be done on the outer surfaces so do not get the ears too thin. The tufts of fur surmounting the ears are quite thick.

13. Go over the forms of the head trying to get them into correct relationship. Keep looking at the illustrations and they should help. The eyes are a special problem to which we will return later, for the present leave a surface in the position so that we may do this.

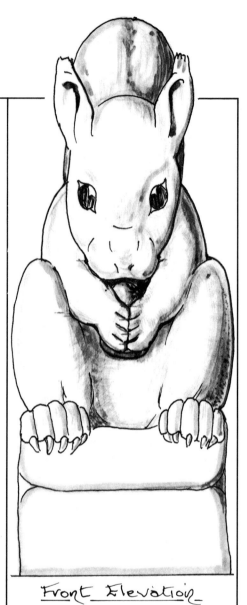

Front Elevation

14. The forepaws: in the reference I have, i.e. sketches in many sketch books filled over the years, one of which survives from student days, and photographic reference to hand, four digits are shown on these paws.

When the basic paw shape has been carved try putting in the details of the, for want of a better word, "fingers". Let them hold the acorn within their grasp.

Be careful when striving to separate the fingers not to overdo this and end up with thin stringy appendages.

At first set in the actual lines which divide them with hand pressure only. Then cut small, slightly inclined planes running into these and gradually gain the effect you want.

Do not carve the acorn within the

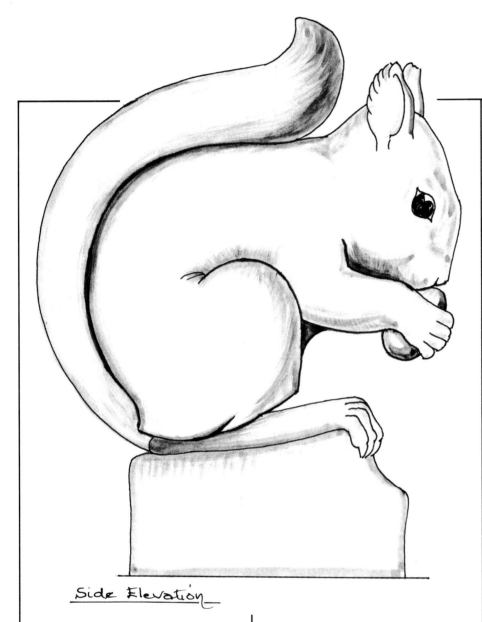

Side Elevation

outer line of the eye. The eye is a ball which must appear to be capable of movement within its socket; strive for such an effect.

Use a small fairly flat section gouge and work over the eye surface until the lids have some slight thickness at the edges and do give the impression that they could close over the curved surface of the eye.

18. Deal with the nose and nostrils, then try carving the acorn within the grip of the forepaws. Complete the details of the rear legs and feet.

19. View the result from all angles and deal with any points requiring attention.

For example the tail will require to be a soft rounded section with some attempt made at texturing the surface along the upward curving flow. Use your own judgment as to how wide it should be when viewed from the rear. Remember, that it is soft and fluffy not stringy; strive for this soft effect.

Do not use a veiner which will only result in a stringy effect unless used with great discretion.

20. The base block can be given a tooled texture by the use of shallow gouges and sawn off square at the size required.

FINISHING

When the whole is completed use a soft wax polish rubbed well into all surfaces and give it a good hard rub with a clean duster. With repetition this will give a pleasant finish.

Baize may be glued on to the under surface of the base if you wish.

clasp of the fingers until later. For now leave that problem and look at the hind legs where they rest upon the base.

15. The outside edge of each has a slight splay being wider at the front. Make a small vertical edge to the lower part of these legs allowing the underside of the haunch to overhang this. There is a fringe of hair which gives this overhang as well as the folding of the limb itself.

Do this at each side of the work, then view from the front to get a correct balance of positions. Allow the toes clasping the edge of the base in the design to spread a little. Treat the toes as described when dealing with the fingers.

16. Returning to the head, the front and side elevations do, I trust, give the information necessary to deal with the shape and form and to gain the result wanted.

Remember the slightly concave shape to show the opening of the ears and the suggestion of the fur tufts to the tops of these, which extend a little down the back edge of the ear as is shown in the design.

17. When the main forms which go to make the head have been resolved, try one eye. Find the appropriate gouges and press in the

TOOLS USED

1 Tenon-saw, 1 Carver's Mallet, 1 Vice and Bench. Gouges: No. 3 or 4 ⅜″, ⅝″ or ¾″ wide; No. 5 ³⁄₁₆″ or ¼″ wide; No. 6 or 7 ⅝″ or ¾″ wide; No. 39 Parting Tool ¼″ wide 60° angle vee. And such others as the work itself may suggest when the work is in progress.

MAKING A WHEELBARROW

There is something special about a wooden wheelbarrow.
It is so much more at home in a garden than a metal one.

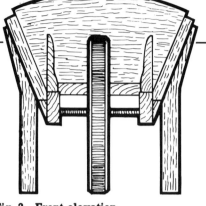

Fig. 2   Front elevation

During recent years most gardeners in need of a wheelbarrow have had to be content with buying a lightweight metal one incapable of carrying heavy loads, or else going to the other extreme of using a heavy builder's barrow. The advantage of making a wooden barrow is that it can be made to whatever dimensions the gardener

Fig. 1   Side elevation of barrow

requires. If made from selected timber and well painted, such a barrow will last a lifetime. Its construction is interesting but quite straightforward despite the fact that there are hardly any right angles.

Drawings should be of a sufficient scale to enable the necessary angles and bevels to be accurately obtained.

FRAMEWORK

The main framework is best made from ash and the two shafts (known as strines) should be carefully selected as they have to take a great deal of weight. The strines are 4'6" long, 2¾" deep by 2" thick (1375mm x 70mm x 50mm). Their ends should be shaped as shown in the side elevation (Fig. 1) so as to fit the hand comfortably.

Three mortises are cut in each strine to accept the tenons on the

ends of the cross rails (known as sloats). The sloats are made from ash 2½" wide by 1½" thick (64mm x 38mm) with bare-faced tenons ¾" (19mm) thick. The top faces of the sloats are set ¾" (19mm) below the tops of the strines to enable the ¾" (19mm) thick bottom boards

(preferably of elm) to come flush with the strines.

The usual method of setting out the framework is to lay the strines on the floor the correct distance apart and place the sloats across them in their respective positions (Fig. 3). Using small cramps to hold them in place the diagonals are checked to ensure that the framework is in truth. The position of the mortises is then scribed on the strines and the shoulders of the tenons are scribed on the sloats. From the marks made on the strines, lines are squared down both sides and the width of the mortises are gauged from the upper edges. It is usual to cut the tenons about ½" (12mm) longer than the thickness of the strines so that the tenon ends project by this amount beyond the faces of the strines.

ASSEMBLY

After cutting the mortises and tenons the framework can be assembled. With heavy stable barrows it is a good plan to pull the framework tightly together by draw-boring. A ¼" (6mm) hole is bored through the centre of each mortise, close to the inner edge. The framework is put together and the ¼" (6mm) twist bit

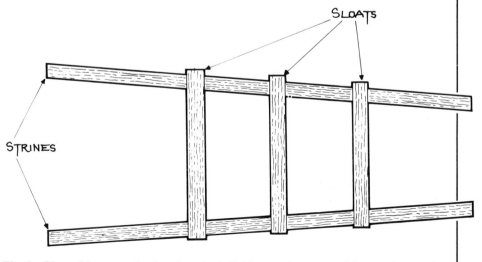

SLOATS

STRINES

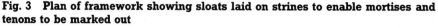

Fig. 3   Plan of framework showing sloats laid on strines to enable mortises and tenons to be marked out

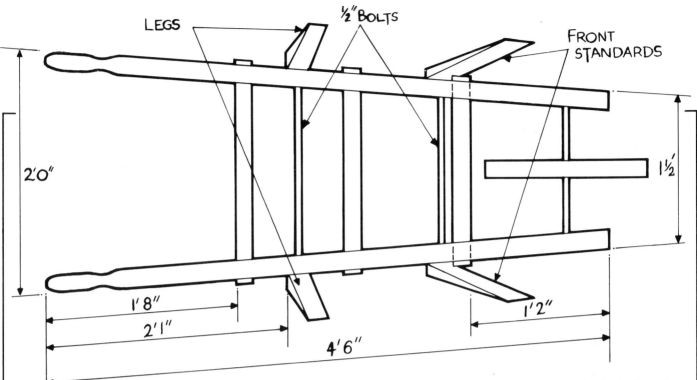

Fig. 4   Plan of framework and principal dimensions

is inserted into the hole in the strine and the point of the bit marks the face of the tenon. The frame is taken apart and with the point of the bit slightly nearer to the tenon's shoulder the tenon is bored through.

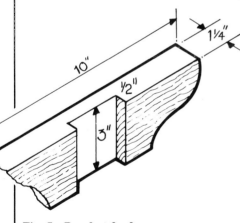

Fig. 5   Bracket for leg

Hardwood dowels are made and their leading ends are given a slight taper. The mortises and tenons are well painted with paint (white lead was always used for this purpose), the framework put together and the dowels driven home. In an ordinary garden barrow draw-boring was often omitted but white lead was always applied to the joints.

When the paint has dried the ends of the tenons projecting through the strines are chamfered off as in Fig. 7.

The bottom boards which are 2′0″ long (612mm) and ¾″ thick (10mm) run longitudinally between the strines and are nailed to the sloats. It is usual to round over the ends of these boards.

LEGS

The legs are 2′0″ long (612mm) and are cut from 4″ x 2″ (100mm x 50mm) ash. The straight portion of the leg is 15″ (383mm) long and this will determine the height of the strines from the ground. The legs are securely held in position by means of the brackets shown in Fig. 5 which are nailed to the undersides of the strines. A long bolt ½″ (12mm) diameter passes through both legs and the strines and is tightened by means of the nuts on the ends.

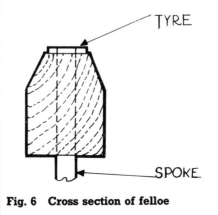

Fig. 6   Cross section of felloe

The leg has a ½″ (12mm) notch cut into it as shown in Fig. 8 so that some of the weight of the load is taken directly by the leg rather than being taken entirely by the long bolt.

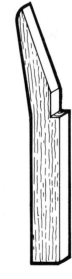

Fig. 8   Shape of leg

If the upper portion of the leg is splayed out so that the top finishes at ⅞″ (22mm) wide this will give sufficient splay to the barrow sides. The outer edges of the legs are lightly chamfered to improve their appearance. If the barrow is to be subjected to heavy use it is advisable to hoop the lower ends of the legs with iron bands 1¼″ (31mm) wide and ⅛″ (3mm) thick.

SIDES

Although the shape of the barrow sides are shown in Fig. 1 their actual dimensions and true shape cannot be taken from the elevation because of their slope. It is necessary to draw a plan of the barrow which shows the sides attached (Fig. 9).

Dotted lines L are drawn where the extremities of the sides cut the front and back of the barrow and at right angles to the base line B. These lines are drawn at all four corners as shown. From the base lines B the true widths of the sides, back and front are drawn. Where the lines denoting the widths cross the dotted lines L, further lines are produced to cut the intersections of the base lines B. These lines are the true bevels for the sides and back and front boards.

The front board which has the greatest bevel is 20″ (512mm) wide, the two sides 14″ (358mm) wide and the back board 9″ (230mm) wide.

Elm 1″ (25mm) thick is recommended for these panels. The sides are nailed to the legs and side stays. The front and back boards are nailed to the ends of the sides and are skew-nailed to the bottom boards. From some more inch thick

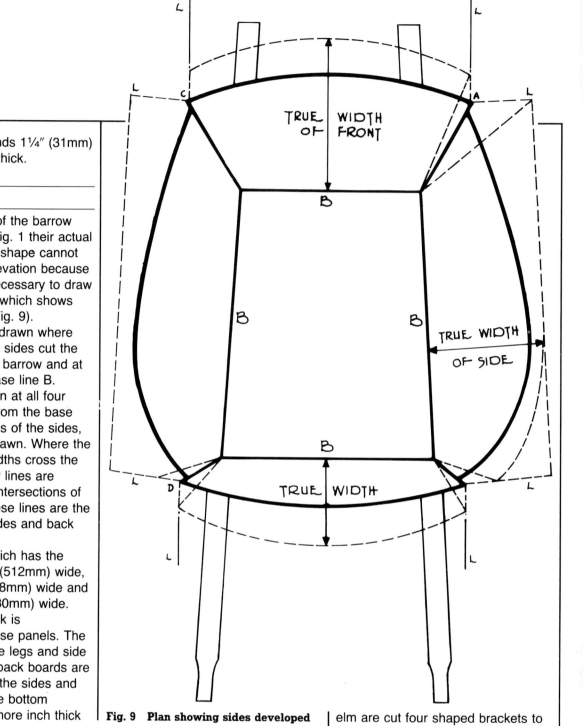

Fig. 9   Plan showing sides developed

elm are cut four shaped brackets to support the front and back boards. These brackets are nailed to the strines and also to the two boards.

WHEEL

Making the wheel calls for careful and accurate work to ensure that it runs truly. It comprises four felloes and two spokes, the lighter one being driven through a mortise cut in the heavier one.

To enable the felloes to be marked out a plywood template is made 2″ (50mm) wide with an outer diameter of 1′ 6″ (460mm). The felloes are

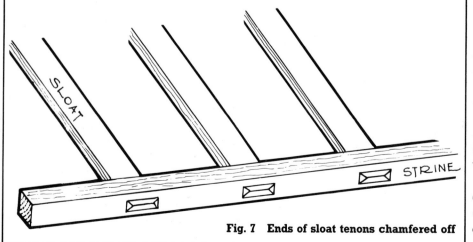

Fig. 7   Ends of sloat tenons chamfered off

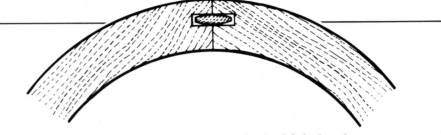

Fig. 10   End of felloe bored to accommodate wheelwright's dowel

sawn from ash 2″ (50mm) thick and are shaped with a bowsaw or preferably a bandsaw. Each felloe end is drilled to accommodate a short dowel as shown in Fig. 10. Note how a Wheelwright's dowel is tapered at its ends. The dowel hole is bored at right angles to the end of the felloe and is not at its centre but nearer to the rim. This minimises the risk of splitting off the lower corners where the grain is short.

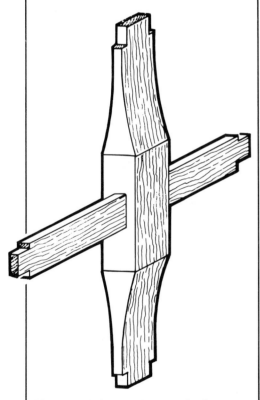

Fig. 11   Lighter spoke mortised through heavier one with ends of spokes shouldered

Having assembled the four felloes and trued the joints at their ends, identifying marks are pencilled on to ensure that when the wheel is finally put together all components are in their correct positions.

The spokes are 2½″ (63mm) wide, one of them is ¾″ (19mm) thick while the other is 1½″ (38mm) thick but reduced to ¾″ (19mm) at the ends as shown in Fig. 11. The ends are also shouldered to fit against the

inner faces of the felloes. The thicker spoke is mortised to accept the lighter spoke and the mortises for the spokes are marked on the felloes. The four felloes are tapped apart prior to being mortises.

When the mortises have been checked for fit, all the joints are painted with white lead and the felloes are driven on to the spokes equal amounts at a time. The four felloes have to be driven simultaneously to enable the dowel in the end of one felloe to enter the hole bored in the end of its neighbour.

AXLE

When all is assembled the hole for the axle is bored at the centre of the wheel. The axle has a solid collar welded to it and the wheel is held tightly against it by means of a washer and a large nut screwed on from the other side. The felloes can now be shaped with a spokeshave as in Fig. 6, not only to lighten the wheel but also to allow a narrow tyre to be fitted. The tyre is best if made by a blacksmith and put on hot so that it contracts on cooling and grips the wheel tightly.

Two pieces of 1½″ (38mm) thick wood are now bored for the axle to run in. The holes are not taken right through so as to prevent the wheel from running out of centre and metal collars are driven into the holes to provide bearings for the axle. As can be seen from the framework plan Fig. 4, the holes are bored at a slight angle on account of the strines not being parallel. The two blocks are secured to the strines with coach bolts.

CUTTING LIST						
PART	DESCRIPTION	L	W	T	MATERIAL	QTY
1	Strines	54″	2¾″	2″	Ash	2
2	Sloats	24″	2½″	1½″	Ash	3
3	Legs	24″	4″	2″	Ash	2
4	Bottom board	24″	18″	¾″	Elm	1
5	Side boards	34″	14″	1″	Elm	2
6	Front board	26″	20″	1″	Elm	1
7	Back board	28″	9″	1″	Elm	1
8	Leg brackets	10″	3″	1¼″	Ash	2
9	Front standards	18″	2″	1½″	Ash	2
10	Front brackets	12″	8″	¾″	Elm	2
11	Rear brackets	6″	6″	¾″	Elm	2
12	Axle blocks	10″	2″	1½″	Ash	2
THE WHEEL						
13	Felloes	12½″	5½″	2″	Ash	4
14	Spoke	18″	2½″	1½″	Ash or Oak	1
15	Spoke	18″	2½″	¾″	Ash or Oak	1

SUNDRIES: Dowelling, white lead, 2 long bolts ½″ diameter, axle, 2 washers and 2 large nuts, 1 tyre made by blacksmith, 2 metal collars, coach bolts, paint.

OLD OAK COUNTRY STOOL

*An ideal starter project for anyone wishing to
try his hand at reproduction type work*

Fig. 1 The completed Old Oak Country Stool

The much copied joined stool goes back to the beginnings of furniture in this country. For the lower classes, it was, for many hundreds of years, the standard form of seating. Today it remains an appealing and useful item of furniture for the modern home. Genuine examples being thin on the ground, making a replica or reproduction is a sensible alternative.

Although oak is the wood most associated with old furniture, any homegrown species could be used. The term oak is used to cover this period and style of furniture because what has survived is largely of oak; and when a wood has the qualities that exude from English oak who needs to find a substitute!

Reproduction making gives us the chance to use up some of the bits and pieces we discard and cut around in our normal cabinet making. These knotty and split bits come into their own in a reproduction giving depth, creating interest and making the piece ooze with character.

One joined stool varies from the next in overall proportions and constructional details. They are given their identity by the decorations that adorn the rails and turnings. The top rails are usually heavily decorated with mouldings or carving. This example is moulded, with a shaped frieze on the pair of long rails, a twin bead on the end pair, and a single bead on the lower stretchers.

Mouldings for reproductions are best achieved with a suitable moulding plane or scratchstock to give a more "country made" feel. The top is either moulded with a traditional "thumb nail" mould or simply rounded over.

The legs are a major feature of a small piece of furniture like this. Most examples are turned, but a chamfered leg is an alternative for the "latheless" amongst us. The style of turning can be copied from an original, out of a book, or a new design.

The stool is joined together by mortice and tenon joints, rails and legs finishing flush. (A mistake often made by fakers is to set the rails back.) In days of old the absence of glue made it necessary to secure the joints with pegs. A hole drilled through the morticed leg and another through the tenon, but slightly closer to the shoulder, would draw the two together when the peg was inserted. Usually two pegs in the top rail tenons and a single one through the lower rails. These pegs are left slightly proud to indicate some movement around them and also pick up some dirt in the finishing stage. The top is also fixed by means of pegs – through the top down into the centre of each leg. This method of fixing allows no room for inevitable shrinkage, and so a piece of wood as dry as possible and in one piece is desirable.

THE EFFECTS OF AGE

What makes a reproduction different from an everyday piece of cabinet making is it simulates a piece of furniture that is possibly 400 years old. So it is inevitable the piece will have suffered damage and wear.

On an item such as a stool the top seating surface will be worn from continual friction from our buttocks. Bottom stretchers will have been the resting place for tired feet and boots and so will be badly worn by their

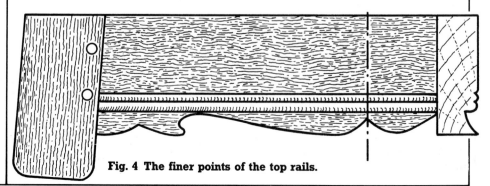

Fig. 4 The finer points of the top rails.

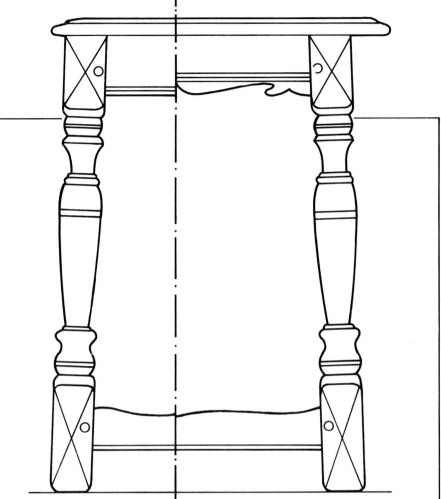

Fig. 2 Scale 1:4

abrasions. There may be the odd breakage to a turning or moulding and the whole will have a "soft" appearance (no sharp edges or corners). The piece will also be covered with dents, marks, scratches. Some areas will be more intensely marked than others.

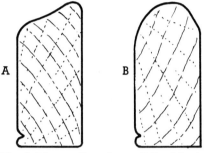

Fig. 3 The resting place of tired feet would result in wear as in "A". "B" is equally worn on outside and inside, which obviously is not possible.

Bottoms of legs, lower rails, the top area and other predominant parts will be the most badly affected.

Another "feature" seen on old furniture is the signature left by the old craftsman's crude and basic tool kit. They had no fancy adjustable planes or the means of keeping them razor sharp as we have today. The tears and ripples left by their tools can be reproduced by using a spokeshave or scrub plane to clean up and allowing it to chatter and create ripples and tears. A good sanding will blend these in to give that worn bedded-in look. Remember on heavily worn areas (bottom stretchers etc.), tool marks on the surface would have long since been eroded. These areas also will be largely free from tears for the same reason.

FINISHING

The finishing process starts with staining to the required colour: a medium brown. Vandyke is the correct pigment. This is mixed with warm water and a dribble of ammonia to give the stain a bit of bite. Water stains have a tendency to raise the grain. So it is necessary to wet the piece with hot water, and then cut down, prior to staining.

Wipe excess stain off with a sponge to create highlights which will coincide with the worn areas. Corners and hard-to-get-at bits will remain quite dark. Once the stain has dried (usually overnight), the surface can be smoothed with some wire wool. Care should be taken on the edges to avoid wearing away the stain and thus producing white lines.

Now the piece is sealed with one coat of button, brushed on. After cutting back, this is followed by two or three coats applied with the fad; just enough to choke up the grain and produce a dull shine. Leave the piece overnight again for the polish to completely harden. Then dull the finish with some 0000 wire wool and wax with a good furniture or floor wax (antique or black).

And there you have a "nearly genuine" traditional 16th Century joined stool. Whether you have just one in the corner of a room as an occasional table, a pair in the kitchen for the kids or a set around a Refectory table, the stools will be much appreciated for their elegance, charm and style.

PART	DESCRIPTION	L	W	T	MATERIAL	QTY
	CUTTING LIST					
1	Top	18"	11"	1¹⁄₁₆"	Oak	1
2	Legs	19¾"	1¾"	1¾"	Oak	4
3	Top Rails*	14"	2½"	1³⁄₁₆"	Oak	2
4	Top Rails*	8½"	2½"	1³⁄₁₆"	Oak	2
5	Bottom Rails*	15¼"	1¾"	1³⁄₁₆"	Oak	2
6	Bottom Rails*	9¾"	1¾"	1³⁄₁₆"	Oak	2

NOTE: Items 3 to 6 include 1¼" tenons to give shorter shoulder lengths.

CREATING A MARQUETRY PICTURE

Step-by-step instructions from the original idea through to the completed picture

Fig. 13. The completed picture.

Many marquetarians start their interest in the craft by buying or receiving a commercial marquetry kit. Having completed a few of these, interest wanes either because the rest of the kits in the range do not appeal or the cutting of marquetry pictures has become just a technical exercise involving little use of one's own creativity.

It is quite a step up the marquetry ladder to produce a picture that is unique and personal to you. There are problems in finding a suitable picture, adapting it, and then knowing what veneers to buy. But for those who wish to go it alone, let us see how the transition from kits to own design can be made.

VENEERS

Some knowledge of veneers will have been gained from the kits but this is usually insufficient for an order to be placed for individual veneers for a particular picture. Fortunately firms such as The Art Veneer Co. Ltd., (Industrial Estate, Mildenhall, Suffolk IP28 7AY. Tel. (0638) 712550) and Abbey Marquetry, (28 Rose Walk, St. Albans, Herts. AL4 9AF. Tel. (0727) 57070) sell packs of veneers which are useful as basic stock. In addition it is advisable to order some larger pieces of sycamore (a white veneer), aspen (useful for skies), European and American black walnut (darker veneers), mahogany/sapele (for borders and backing etc.) and an assortment of burrs if there is any foliage in the picture.

Not all packs of veneers will have the individual veneers named. This is not very important when the picture is being made as the veneers can be chosen for their effect but it does make it difficult when it becomes necessary to re-order the veneer. Boxes of named samples can be bought and some catalogues do have colour illustrations of the

veneers but unfortunately the colour reproduction cannot always be relied on. As experience is gained more veneers will become known and the problem of identifying veneers will ease.

Assuming the original kits instructed you to use the "window method" (see *Woodworking Crafts* No. 3 May – July 1982 and the fuller explanation of the method in "Marquetry for Beginners" by Ernie Ives, available from the the author at 63 Church Lane, Sproughton, Ipswich IP8 3AY, price £1.60 inc. post) then the techniques and tools used will be similar. The real difference is that the kit gave you a design with a key to each piece; you will have to produce the design for yourself. There is no need to make up a key as this is done as the picture progresses.

IDEAS

Where do you get ideas for a design from? Almost anywhere! Cards, calendars, books, adverts, wrapping paper, colour supplements, carrier

bags, holiday slides, etc. Start a file of pictures that could be adapted for marquetry and don't let your friends and relations throw away their Christmas cards and calendars until you have inspected them.

This file will be the source of ideas for many pictures. Of course, if you have the artistic ability, you can draw your own pictures from scratch. Few of the pictures in the file will be usable without some degree of adaptation. Many will have bright reds, blues and greens, colours which are not in the marquetarian's palette; the size or shape may be wrong; or again there may be unwanted detail or detail may have to be added. All, or some, of these will have to be dealt with at the design stage and before the cutting can begin.

COMPOSITION

In general it is easier to work from a painting or drawing rather than a photograph as the artist has already worked out the composition and left out unnecessary details. The camera

Fig's. 1 & 2 Cardboard L's used to frame a picture. More than one shape can be found.

sees and records everything in front of its lens. You will have to move or remove some items and add detail where this is lacking. For example, trees may have to be planted, transplanted, pruned or uprooted; they may have to be given leaves if there are too many bare twigs to cut and the season of the year changed from winter, or spring when the leaves are green, to autumn when they are reddish and near to the colour of the veneers; distant figures can be brought forward to give interest to a bare foreground. This is where your own artistry and creativity play an important part.

Book and calendar illustrations are often made to fit the space available, or to conform to a predetermined format, rather than to the proportions that aesthetically suit the picture. Scenic calendars in particular frequently have a wide expanse of lawn or road in the foreground which would be uninteresting when translated into wood and a decision has to be made where to cut it. An easy way to see the effect of any alteration in shape or cropping of a picture is to cut two large L's from hardboard or stiff card and use them to 'frame' the picture. The arms should be about 18″ and 14″ long. These L's will also be useful later when the borders and margins round the completed picture are decided on. Very often more than one picture can be found in the original. (Figs. 1 & 2.)

SIZE

Turning now to the question of size. We would be very limited in our choice of design if the finished picture had to be the same size as the illustration being copied, especially as book illustrations are normally reduced and intended for viewing from a distance of only a few inches, whereas a marquetry picture is usually hung on a wall and viewed

from a few feet away. If you are lucky in finding a picture that is the right size then skip the enlargement stage.

How you enlarge your particular picture will depend on your skill and facilities. A pencil and sheet of paper are all that are required by those who have draughting skill but most will need more mechanical methods to assist them.

Small squares can be drawn over the original (or alternatively the

squares can be drawn on clear acetate film and the film placed over the original) and proportionally larger squares drawn on the paper. Wherever a line crosses the grid on the original this is plotted on the paper. This should get the proportions correct but the method still needs some skill and is time consuming if the picture is complex. Pantagraphs will do a similar job but don't buy a cheap plastic one as the arms bend and twist and give a

Fig. 3. Using a projector to enlarge a transparency. The projector must be level.

distorted image. A good wooden or metal pantagraph will work well if you can co-ordinate the movement of the hand guiding the pencil while watching the point moving over the original picture. It takes a little practice.

PHOTOGRAPHS

Photographers won't need telling that the easiest way to enlarge the picture is to copy it photographically and then produce black and white prints of the required size. These prints will give all the tones of the original without the distraction of colour. One can then choose the veneer for its tonal value without worrying about it not being blue or green.

Two prints should be made, one is kept for reference and the other outlined in with Indian ink. When the ink is dry, the print is immersed in a bath of Farmer's Reducer (from photographic shops) and this will bleach away the image and leave a line drawing.

PHOTOCOPIES

Some photocopying services can enlarge or reduce. Their copying machines work best with a clear, black line drawing; so an ink tracing should be made of the original if it is a coloured print. Enlargement may

have to be in more than one step but at least you will get an accurate enlargement without having to employ expensive photographic equipment.

TRANSPARENCIES

Colour transparencies are easily enlarged by projecting the slide on to paper instead of a screen. The image can then be pencilled in. Make sure that the projector is level, i.e. that the centre height of the lens is the same as the centre of the projected image otherwise the picture will be noticeably distorted. (Fig. 3.)

This method has the advantage that the magnification of various parts of the picture can be varied by altering the projector – paper distance. In this way the general background can be put in and then figures that were too small in the distance to be of interest can be further enlarged and placed more prominently in the foreground. The projector method was used for "The English Village", taken from a holiday slide of Wendens Ambo, Essex, (Fig. 4), the subject I chose for this project.

CHOICE OF DESIGN

If you have completed only a few kit pictures your choice of design may

be limited by the skill, equipment and stock you have acquired. As far as skill is concerned, don't be too faint hearted. Don't immediately look at a picture and say, "I can't do that!" when in reality, although there may be a great deal of work in the picture, no more skill may be required than in a simpler looking piece. Don't confuse the amount of work with the difficulty of it. Try and work out where there may be any real cutting or other problems and see if they can be overcome. Why worry that the picture will take a long time – the pleasure of marquetry is surely more in the making than the owning of the finished product.

Lack of equipment and stock may also influence your choice of design or your treatment of it. For instance a marquetry picture may require a specially figured piece of veneer for the sky or sea without which the picture would loose so much of its impact that it is worth waiting until the right piece is found. I certainly wouldn't have put all the trees in "The English Village" if I hadn't the burrs in stock for it and I wouldn't have made the shapes quite so curly if I hadn't a fretsaw to cut them.

EXECUTION

Now let us look at the way I went about making the picture as the methods used are applicable to most marquetry pictures.

Initially I produced quite a rough pencil drawing (Fig. 5) but even at this stage I tried to eliminate unwanted detail and to translate some of the shapes into actual pieces. The shadows too were pencilled in to give the drawing some depth and help determine the direction of the light. Without the shadows the picture will look flat and lifeless. It will lack any three-dimensional quality. This is another instance where difficulty may be experienced if you are working from

Fig. 4. Wenens Ambo taken from a holiday transparency.

Fig. 5. The rough line drawing made using the projector.

Fig. 6. Using the L's to determine the shape of the design.

Fig. 7. An ink tracing made of the design.

a photographic calendar. Many of the pictures are taken with flat frontal lighting with few shadows; so for the marquetry design you may have to move the sun around to give more light and shade and contrast to the design.

At this stage some attempt at shading and breaking up of the tree areas was made although the final shapes of the pieces would be largely governed by the figure in the burrs used. Quite a lot of freehand sketching was done on the tree areas as they were fitted in. I didn't like the builder's lorry in the road and tried to sketch in a man with a wheelbarrow instead – not too successfully but that could be altered at a later stage.

TRACING

Before making a tracing of the design, the hardboard L's were used to visualize the limits of the picture

area (Fig. 6) and these were marked on the drawing. A tracing of all the outlines was then made (Fig. 7). With this type of picture a certain amount of freehand sketching is done as the work progresses, so some of the lines on the tracing are only approximate. A more accurate drawing would have to be made for marquetry portraits of people, animals and birds, etc.

A piece of aspen was found for the sky and as this was large enough to cover the whole picture it was used as the waste veneer as well. Wherever possible I work from the background to the foreground. As the church was behind everything else, this is where I started.

Four registration marks were made on the tracing and these, together with the borderlines and the outlines of the church, were transferred on to the sky veneer. The registration marks allow the removal and replacement of the tracing from the

background veneer. It can be hinged to the top of the veneer but it does get in the way especially when fretsawing. I also work from the right (face) side of the veneer as it allows me to see exactly the grain effect of the veneers used. Many of the more highly figured ones are markedly different on each side. Working from the face side also saves me from having mentally to reverse the picture when comparing it with the original.

As the work progressed on the tower, other details like the windows were put in but they were kept a little vague especially in the shadow areas (Fig. 8) – the shadow area being the most conspicuous feature on the tower. Had the church been even further away the details would have been less distinct and also the colours chosen would have been softer and less contrasty so as to help the illusion of depth; the aerial perspective of the picture, where the

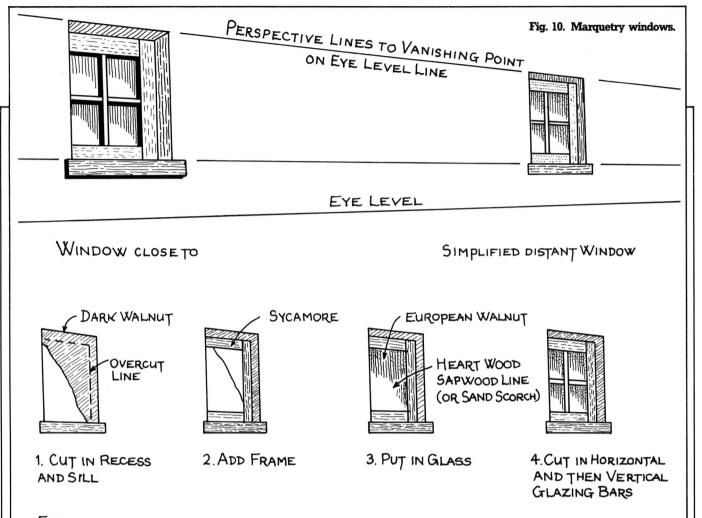

PERSPECTIVE LINES TO VANISHING POINT ON EYE LEVEL LINE

Fig. 10. Marquetry windows.

EYE LEVEL

WINDOW CLOSE TO

SIMPLIFIED DISTANT WINDOW

DARK WALNUT

OVERCUT LINE

1. CUT IN RECESS AND SILL

SYCAMORE

2. ADD FRAME

EUROPEAN WALNUT

HEART WOOD SAPWOOD LINE (OR SAND SCORCH)

3. PUT IN GLASS

4. CUT IN HORIZONTAL AND THEN VERTICAL GLAZING BARS

FOR THE LARGER WINDOW THE PANES WOULD BE PUT IN INDIVIDUALLY AND THEIR REBATES SHOWN.

foreground colours are strong and bold and the features detailed and the distant colours pale, tending to bluish and with details only suggested.

The trees were then sawn in, a hotchpotch of mainly walnut burrs (Fig. 9) which changed the seasonal look of the picture from summer to autumn. Had I have chosen green dyed veneer, the result would have looked unnatural and the green would have stood out too prominently in a picture made of natural veneers. Readers will no doubt spot the differences between the photos of the trees and the original drawing.

My technique for largish areas like the road and the banks on either side, is to cut the whole of each area out as one piece and then search through the stock of veneer to find the most suitable piece. Sometimes a veneer with just the right markings

can be found to fill the space without further work but usually other pieces have to be cut into it. Even then one has to be prepared to change the whole area at a more advanced stage if it doesn't blend in with the rest. I had to change the road as the original piece seemed too dark for the surroundings.

Use a soft pencil (BB or BBB) to do any freehand sketching directly on to the veneer. The line shows clearly and mistakes are easily rubbed out. Remember, the original drawing is only a guide, it doesn't have to be followed slavishly. The veneer markings may suggest better ways of doing the parts and you can still add or omit details as you go along. You are in control. I debated mentally whether or not to leave out the iron railings on the right hand side of the road but in the end decided their diminishing perspective helped to give the picture depth.

DETAILS

The work on the houses and other details was quite straightforward, only the windows needed a special mention. The method I use is shown in Fig. 10. This gives quite a fair result for small windows that are viewed from an angle and isn't difficult provided the glue on each piece is allowed to dry before the next is cut. If you are doing a row of houses, the thickness of the bars will increase as they get nearer to you (and so will the size of the window). It is no good just putting the edge of the veneer in for all of them!

FIGURE

After 34 hours and almost 300 pieces, the cutting of my village was complete. The face side was rather dirty from the glue but it had more atmosphere than the clean underside

Fig. 8. The tower cut in. Note the registration marks in the four corners.

Fig. 9. The trees cut in mainly from walnut burrs.

Fig. 11. Paper cut-out of the figure used to decide on the final position of the figure.

Fig. 12. Strips of the border veneer are used to decide on the width of the white margin.

and I knew that all the dirt would clean off to give a pristine scene.

I was still undecided about the figure. Without him the picture seemed lifeless but I was not sure that I had him in the right place. I have found the most practical way of experimenting on such occasions is to make a paper cut-out and move this around directly on the wood (Fig. 11). Once the best position is found the cut-out is sellotaped to the veneer and transferred on to the wood with carbon paper in the usual way. This is quite a useful method for positioning movable details but one does have to be careful not to move the detail too far in or out of the picture as the perspective difference will alter the size. In my case I only moved the figure laterally.

BORDERS

Borders on a picture are largely a matter of personal preference. I like a wide, white margin (with or without a stringer) and then a narrow dark border. Whenever I can find a piece of sycamore wide enough I let the picture into it rather than putting strips round and mitreing the corners as the mitres tend to show up more in light veneers. It is not really a wasteful method as the piece that is taken out is still a useful size to use for another picture. To determine the width of the margin I cut the borders and loosely place them on the

margin and adjust the distance until I get the effect I want. The sycamore is then squared up and the border fitted.

Pressing, cleaning up and finishing will follow the methods previously used for the kits.

The end result should be infinitely more satisfying to the maker. An individual and unique piece of work that will bring praise from those who view it.

Marquetarians wishing to develop their skills will find it rewarding to join the Marquetry Society. Details from the Hon. General Secretary, Mrs. Pat Aldridge, 75 First Avenue, Breach Barns, Galley Hill Road, Waltham Abbey, Essex EN9 2AN. Tel: Lea Valley 769433 – Ed.

A beautifully balanced design that makes the work involved well worthwhile

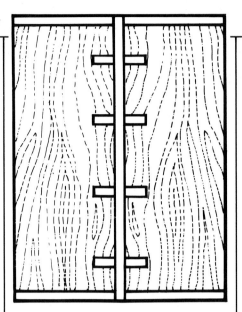

When one thinks of a desk, the study, office or library is usually the setting that is most obvious, but a desk can also be a useful addition to any home that has a bit of "spare" room. A desk in the home will be something you wondered how you managed without. It houses and keeps together all the important bits and pieces every household seems to accumulate while, as a piece of furniture, adding extra interest to the room.

The desk illustrated here is based largely around a mahogany example belonging to a member of my family. When I first saw the desk my eye was caught by its excellent proportions and style. Much furniture made today and in the past lacks that certain something that guarantees a second look. This piece is sure to hold the attention, so when it came time for me to make a desk (something I had always promised myself) a copy of this one was the obvious choice.

When you stumble upon a piece of furniture where the maker or

1. The veneer joint is first "tied" together with short strips of tape, then one long length covering the join, finally tape the ends to prevent splitting.

designer has got it right, it is always worthwhile making notes of size and proportions, details of mouldings and perhaps taking a photograph to give an overall impression (asking permission is polite, if you are not the owner) even if you have no

immediate plans for such a project. As this piece was mahogany and I desired an oak pedestal desk, some minor changes were necessary (shapes of mouldings etc.) to suit a period oak style.

The desk, as with most pedestal desks, is made up of three sections, the top three-drawer section sits on the pair of pedestals each containing a further three drawers, and the whole is located together by blocks or dowels. Sometimes it is desirable to have a deep file drawer incorporated in a desk in place of the two bottom drawers. To avoid altering the graded effect of the drawers, the two bottom fronts are framed up into one "false front" and fixed to the large file drawer to give a conventional appearance.

VENEERING

The main body of the desk is to be veneered, that is, two pairs of pedestal ends and their respective back panels, and the one long side and two short ends of the top

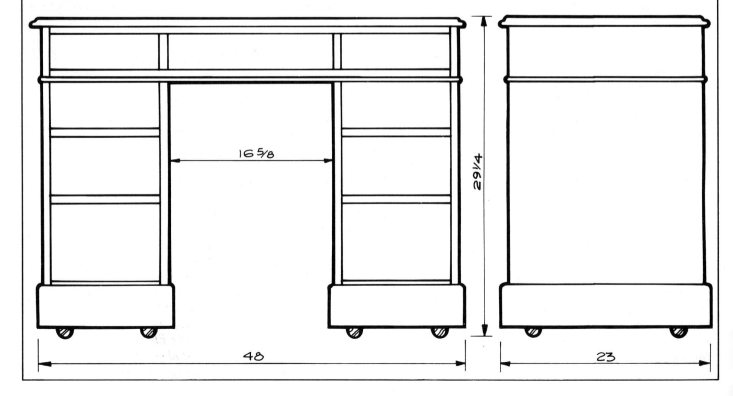

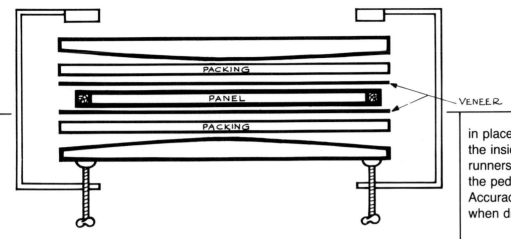

PACKING

PANEL

VENEER

PACKING

2. Cramping arrangement for successful veneering.

section. The groundwork for this veneering is of plywood, cut out so that the grain direction is at right angles to the intended veneer, thus maintaining a stable panel and insuring against surface checking. Lippings ¾ × ½ are applied to all visible front and back upright edges, and carefully flushed level with the panel.

Veneer of a matching grain pattern is required around the pedestals; to accomplish this, ten 12″ wide leaves were needed for the face veneer. Two pieces of veneer make up the pedestal ends, the joint being planed and held together with paper tape, Fig. 1. All other pieces require a single piece of veneer. All panels must be balanced, either with oak or a cheaper backing veneer. For the face, crown cut oak veneer was used in preference to the medullary ray figure of quarter cut stuff.

The drawing in Fig. 2 shows a suitable method of laying the veneer by hand using PVA adhesive. Polythene or newspaper must be placed between each panel to avoid ending up with a solid lump of wood, as glue seepage is quite high with oak, (two pairs of hands are useful when laying and cramping takes place). Leaving in cramp overnight, and then out of cramp for a further day, is a worthwhile policy to ensure complete dryness.

After trimming to size, the next task of sanding requires the removal of the veneer tape used in jointing. Anyone who has been tempted to use masking or Sellotape will have found to his cost that it doesn't come off without a fight, and only then

hanging on to fibres of wood. The only tool for the job is gummed paper tape, this can be scraped off dry or with the help of some warm water.

PEDESTALS

The pedestals are each made up of a pair of ends, with a back and four drawer rails separating them. The back panel is fixed by a loose tongue, and groove joint, and the drawer rails are either tenoned or doweled, all finishing flush.

After assembly the whole should be flushed off and cleaned up, before the base is fitted. This has an ovolo worked along the top edges; mitred at the corners it can be fixed

in place by glue and screwed from the inside. The fixing of drawer runners and kickers to the inside of the pedestals completes this stage. Accuracy here will be rewarded when drawer fitting time comes.

TOP SECTION

This is made in two parts. The drawer section is constructed in much the same way as the pedestals, except that the drawer runners/kickers and dividers are an integral part of the construction. The top writing surface is made up of a piece of plywood the same size as the intended leather which has lippings, tongued, grooved and mitred around its edges, forming a border for the leather. A suitable moulding softens the edge.

After cleaning up and fixing drawer guides in place the two can be joined together by screws to form the top section complete. The cock bead fixed around the lower edge is a useful addition that disguises the joint with the pedestals.

4. **Dovetailing by hand, a sign of quality and skill.**

CASTORS

Giving the desk "wheels" is a small but useful addition that will surely make the housewive's work a little easier when it comes to spring-cleaning. But although the castors will be appreciated they will rarely be seen, so using the cheap but very good plastic models currently available will save a few pennies over the cast brass variety. Mounting blocks are fixed inside the corners of the base to give a ¾" floor clearance.

Fitting of castors is best left to the very last job, as it can become quite an annoyance working on something that is constantly trying to escape across the workshop!

DRAWERS

The overall impression of the desk is "all drawers" and so getting down to some serious dovetailing is the order of the day. Of the nine drawers there are five variations in size, all measurements being taken from the finished carcases and the "bits" numbered according to their location to avoid confusion.

Make a point of using wood with the same figuring for all the fronts, a priority being that the three top drawers come out of one length and are maintained in this position, so when completed the grain runs through nicely.

Half inch chestnut is the stuff for the sides and backs, thicknessing it down to around ⁵⁄₁₆". The drawers are dovetailed in the traditional time-honoured manner (sharp chisels and a keen eye). Remember to keep the front dovetails short to allow for the fielding, which is best left till after dovetailing (or even after fitting) to maintain some support while chopping the sockets.

A groove is worked along the bottom edge of the sides and front to take a plywood bottom, which is slid in from the back after assembly and fixed by a couple of screws up into the back. The drawers are individually fitted to their respective locations, numbering drawer and compartment permanently as each is fitted. (ABC, I II III or some other obvious mark on drawer bottom and inside corresponding compartment.) Locks can be added to the drawers if required. My personal preference is to omit locks unless a specific situation calls for "lockability". In most homes things shouldn't need to

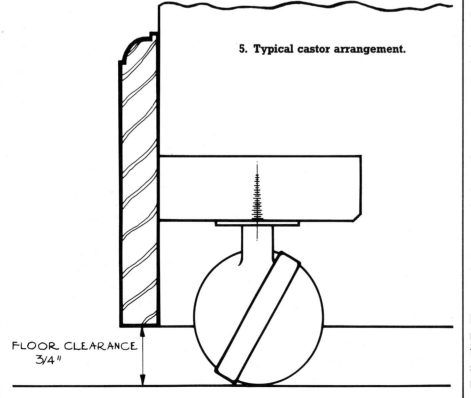

5. **Typical castor arrangement.**

FLOOR CLEARANCE
3/4"

be locked away from other members of the family (except the booze). But if some intruder became interested in the contents of a locked drawer, far more damage could be done opening it than the contents might be worth. Also, from a commercial point of view, the price of locks and the time taken to fit them makes it difficult to justify the cost to a customer for such a seemingly small addition.

Choice of handles is a matter of personal preference. The swan neck

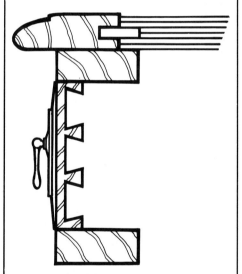

3. Typical drawer arrangement.

handle is the obvious choice, being a matter of choosing one of the many variations on this theme. Most brassware can be purchased in an antique finish, but if the only ones available are bright, these can be aged by fuming with ammonia, after first soaking in cellulose thinners to remove the protective lacquer.

FINISHING OFF

This desk will be stained to fit in with other furniture of an antique appearance, and will be distressed accordingly. There are various methods open to us in achieving this type of finish; personal choice and

experience are the deciding factors. In finishing, use of the best materials will pay dividends time and time again. That means brushes and rags as well as the stain, polish and wax. Good polishing comes with practice and careful preparation. There are no short cuts to a good finish.

With the piece now echoing craftsmanship at its finest, all that remains is the completion of the writing surface. As the skill and equipment for this is outside the scope of most woodworkers, it is

best "contracted out" to a specialist. From the range of leathers and tooling, a scheme that complemented the colour of the wood and the situation of the desk was chosen. A professional job was done for a very reasonable charge, the effect being better than I had imagined. A flick through the Yellow Pages will locate a suitable craftsman in your area.

Now there is no excuse for Great Aunt Maude not getting that letter. "Ah, where did I leave my pen?"

PART	DESCRIPTION	L	W	T	MATERIAL	QTY
	CUTTING LIST					
1	Ends	22½″	21½″	¾″	Veneered Ply[1]	4
2	Backs	22½″	10″	¾″	Veneered Ply	2
3	Drawer rails	11½″	1¾″	13/16″	Oak[2]	8
4	Bases	75″	3¾″	9/16″	Oak	2
5	Ends	21½″	5″	¾″	Veneered Ply	2
6	Back	38¹⁵/₁₆″	5″	¾″	Veneered Ply	1
7	Drawer rails	39¹⁵/₁₆″	1¾″	13/16″	Oak[2]	2
8	Runners/kickers	20″	1¾″	13/16″	Oak[2]	4
9	Drawer divisions	4⅜″	1¾″	13/16″	Oak[2]	2
10	Top panel	36⅜″	17⅜″	¾″	Ply	1
11	Lips	42⅛″	2¾″	13/16″	Oak (mitred)	2
12	Lips	23″	2¾″	13/16″	Oak (mitred)	2
13	Drawer front	16⅜″	3⅜″	¾″	Oak	1
14	Drawer fronts	10½″	3⅜″	¾″	Oak	2
15	Drawer fronts	10½″	4½″	¾″	Oak	2
16	Drawer fronts	10½″	5½″	¾″	Oak	2
17	Drawer fronts	10½″	6⅝″	¾″	Oak	2
18	Drawer back	16⅜″	2½″	5/16″	Chestnut	1
19	Drawer backs	10½″	2½″	5/16″	Chestnut	2
20	Drawer backs	10½″	3⅜″	5/16″	Chestnut	2
21	Drawer backs	10½″	4⅝″	5/16″	Chestnut	2
22	Drawer backs	10½″	5¾″	5/16″	Chestnut	2
23	Drawer sides	19″	3⅜″	5/16″	Chestnut	6
24	Drawer sides	19″	4¼″	5/16″	Chestnut	4
25	Drawer sides	19″	5½″	5/16″	Chestnut	4
26	Drawer sides	19″	6⅝″	5/16″	Chestnut	4
27	Drawer bottoms	10½″	19″	¼″	Plywood[4]	8
28	Drawer bottom	16⅜″	19″	¼″	Plywood[4]	1
29	Leaves		12″		Oak veneer[5]	8

[1]Including ½″ lips to Long Edges. [2]Including ½″ tenons. [3]Including ½″ lips to Short Edges. [4]Take exact measurement from finished drawers. [5]Crown Cut Oak Veneer.
SUNDRIES: Material for loose tongues, runners, kickers, guides, battens, etc. can usually be found in the form of off-cuts, and are thus omitted from the above.
HARDWARE: 10 Brass Swan Neck Drawer Handles, 8 Castors.

DRAW-BORING THE MORTISE AND TENON JOINT

A delightfully clear explanation of a technique which deserves to be more widely known.

The mortise and tenon must be one of the best known and frequently used woodworking joints. Having assembled the joint it can be prevented from coming apart by various means. It can be glued, wedged or draw-bored. The last named method is most suitable for maintaining tight joints in large entrance gates or heavy frames and examples of its effectiveness and durability can be seen in the framework of Elizabethan buildings.

The joint is cut in the usual manner. The mortised piece has a hole for the wooden pin bored close to the edge against which the shoulders of the tenon will fit. It is essential to site the wooden pin near the tenon shoulders to allow for the possible shrinkage across the width of the wood. If the hole were bored centrally and shrinkage occurred, a gap would appear between the tenon shoulders and the edge of the mortised piece.

Having bored the hole for the peg in the mortised piece, it is now necessary to assemble the joint and drive it tightly home. Place the bit in the hole and mark the side of the tenon with the point of the bit. Carefully tap the joint apart. It will be as in Fig. 2 with the hole for the peg marked "A" and the mark of the bit point "B". The bit point is not placed on this mark but is moved ⅛″ (3mm) closer to the tenon shoulders to point "C" where the tenon is bored through. The joint can now be finally assembled and if a section were taken through the joint it would appear as in Fig. 3.

TAPERED PIN

By driving a tapered pin through the joint the tenon shoulders will be forced tightly together. Sometimes a tapered steel drift is used to draw up the joint when a round wooden peg of the appropriate diameter is driven through and then trimmed to length.

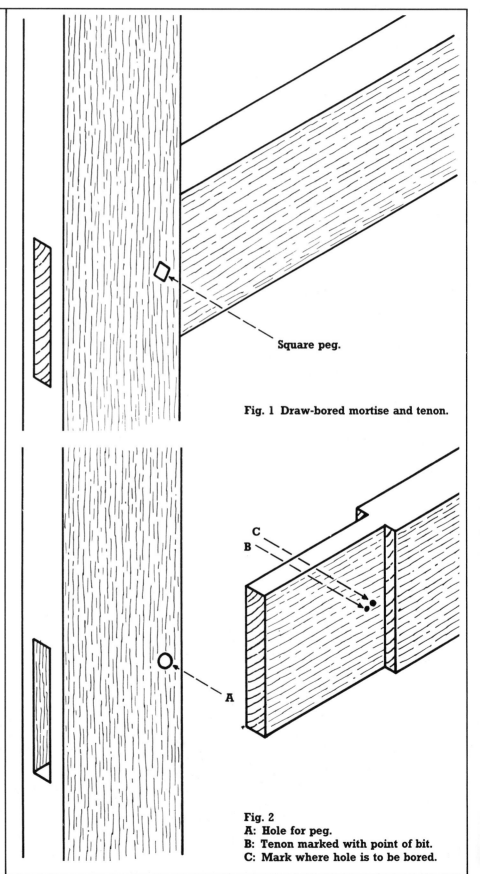

Square peg.

Fig. 1 Draw-bored mortise and tenon.

Fig. 2
A: Hole for peg.
B: Tenon marked with point of bit.
C: Mark where hole is to be bored.

Having driven out the steel drift it can be used to draw up the next joint.

The disadvantage of using a round peg is that if shrinkage occurs it will take place across the grain of the pin so that the drawing up action will be lost and the joint will loosen.

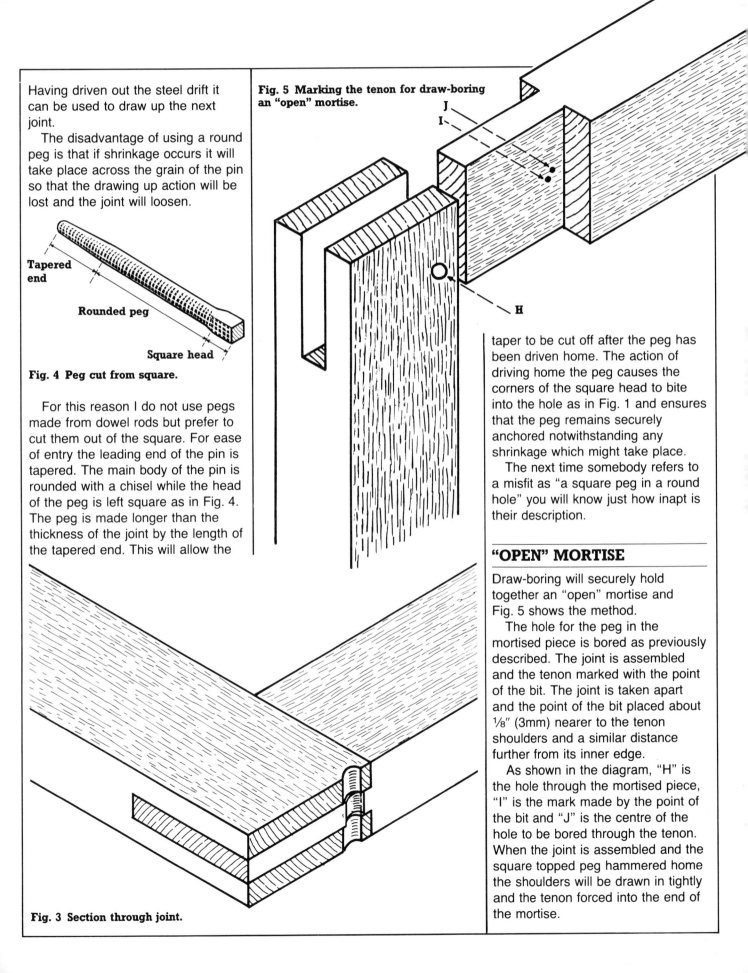

Tapered end

Rounded peg

Square head

Fig. 4 Peg cut from square.

For this reason I do not use pegs made from dowel rods but prefer to cut them out of the square. For ease of entry the leading end of the pin is tapered. The main body of the pin is rounded with a chisel while the head of the peg is left square as in Fig. 4. The peg is made longer than the thickness of the joint by the length of the tapered end. This will allow the

Fig. 5 Marking the tenon for draw-boring an "open" mortise.

J
I
H

taper to be cut off after the peg has been driven home. The action of driving home the peg causes the corners of the square head to bite into the hole as in Fig. 1 and ensures that the peg remains securely anchored notwithstanding any shrinkage which might take place.

The next time somebody refers to a misfit as "a square peg in a round hole" you will know just how inapt is their description.

"OPEN" MORTISE

Draw-boring will securely hold together an "open" mortise and Fig. 5 shows the method.

The hole for the peg in the mortised piece is bored as previously described. The joint is assembled and the tenon marked with the point of the bit. The joint is taken apart and the point of the bit placed about ⅛" (3mm) nearer to the tenon shoulders and a similar distance further from its inner edge.

As shown in the diagram, "H" is the hole through the mortised piece, "I" is the mark made by the point of the bit and "J" is the centre of the hole to be bored through the tenon. When the joint is assembled and the square topped peg hammered home the shoulders will be drawn in tightly and the tenon forced into the end of the mortise.

Fig. 3 Section through joint.

MAKING A BIRD TABLE

*This table will look its part in the garden,
and will allow you to observe the birds.*

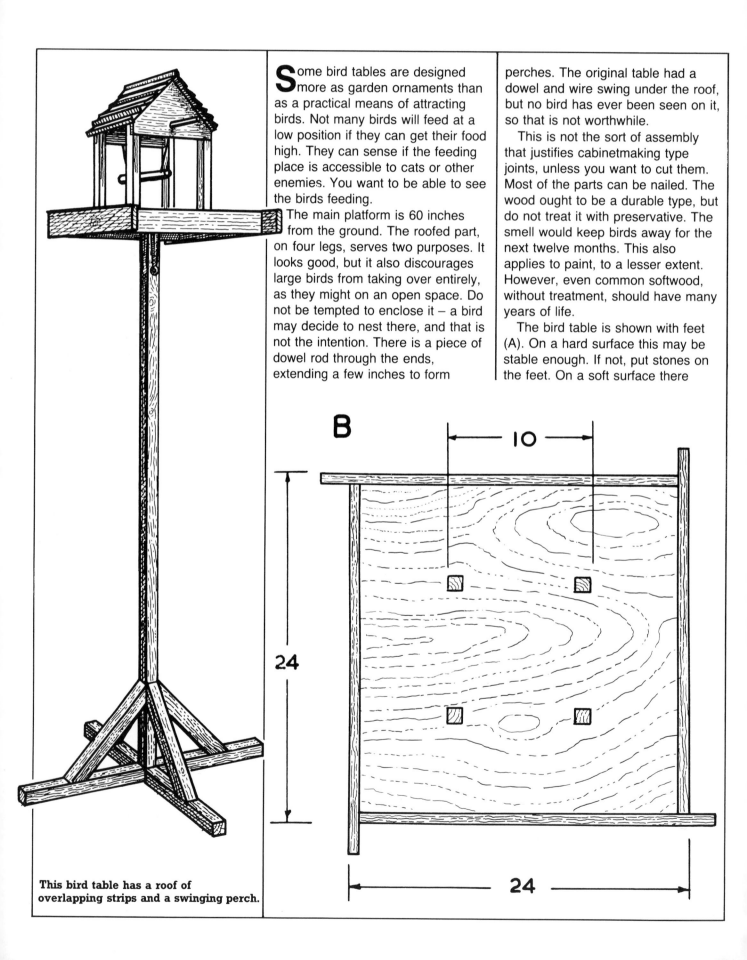

Some bird tables are designed more as garden ornaments than as a practical means of attracting birds. Not many birds will feed at a low position if they can get their food high. They can sense if the feeding place is accessible to cats or other enemies. You want to be able to see the birds feeding.

The main platform is 60 inches from the ground. The roofed part, on four legs, serves two purposes. It looks good, but it also discourages large birds from taking over entirely, as they might on an open space. Do not be tempted to enclose it – a bird may decide to nest there, and that is not the intention. There is a piece of dowel rod through the ends, extending a few inches to form perches. The original table had a dowel and wire swing under the roof, but no bird has ever been seen on it, so that is not worthwhile.

This is not the sort of assembly that justifies cabinetmaking type joints, unless you want to cut them. Most of the parts can be nailed. The wood ought to be a durable type, but do not treat it with preservative. The smell would keep birds away for the next twelve months. This also applies to paint, to a lesser extent. However, even common softwood, without treatment, should have many years of life.

The bird table is shown with feet (A). On a hard surface this may be stable enough. If not, put stones on the feet. On a soft surface there

This bird table has a roof of
overlapping strips and a swinging perch.

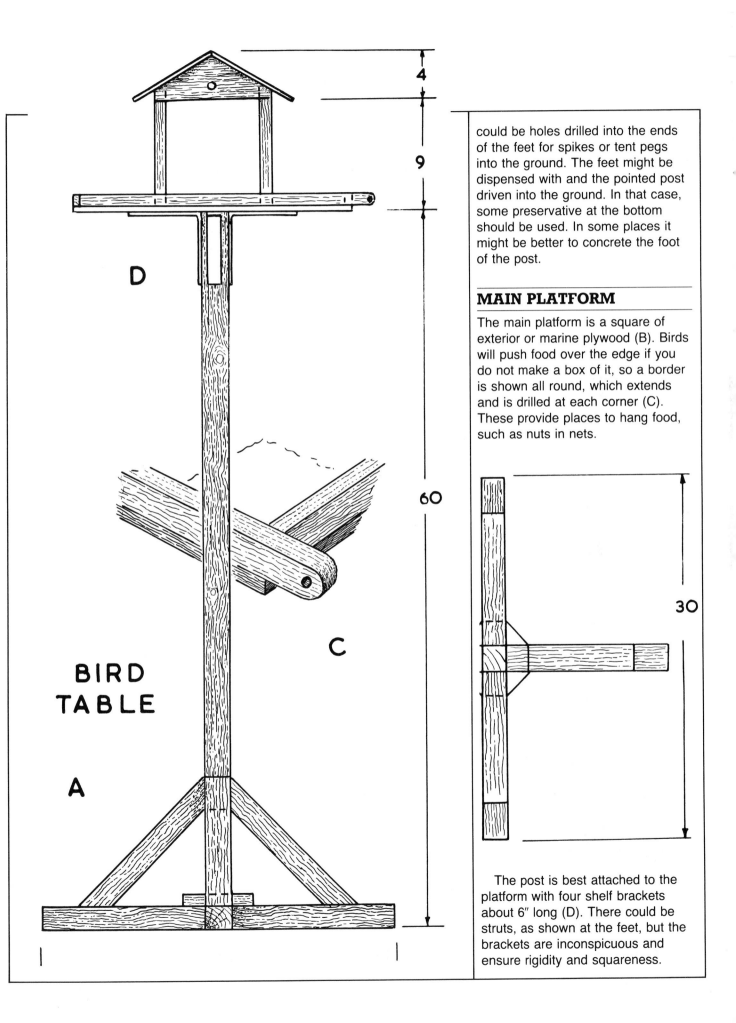

4

9

60

**BIRD
TABLE**

D

C

A

could be holes drilled into the ends of the feet for spikes or tent pegs into the ground. The feet might be dispensed with and the pointed post driven into the ground. In that case, some preservative at the bottom should be used. In some places it might be better to concrete the foot of the post.

MAIN PLATFORM

The main platform is a square of exterior or marine plywood (B). Birds will push food over the edge if you do not make a box of it, so a border is shown all round, which extends and is drilled at each corner (C). These provide places to hang food, such as nuts in nets.

30

The post is best attached to the platform with four shelf brackets about 6″ long (D). There could be struts, as shown at the feet, but the brackets are inconspicuous and ensure rigidity and squareness.

ROOF

For the roofed part, two end pieces are cut at about 30°, with enough below the cuts for nailing to the uprights (E). The bottoms of the uprights are merely nailed up through the platform, but make sure the parts finish vertical. It may not bother the birds, but you would feel unhappy about a cock-eyed appearance. Drill the roof ends for ½″ dowel rod to go through – anything thinner would be difficult for claws to grip. Use your own ideas for roof covering. There could be two pieces of thin plywood. There could be several thin pieces of wood overlapping like slates. Waney-edged strips look good. There could be pieces of metal or slate. *(Roofing felt might also be considered. – Ed.)*

FEET

The feet should cross level, preferably with a halving joint (F). Make a block to go over the joint, with a hole for the foot of the post. There could be a narrower mortise and tenon joint, but the hole is shown fullsize (G). The four struts are drawn at 45°, but they could be at a steeper angle. Make sure the cut ends are square to each other. As you assemble opposite struts, check squareness by measuring from the end of the foot each side to the top of the post. If these diagonals are the same, your post will be upright that way. You could use a waterproof glue between the parts at the bottom of the assembly, but nails driven diagonally through the meeting parts should provide adequate strength without glue.

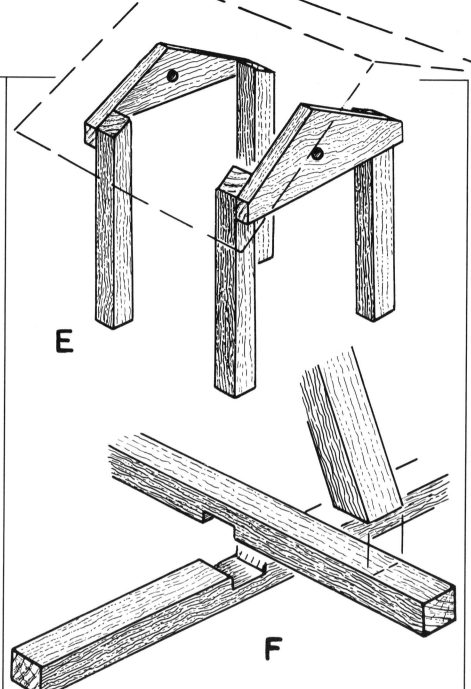

CUTTING LIST						
PART	DESCRIPTION	L	W	T	MATERIAL	QTY
1	Platform	24″	24″	½″	Plywood	1
2	Platform edges	26″	1½″	½″	Softwood	4
3	Roof legs	11″	1″	1″	Softwood	4
4	Roof ends	11″	6″	½″	Softwood	2
5	Roofs	14″	9″	¼″	Plywood	2
6	Post	60″	2″	2″	Softwood	1
7	Feet	31″	2″	2″	Softwood	2
8	Struts	18″	2″	2″	Softwood	4
9	Pad	7″	7″	1″	Softwood	1

SUNDRIES: ½″ Dowelling, 4 tent pegs (optional), 4 shelf brackets and screws, waterproof glue or nails.

BUILD A WENDY HOUSE

*The Wendy House suggested here may not be as grand as J. M. Barrie's conception but,
if my daughter (now full-grown) is any guide, the reader can be assured
that it will be received with no less enthusiasm.*

As this can be classed as a
building of limited life we will
dispense with housed joints and
other such sophistications and just
get on with it.

Cut all the materials to length and
lay aside in separate lots.

A dry course of bricks should be
laid level to take the floor and a DPC
laid on top. Strips of roofing felt will
do nicely.

FLOORING

The floor-joists are nailed together
and checked for square. Face nail
the first floor-board around its edges
and then through the feather into the
intermediate joists. Carry on nailing
the rest of the flooring using 2½"
galvanised or sheridised round wire

nails but only face-nail where the
heads will be hidden by the walls,
otherwise always through the
feather. We don't want the finished
floor to look like a currant cake. The
final board will have to be ripped to
about 3" but it's best to leave this to
the last in case the flooring 'creeps'
a little as it's laid. If you are working
'al fresco' the floor will give you a
surface to assemble the other
sections on.

WALLS

Nail together the studs and runners
for the front and nail in the dwangs
at the door and window. Check for
square and stitch nail the first length
of cladding to the studs with the
bottom edge of the cladding

projecting 4½" below the bottom
runner. When the walls have been
positioned this bottom length of
cladding will be nailed to the edge of
the floor section and the stitch nails
drawn. Assemble the window and cut
the head and sill to leave the
projections on either side. Fix the
door-head and the 1¼" × 1¼"
pieces in position. (See section B-B.)
Make the door and hinge in place.

Assemble the back wall in the
same way.

When you have assembled the
gable framing and checked for
square, apply the bottom length of
cladding as with the front and back.
The cladding will project 2" beyond
the framing at each end.

Stand the back section in position
on the floor and nail to the floor. Do

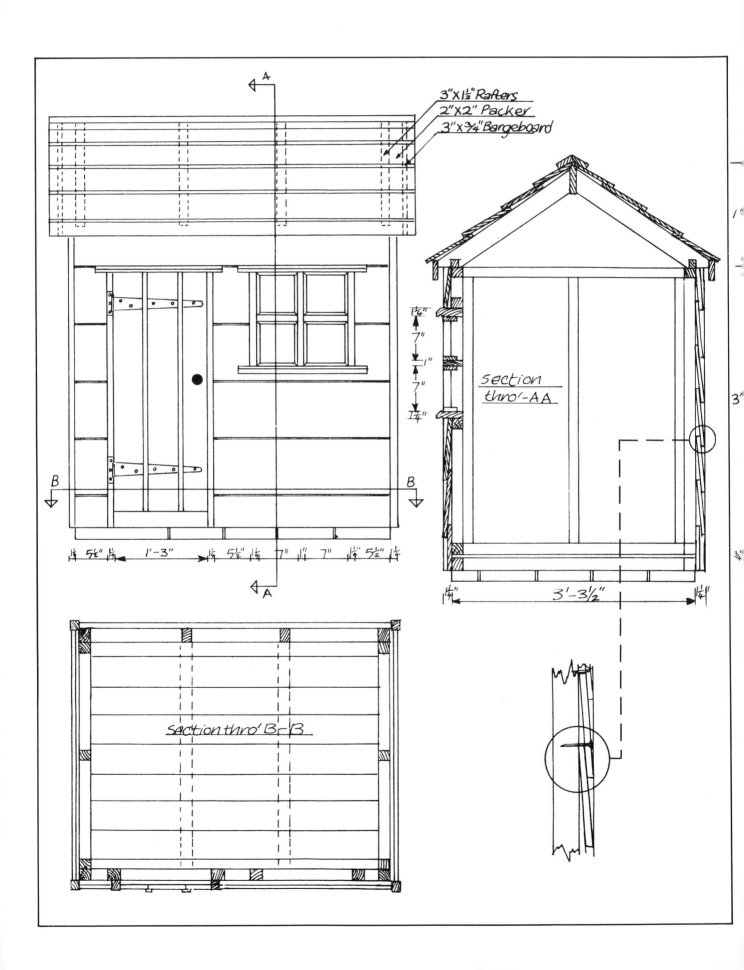

3"x1½" Rafters
2"x2" Packer
3"x¾" Bargeboard

section thro'-AA

section thro' B-B

3'-3½"

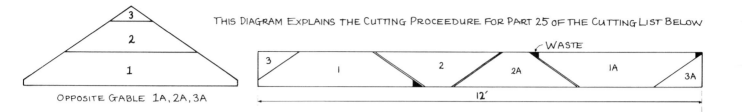

THIS DIAGRAM EXPLAINS THE CUTTING PROCEEDURE FOR PART 25 OF THE CUTTING LIST BELOW

OPPOSITE GABLE 1A, 2A, 3A

the same with the gables and nail them to the back section through the studs. Position the front, nail to the floor and nail the gables to it through the studs.

ROOF

Nail the pole-plates in position and you are now ready for the roof. The roof shown is ⅓ pitch calculated on 'effective span' and the top cut is 56% and the bottom cut 34. The long point length of the rafter is 2' 4" and is blunted to take the fascia board and checked to fit over the pole-plate. Nail barge-board packers to the face of the rafters to be used at the gables keeping them flush with the top edge of the rafters and cut off in line with the top and bottom cuts of the rafters.

Mark the positions of the rafters on the pole-plates and transfer the marks on to the ridge. Stand the rafters up in pairs, nail them to the wall-heads, slip the ridge up between the pairs of rafters and nail to the marks on the ridge. Complete the gable cladding. Nail the fascia-boards to the rafters. Nail the bottom of the first length of roof cladding to the top edge of the fascia and the rest to the rafters in the same way as the side cladding was fixed. Make the ridge cap as shown and cut and fix the barge-boards. A cutting of the cladding which was taken out at the window is now ripped to 4¼" and nailed to the edge of the floor and joist at the bottom of the door.

Glaze the window using some type of safety glass. (I used Georgian plate.) A sham handle and a very easily operated cupboard catch should be fitted to the door.

An extra bit of style could be given to the roof in various ways. If a Tyrolean touch is wanted, sprockets or tilting-fillets could be fitted to give the roof a bell-cast. Tiles, slates or shingles could be applied to the

cladding but if this is done felt soakers should be used.

Apply some preserving liquid and the job is done. The new owner will attend to the furnishings and the internal decor.

When I built my daughter's Wendy House I took a look inside after a few days and was surprised to see what appeared to be a poster of a piano with the lid up. On closer inspection it proved to be a photograph of a young gentleman called Donny Osmond.

CUTTING LIST						
PART	DESCRIPTION	L	W	T	MATERIAL	QTY
FLOOR						
1	Joists	4' 3½"	2"	2"	Softwood	2
2	Joists	3' 3½"	2"	2"	Softwood	4
3	Floor surface	4' 3½"	4½"	¾"	Tung and groove	9
FRONT						
4	Runners	4' 3½"	2"	1½"	Softwood	2
5	Studs	3' 6"	2"	2"	Softwood	6
6	Dwangs	1' 3"	2"	2"	Softwood	3
7	Cladding	2' 4½"	9"	½"	Softwood	4
8	Cladding	4' 3"	9"	½"	Softwood	1
9	Cladding	5½"	9"	½"	Softwood	7
10	Poleplate	4' 3½"	1"	1"	Softwood	1
WINDOW						
11	Dressed head and cill	1' 9"	4½"	1⅛"	Softwood	2
12	Dressed head and cill	1' 3"	3"	⅛"	Softwood	1
13	Dressed head and cill	7"	3"	⅛"	Softwood	2
14	Glazing beads	7"	¾"	½"	Softwood	32
DOOR						
15	Planking	3' 1½"	5"	½"	Softwood	3
16	Beading	3' 1½"	1"	½"	Softwood	2
17	Dressed head	1' 9"	4½"	1⅛"	Softwood	2
BACK						
18	Runners	4' 3½"	3"	1½"	Softwood	2
19	Studs	3' 6"	2"	2"	Softwood	2
20	Studs	3' 6"	2"	1½"	Softwood	2
21	Poleplate	4' 3½"	1"	1"	Softwood	1
GABLES						
22	Runners	2' 11½"	2"	1½"	Softwood	4
23	Studs	3' 6"	2"	1½"	Softwood	6
24	Cladding	3' 3½"	9"	½"	Softwood	12
25	Cladding	12'	9"	½"	Softwood	1
26	Corners	4' 0"	1¼"	1¼"	Softwood	4
ROOF						
27	Rafters	2' 3"	3"	1½"	Softwood	8
28	Packers	2' 3"	2"	2"	Softwood	4
29	Bargeboard	2' 6"	3"	¾"	Softwood	4
30	Fascia	5' 0"	3"	¾"	Softwood	2
31	Sarking	5' 0"	9"	½"	Softwood	8
32	Ridge cap	5' 0"	3"	¾"	Softwood	2
33	Ridge	4' 8"	5"	1"	Softwood	1

SUNDRIES: 4 panes of safety glass 6⅞"×6⅞", 2½" galvanised or sheridised round wire nails, 1 sham handle, 1 cupboard catch, 2 door hinges, wood preservative.

An unusual and interesting project from a more leisurely age.

Book rests type A (above) and B

Reading at meals was one of the idiosyncrasies of the Rodd boys when the family came to Canada in the twenties and so for my own convenience – and later for my brothers' – I devised and made the type of book rest illustrated in B. They made very satisfactory and inexpensive presents and found a place for odd scraps of material which seemed too nice to throw away. I must have made a good many of them; some with lip and back bracket hinged so that they could be folded flat.

Evidently the demand for them is not yet dead for, the grandchildren having latched on to the remaining examples, my daughter suggested that I make her one for a birthday or Christmas present.

After some thought it occurred to me that a higher model set at a steeper angle would make at least an interesting variation and might prove to be more convenient than the original design and so I made the drawings shown.

I happened to have some pieces of marquetry which had been cut in 1910 and among them were two small pieces probably intended for the side panels of the front of an upright piano. In the centre of each would have been mounted a swinging brass candlestick for illuminating the music and it will be seen from the photographs that there is a blank space in the centre

appropriate for this purpose. The old newspaper backing used for holding the pattern together contained some interesting items including the release from prison of some suffragettes after having served their term. Miss Dorothy Shallard, Miss Bryant, Miss Pitfield and Miss Lily Asquith: they complained of the forced feeding.

PREPARING THE MARQUETRY

After making a set of cardboard patterns, the next step was to prepare the ground for the marquetry

out of ½" plywood. Instead of veneering the edges I faced them with solid walnut strips as shown in drawing C. The top strip shows 1¼" for the curve plus ¼" for a tongue which is shown with a dashed line. The side ones show ½" plus tongue. Having cut them out I rebated each side of the strips with a table saw so as to make a tongue about ³⁄₁₆" thick and then grooved the plywood with the same tool to receive them, making the fit fairly snug so that they could be glued without having to bother with cramps. The bottom did not need facing because it would be covered by the ledge which is rebated as shown to the right.

LAYING THE MARQUETRY

Laying the marquetry on the front and a plain piece of walnut veneer on the back is easy enough for the old hand but some hints for the beginner may be helpful. The adhesive to be used will probably come under one of two classifications; the first achieving its greatest strength after its solvent, usually water, has been first absorbed by the porous wood and then has evaporated. The second and more recent ones are hardened by the addition of a chemical, usually labelled 'Hardener', which is mixed in certain proportions and do their work in a specified time. For this reason one should always read and follow the instructions which come with any new or unfamiliar product. With both kinds it is essential for the veneers to be pressed firmly against the ground until the glue has set up.

Being ancient and set in my ways I used what used to be called Scotch glue; an animal glue which is applied hot. I sandwiched the veneers and ground between two squares of ¾" plywood called cauls and applied the pressure with my bench holdfast.

In using the holdfast for this purpose, there is a tendency for it to

C

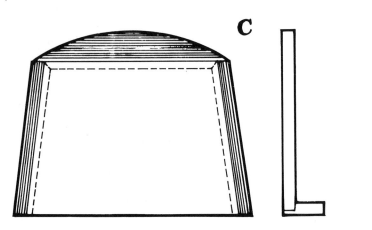

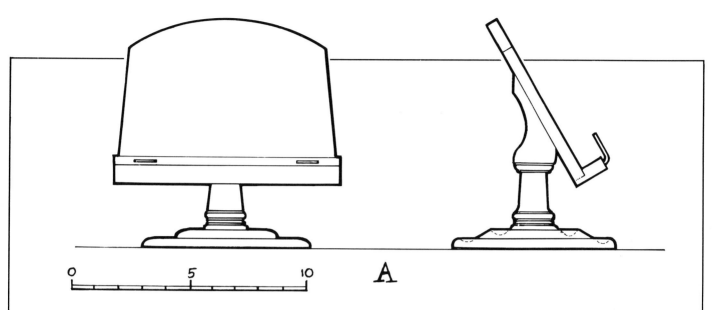

0   5   10   A

draw the upper caul towards the hole in the bench as the pressure is being increased with the result that the veneer, well lubricated with the glue, will slide out of place. To cope with this I cut the back veneer an inch longer than the ground and laid it on the lower caul with the side to be glued up and the centre beneath the foot of the holdfast. To make sure the marquetry would be centred on the ground I first cut the lower edge in relation to the pattern and then attached this edge to the ground with masking tape; newspaper backing,

up. I then turned it over and pencilled around it so that I could check the border distances. All being well I added a second tape on top of the first and also tacked a strip of lath beneath a long edge of the upper caul.

Now the procedure was as follows: first a trial run. The lower caul and back veneer is already in place. Add the ground with attached marquetry on the veneer with the top towards the holdfast and the bottom barely covering the veneer. Put on the upper caul with the lath against the

taped bottom of the marquetry. Swing over the holdfast and tighten. Make any necessary adjustments.

Now slacken and carefully dismantle. Mark the position of the lower caul on the bench with chalk. Heat the cauls; lift the marquetry on its hinge of tape and glue both it and the ground. Close it and glue the back and the plain veneer and assemble as before. The panel, as expected, will slide on the backing veneer but the extra inch should take care of this. Because of the water content of the glue, the cauls were removed about two hours later and the panel exposed for drying.

With most other glues it is easier because you don't have to bother with heat and they take longer to set up giving you more time to work. There are of course plenty of other ways of applying pressure; putting the sandwich of ground, veneers and cauls in the vice with some G-cramps on the part projecting, for instance. Putting weights on them is an idea that comes to mind but it is not easy to find a handy substitute for the several hundred pounds provided by the handscrews.

CUTTING GAUGE

The rebates for the boxwood borders were worked with a cutting gauge. Mine is a home-made one and uses a blade made out of a broken $7/32''$

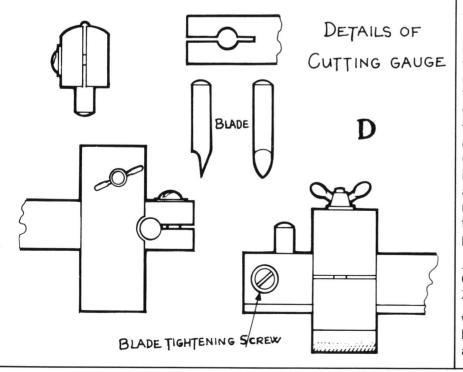

DETAILS OF
CUTTING GAUGE

BLADE

D

BLADE TIGHTENING SCREW

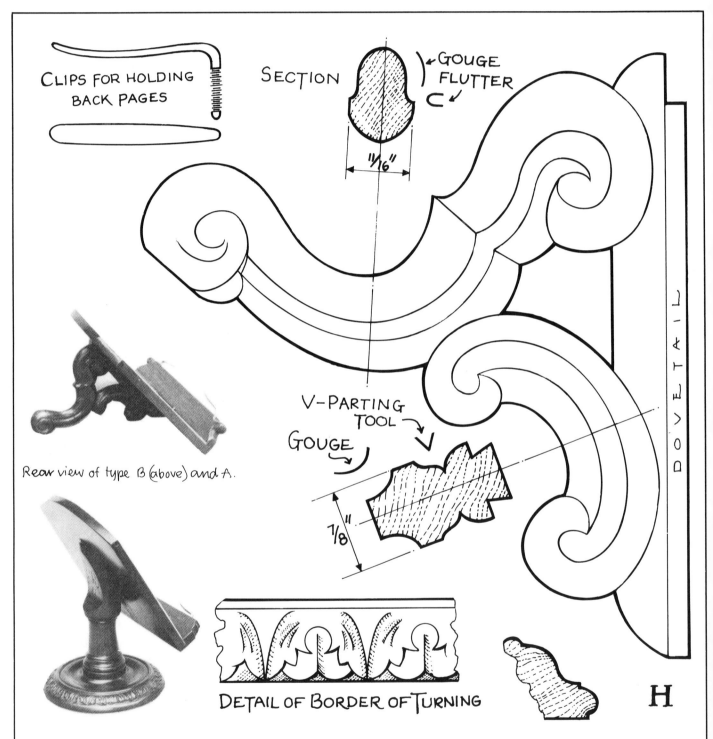

CLIPS FOR HOLDING
BACK PAGES

SECTION

GOUGE
FLUTTER

¹¹/₁₆"

V-PARTING
TOOL

GOUGE

⁷/₈"

Rear view of type B (above) and A.

DETAIL OF BORDER OF TURNING

DOVETAIL

H

twist drill. The advantage of this is that the blade can be aligned exactly with the fence with the vertical face in either direction. For this job, or for cutting back the edge of the veneer on a panel for cross-banding, it would be with the face out as shown. For cutting the banding itself, or for cutting the outer edge of a groove for inlay across the grain, it would be reversed.

Details of the tool are shown in D. The blade-tightening screw can be either a wood screw or a metal one with a nut let in on the opposite side. The fence is locked by the same principle but uses a wing-nut instead of a screw. In order to grind the face of the drill flat, it should be held in vice-grip pliers resting on a level surface and using the flat face of the grinding wheel: the bevelled side is slightly rounded: both should be finished on a fine stone.

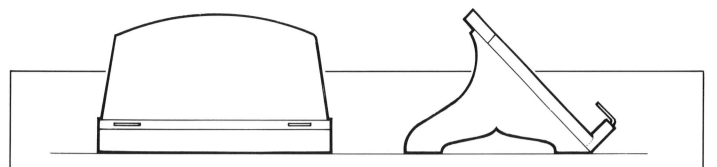

B

E, F and G show the three steps for cutting the rebate. In E, the limit (size of boxwood square) has been marked with a light cut. In F, the corner has been bevelled with a block plane and then in G the triangular strip has been removed with alternate firm cuts.

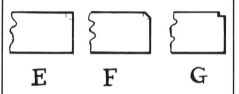

E F G

In the olden days we used to hold the inlay in place with string while the glue dried; often round strategically placed nails in a board cramped to the panel, on one or both sides. Now we find masking tape both better and quicker, especially if four hands are available; two to hold the inlay in place and the other two to handle the tape like a band-aid.

BRACKET

Following the drawing B would be fairly straightforward. The bracket should be secured with a long dovetail entered from the lower edge. If one is available it can be easily cut with a router; the ledge, which is the last piece to be glued can be simply rubbed in place.

The carved bracket seen in the photo and pencil drawing was made of ⅞" walnut and fitted with hand tools. Because of this the dovetail was cut on a taper as a good fit is more easily achieved that way, especially when one's vision is failing. The turned pillar could have been simply glued to the back of the panel but a lifetime of repairing glue joints which have failed has robbed

me of the confidence young people seem to have in glue and so I added three screws with their heads covered with cross grained walnut plugs.

The carving is of course redundant but when the object is mainly amusement; why not? The design of the bracket is derived from the front legs of William and Mary chairs; a form of scroll which in turn likely came from Renaissance Florence. After sawing out, the leg part was shaved down on each side just behind the foot with a spokeshave so as to give a trim ankle; the scrolls were then traced on each side.

The section is shown in two places as well as the imprint of the carving tools used. First the scrolls were set in with the gouges held vertically. The upper edges of the sweeps were then followed with the fluter and the lines of division with the V-parting tool. The concave side of the small scroll was of course done with the gouge. Spokeshave, gouges and files were used for much of the remainder, the gouge beside the fluter being used to produce the reverse curve seen in the section.

CARVED BORDER

The carved border of the base of the other stand is shown below. The

division plate on the lathe was used to mark this area into 32 divisions and a thin cardboard pattern was used to mark each leaf. This is best cut with the gouges which are available to set in the carving.

The modelling should be simple, consisting of two V-tool cuts for the centre rib; then the sides rounded into them and a pair of veins each side as shown. During the Queen Anne period something very like this was a common feature as a gilt border between a mirror and the cross-banded moulding of the frame. It was usually carved in pine and then the gilder built up a layer of gesso on which to lay his gold leaf. This created a very smooth and rounded effect.

The brasses for holding back the pages were made of ⅛" bronze welding rod 2¼" long, 1½" was flattened by hammering on a steel block and then the end was rounded with a file. Half inch of the opposite end was threaded and then bent at right angles; the end also curved out a bit. A little work with emery cloth and buff and it was ready for lacquering. The hole should be a little bit small and should receive a drop of oil before the clip is screwed in. Experience has shown that they are easily adjustable yet stay where they are put for a great many years.

CUTTING LIST						
PART	DESCRIPTION	L	W	T	MATERIAL	QTY
1	Board	10"	7½"	½"	Plywood	1
2	Lip	10"	1¾"	½"	Walnut	1
3	Post	7"	2"	2"	Walnut	1
4	Disc	7"	7"	¾"	Walnut	1

SUNDRIES: 2 Brass leaf holders ⅛" × 2¼", walnut veneer, suitable marquetry, scotch glue, masking tape, 3 screws.

A MODEL WELSH DRESSER

*As a woodworker, I found making a miniature Welsh dresser an ideal way to keep busy
in the workshop when in my mid-70s failing physical ability stopped me handling
full-scale furniture. Such a compromise is no defeat, for modelmaking
challenges the woodworker's skills.*

Fig. 1 Model Welsh Dresser. Quarter scale.

First there is the matter of converting your timber down to dimensions of ⅛″ and less; there is the tricky turning of knobs for doors and drawers at something under ½″ diameter; the fashioning of fine beadings for skirt and canopy; the hinge problem, not to mention the basic style or period of the dresser to be constructed. For instance, some have three drawers with an open space below, in which case the supporting legs are usually turned, and turning down to a maximum diameter of ⅜″ may prove a deterrent. Furthermore, here in mid-Wales it is the custom for dressers to be closely hung with lustre jugs, and so closely is this convention followed that a collector of lustre may find himself facing the necessity to buy the dresser. If the model-maker should pursue this pattern he would need to find miniature jugs and equivalent hooks, which in this case is somewhat outside the object of the exercise.

I decided on a scale of 3″ to the foot as being of a size that is both useful and ornamental, and in which normal woodworking techniques can be used. As I was anxious to fit the doors and drawers with fielded panels, I settled for a dresser with three drawers and two cupboards with a dog-kennel between, the whole being surmounted by a rack of two shelves and a canopy.

CHANCE TO LEARN

Furthermore, because my experience had been almost entirely confined to hand-work assisted by small power tools, and because I believed I was still not too old to learn something of mechanised processes, I saw possibilities in a day-session at the local College of Further Education where I could combine my project with new experience, and take the sweat and toil out of the conversion of my 1″ oak to the range of smaller

dimensions. In the event, the circular saw and the bandsaw proved beautifully accurate, but the thicknesser was less trustworthy and the sander tended to take more than its share. And there was some frustration arising from the fact that the instructor, in his anxiety not to sacrifice his pupils' fingers, insisted on using most of the machines himself!

MAKING CONCESSIONS

At this stage it might be appropriate to comment on appearance in relation to practicality in scaling down. By this I mean that whereas accurate quarter-scale is generally desirable, there are occasions on which one may make slight concessions which can ease the work without affecting the appearance. To take an example, the doors, which full-size would be 1″ nominal or ⅞″ actual, would appear rather on the thin side when reduced to 7/32″. At 5/16″ the appearance is not marred and that slight extra thickness considerably eases the morticing.

By the same rule the top of the cupboard section which would normally be only 1″ thick looks over-light when fully scaled down. In fact, particularly with a nosed edge, a bare ½″ does not appear too heavy.

Except for minor differences the construction of the model follows the pattern of the full size article. The carcass of the lower portion might normally have had framed and

Fig. 3 Base showing grooves to locate the shelves. (See Fig. 4)

panelled ends and partitions, but in the model these were made solid. This in turn obviated the necessity for drawer-guides, though drawer-runners had still to be fitted. Following the conversion of the timber, only normal hand tools were used throughout, with the exception of a carving chisel of something under ⅛″ to clear the mortices after drilling. In making the door-frames ¾″ wide I erred on the generous side, but this was to allow workable space for the mortices after cutting the grooves for the panels. The narrowest blade of the grooving

Fig. 2 Doors and drawers open.

plane was not too wide for these channels, as the panels which started at a thickness of ⁷⁄₃₂″ were bevelled down to a bare ⅛″.

Door and drawer knobs were turned on the lathe to a maximum of ⁷⁄₁₆″ for the cupboards, and slightly less for the drawers, leaving a shank of around ⅛″ long enough to enter an appropriately drilled hole.

HINGES

Hinges presented an initial problem. The smallest I had were ¾″ cigar-box hinges in brass, a trifle

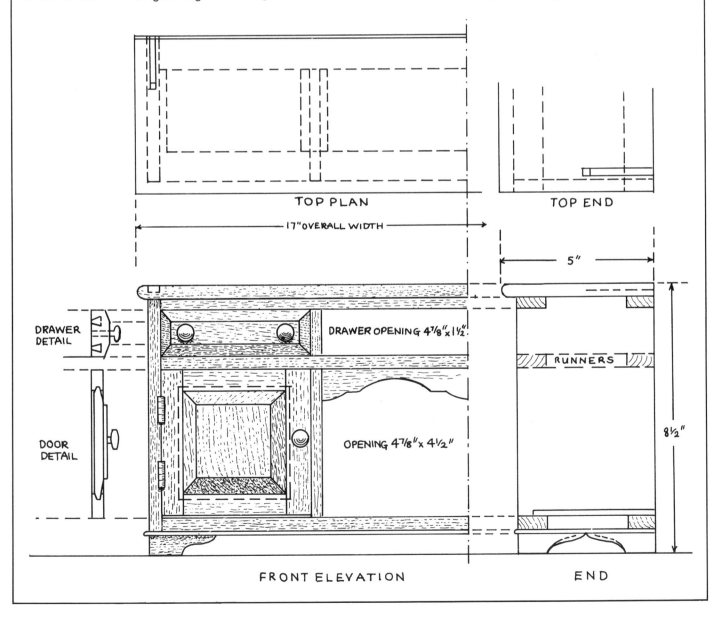

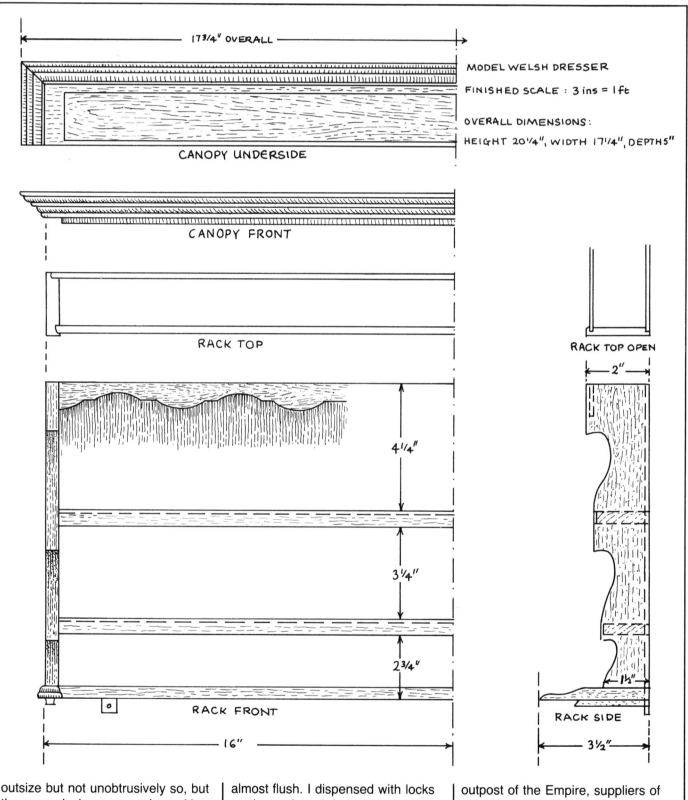

17³/4" OVERALL

MODEL WELSH DRESSER

FINISHED SCALE : 3 ins = 1 ft

OVERALL DIMENSIONS :
HEIGHT 20¹/4", WIDTH 17¹/4", DEPTH 5"

CANOPY UNDERSIDE

CANOPY FRONT

RACK TOP

RACK TOP OPEN

2"

4¹/4"

3¹/4"

2³/4"

1¹/2"

RACK FRONT

RACK SIDE

16"

3¹/2"

outsize but not unobtrusively so, but they gaped when screwed on with even the smallest screws. This was overcome by tacking them on with tiny copper tacks and filing the heads almost flush. I dispensed with locks on the cupboard doors but glued to the leading edge of each a carefully fitted wedge which tightened just enough to hold the door shut. In this outpost of the Empire, suppliers of specialised knick-knackery are few and far between, and one is obliged to fall back on his own ingenuity and bit-box.

Fig. 4 Shelves upside down showing method of fixing to base. (See Fig. 3)

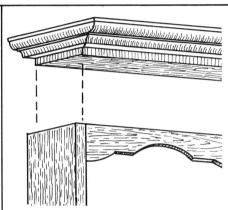

Fig. 7 Detail of canopy.

AIRCRAFT PLY

The drawers followed the usual structural procedure with the sides being dovetailed to the fronts, but material thin enough yet strong enough for the bottoms gave some food for thought, until I recalled some tiddly bits of aircraft ply which had fallen off a cart during the war. There was just enough. Beautiful stuff, and so thin that it gently slotted into the fine tenon-saw cuts in the sides and fronts.

Fig. 6 Exploded view of housing of plate rack into base.

Setting the shelf rack on to the base called for an anti-topple device. This was achieved (as shown in the drawing) by carrying two small tongues from the backing of the plate rack down over the horizontal back

member of the cupboard section and fixing with two small screws, and also recessing the undersides of the feet into slots in the top, undercut at the toe to prevent them lifting out.

The canopy was made as a loose item and dropped into the open top of the rack. This would normally be hollow, showing the mouldings only, but was made solid as the model would probably stand below eye level.

It was built up from laminations of different thicknesses each with its own beaded edge.

The fronts of the shelves were clad with a very thin facing, showing a shallow lip to prevent the plates slipping off. An alternative would be a shallow groove in each shelf, but this could be out of proportion. The pelmets over the shelves and over the dog-kennel were worked out with rule and compasses to the designs shown in the drawings. A fine bead was set around the base and the feet shaped to the conventional pattern.

Finally, a medium oak stain and wax polish finish produced a colour and patina which set off the furnishings of miniature china.

Fig. 5 Shelves showing canopy lifted out of position.

A TRADITIONAL CRADLE

By the author of the book 'Making Family Heirlooms'

Photo. 1 The completed cradle.

particular subject. Its design incorporates panelled sides and ends with a surrounding open-top rail of short, turned spindles and the top of each corner post has a ball finial turned on it. The contrast in colour between the light sapwood and the darker heart of yew was used to advantage wherever possible.

As yew of satisfactory quality is not always easy to obtain in sufficient quantity, it is as well to begin by getting together all the yew required and sort it through for colour matching etc. A timber other than

The name cradle comes from the Old English *cradol* and is related to the Old German *kratto* which meant basket. Early cradles would no doubt have been of rush or osiers (willow) woven like a basket – in fact, the biblical basket in which the baby Moses travelled was probably a cradle. Such cradles would have been easy and cheap to make. Moreover, when one had held a child afflicted by some terrible illness, it would be no great loss to burn the cradle as a safeguard against further infection.

The earliest cradles which have survived were made mainly in oak, with panelled sides and a solid hood at one end, often richly carved. Rockers formed part of the end panels or were inserted into the base of the corner posts. Later cradles, more lightly built and without hoods, had rockers screwed into the base of the framework and are to be found made in a variety of woods, including beech and some fruitwoods. Turned finials on the corner posts have long been popular, providing a convenient place to hold on to when rocking the baby.

Photo. 2 End section panels and rails.

YEW

Yew was the wood chosen to make the cradle described here, its mellow tones seeming most fitting for this

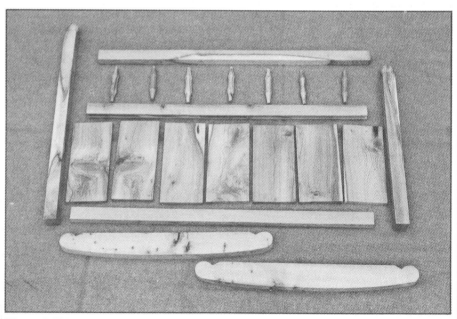

Photo. 3 Side components and prototype rockers.

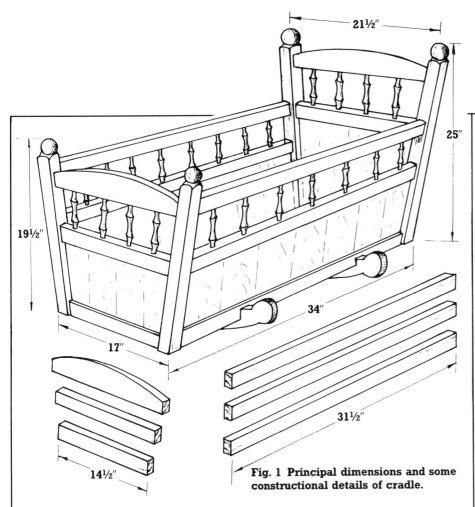

Fig. 1 Principal dimensions and some constructional details of cradle.

Photo. 4 Hand scraping.

yew could be used. *But, needless to say, whatever material is used it must be properly seasoned and thoroughly dry before the work begins.* A total of 18 pieces measuring 9½" x 4½" x ¼" are required for the side and the lower end panels and a further four, 15" x 4½" x ¼" for the longer upper end panels. The materials for these were machine planed before the individual pieces were cut to length, after which they were scraped by hand and sanded smooth.

SIDE AND END RAILS

The side rails, three each side, and the end rails, three each end, are next to be prepared. All except the two end top rails are made from 1½" x 1"-section material, planed to 1⅜" x ⅞". The two end top rails have curved top edges and are cut from 2½" x 1" material. The six side rails are cut to their exact length, but the six end rails are all left overlength to begin with to allow for the later angled cutting at the different lengths determined by the sloping sides of the cradle (see Fig. 1). Lower and middle side rails and lower and middle end rails are slotted all along one edge to accommodate the panelling, the slots being ¼" in depth, the width matched to the thickness of the panel pieces (⅜" in the one made).

CORNER POSTS

The four corner posts are then cut to length – don't overlook the extra length of the two top posts – and

planed to 1⅜" square. Mounted in the lathe, each post has a ball finial turned on its upper end as shown, after which each post is hand scraped and sanded smooth.

Now the corner posts are marked out to locate the positioning of the side and end rails. Fig. 2 shows this marking out in detail. Side and end rails are dowel jointed into the corner posts, a simple but adequate method which can be replaced by some

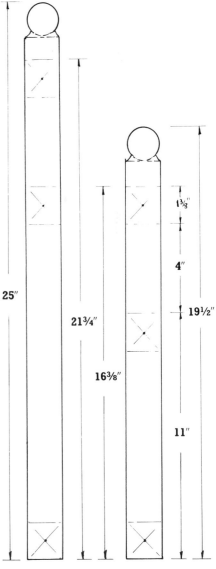

Fig. 2 Overall length and detailed marking out for corner posts. Mark out as shown on two adjacent sides to locate the position of side and end rails.

Photo. 5 Drilling spindle holes in rails.

difficult mortice and tenoning by those who wish to do so. The jointing of the corner posts to the side rails is quite straightforward, but a different approach and a little extra care is necessary when drilling for the joints between the corner posts and the end rails due to the angles at which they meet each other.

DOWEL JOINTING

As a first stage, drill all the dowel holes square into the ends of all the rails irrespective of whether they are side or end rails. Be generous with

depth in the case of the six end rails as some wood will be lost in making the angled cuts later. In order to ascertain the true length and the correct angle of each of these end rails it is best to make a full-size drawing of the top end of the cradle from the dimensions given in the diagram. Measurements taken from this will give true lengths. The angle used throughout is 95° and a sliding bevel should be set to this for marking-out purposes. *Note that it is necessary to mark out the outer pieces of end panelling to the same angle.* End rails and the outer panels

can then be butt to the correct length and angle (see Fig. 3).

Now the dowel holes are drilled into the corner posts at the previously marked positions. For the side rails these go in square and will present no problem, but those for the end rails must be drilled at an angle of 95°. Use the sliding bevel at the same setting as before to mark this angle at each drilling position. A dry assembly of end panels into rails, and rails to corner posts, is a good idea at this stage to check that all will eventually go together correctly.

SPINDLES

With one small turned spindle to each piece of panelling a total of 22 spindles is required. These, which may be to any design of your choice, were turned mainly from offcuts, mostly single but in some cases, where the piece was long enough, two were turned end to end and separated afterwards. Pieces 5″ long

Fig. 3 Details of dowel jointing of rails into corner posts and dimensions and spacing-out of turned spindles.

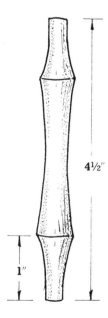

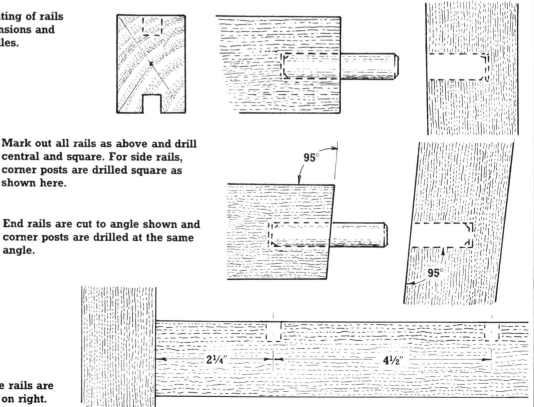

4½″

1″

For spindles, top and middle rails are drilled at centres as shown on right.

Mark out all rails as above and drill central and square. For side rails, corner posts are drilled square as shown here.

End rails are cut to angle shown and corner posts are drilled at the same angle.

95°

95°

2¼″   4½″

and 1″ square are needed to make a single spindle. The turned tenon at each end of each spindle is ⅜″ in diameter and parallel for ½″ before flaring out to form the spindle shape. Polish the spindles while they are still on the lathe. Part off on the lathe or saw to finished length, which is 4½″ overall.

When these are finished drill the holes into which they are to fit into the top edge of the middle rails and the lower edge of the top rails. The drilled holes are ⅜″ in diameter and ¼″ in depth. The top edges of all the top rails are rounded over so as to leave no sharp corners.

FINAL ASSEMBLY

Final assembly of the cradle body begins with the gluing up of the two end sections. First, dowels are glued into place in the holes drilled in the end rails. Then a little glue may be placed in the slots cut to accommodate the pieces of panelling and the panel pieces correctly assembled between the bottom and middle rails. Glue in the spindles

Photo. 7 **End section ready for gluing.**

Photo. 8 **End section in cramps.**

Photo. 6 **Checking position of spindles.**

between middle and top rails; then, with glue in the dowel holes in the corner posts and on the ends of the rails, the whole section is brought together. Cramp up with sash cramps, and with the surplus glue cleaned off leave until set, then remove the cramps.

The assembly is completed by gluing the dowels into the side rails, and the side panels and spindles into their respective slots and holes. Glue

is placed in the dowel holes and on the ends of the side rails, the sides then put together with the two end sections and cramped up. *Check that the cradle body goes together squarely while doing this.*

Measurement taken across the inside of the lower part of the cradle will give the precise measurements for the piece of ply which forms the bottom of the cradle. Anyone with an abundance of yew can make the bottom from solid material, but ply is quite suitable. The bottom should be a snug fit down on to the inside edges of the bottom rails. It is held in place by means of the screws which pass through it and into the rockers, as will be seen in Fig. 4.

ROCKERS

The final job is to make and fit the rockers. These are marked out with the help of the pattern given in Fig. 4. But check its measurements against your own cradle and adjust for any differences, especially in the shaping of each rocker to accommodate the bottom side rails. Cut to the correct shape and test for fit by having a trial, dry assembly. If all is well, drill and countersink holes through the bottom of the cradle, as shown; glue the rockers into position and screw down into each through the cradle bottom. This has the effect of sandwiching the bottom rails

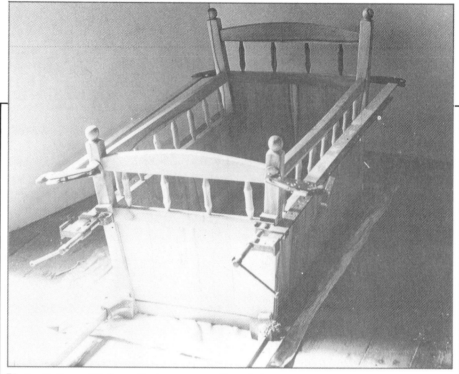

Photo. 9 Assembled cradle in cramps after gluing-up.

between the cradle bottom and the rockers, thus locking everything securely together.

FINISHING

After a light sanding down, a clear finish is applied to the cradle in order to preserve and enhance the appearance of the yew. A wax finish over a suitable clear sealer makes a nice job, but some, anxious to have a finish less susceptible to finger marking and the effects of moisture, might prefer to use polyurethane varnish or a pre-catalysed lacquer.

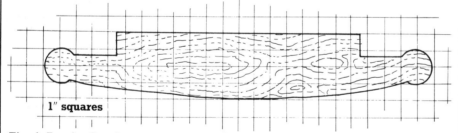

1″ squares

Fig. 4 A pair of rockers are cut out to the profile shown above.

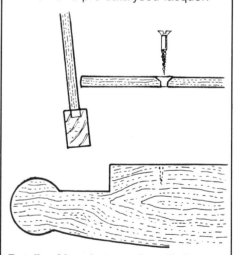

Details of how bottom of cradle is screwed through into rockers.

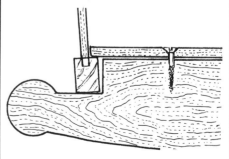

PART	DESCRIPTION	L	W	T	MATERIAL	QTY
\multicolumn{7}{c}{**CUTTING LIST**}
1	Corner posts (head)	25″	1½″	1½″	Yew	2
2	Corner posts (foot)	20″	1½″	1½″	Yew	2
3	Side rails	31½″	1½″	1″	Yew	6
4	End rails	18″	2½″	1″	Yew	2
5	End rails	16¾″	1½″	1″	Yew	2
6	End rails	14½″	1½″	1″	Yew	2
7	Panels (head)	15″	4½″	¼″	Yew	4
8	Panels (side and foot)	9½″	4½″	¼″	Yew	18
9	Rockers	24″	4″	1″	Yew	2
10	Bottom	32½″	18½″	½″	Plywood	1
11	Turned spindles	5″	⅞″	⅞″	Yew	22

SUNDRIES: Dowelling, wood glue, screws. To finish: polyurethane varnish or pre-catalysed lacquer or clear sealer with wax finish.

TURNING IN MINIATURE

With these exercises, plus a little ingenuity, you can make your own miniature tableware

The big advantage of turning in miniature is that you need only small pieces of timber of a kind readily available to everyone, whether living in the city or country.

Timber comes from the felled tree, mostly the limbs. City dwellers walking through the park will often come across small branches that have broken off old and decaying trees. Rubbish tips are also a useful source; you may be lucky enough to come across the odd piece of furniture that has been thrown away.

Friends save me bits and my timber store contains every type of species, including yew, ebony, holly, oak, lilac and other trees of the garden and hedgerow. Yew is one of the best, having close grain, beautiful colours and great strength. It polishes from the tools when correctly sharpened and applied – a

real adventure in turning. Ebony is expensive but is ideal for small work and polishes like glass. Turning lilac can be compared to turning box; most lilac trees are grafted to hawthorn stock, the timber is similar with long close grain and a beige to white colour. Oak is splendid in miniature work, and most of the fruit trees can be used.

Always check the timber for beetle and other attack. Timbers of the hedgerow may have wire, nails and leadshot embedded in them. Examine old furniture woods with great care to preserve the fine teeth of saws and the edges of turning tools. Offcuts from turners often find their way to the bonfire. Make sure they know about you, since they are usually generous people. Don't ignore the shipbreaker's yard and similar places.

Exotic timbers will generally need to be purchased. There are a number of specialists in this field who will find the exact material for you, but try all those from the countryside. If you haven't turned yew or laburnam then you have a great pleasure in store; and often at no cost. Turnings can also be made using ivory and bone. The techniques of cutting are a little different but this work is so delicate and a pleasure to execute.

Bones are no problem. Old bleached ones are best, but don't rob the dog or kill the mother-in-law – visit the butcher. Ivory will not need an elephant safari – old snooker balls, piano keys, hairbrushes are the best sources. If the bones need cleaning, first bury them in the garden for a while – nature is a good scourer – then scrub them and store to dry.

Fig. 2

SEASONING ESSENTIAL

Timber must be seasoned, even the small offcuts. A high moisture content may make easy work of turning but drying out will bring disaster. Timber in planks must be stored with stickers, in the flat, kept dry and with plenty of air circulation. Allow a year per inch of thickness. Seal the bends and branch cuts with paraffin wax, old paint, pitch or tar substitute – anything which will seal and leave the bark on. Small tree limbs (up to 2″) can be sawn into billets 1-2′ long or even smaller. Seal as for planks and name and date each piece. The billets can be stored in hessian sacks or spread in an outhouse on shelves. Heat should be avoided. Check periodically and keep adding new stuff as the seasoned material is used. (See Fig. 1).

Fig. 1

LATHE

The lathe need not be highly sophisticated and only the simplest of holding devices is needed. The Coronet Major is used for most work but when demonstrating in public the miniature lathe of Elliott or Toyo take the eye, and both are highly portable. For holding, a small chuck is available. Firm holding and accuracy in turning is a prerequisite for this work. For simple turning between centre a tiny driving fork, or a square hole cut in a block inserted or attached to the headstock, will give an effective drive.

TOOLS

Turning tools for this work, bought in the market place, seem never to be quite right for weight or style. The standard tools are too heavy. Making them to suit seems the answer. A good quality tool steel is essential and small lengths can be purchased from any fine tool merchant or bar stores.

A set of four meets the need.
1 Skew Chisel – *planing and shaping*
1 Parting Tool – *parting off and tiny beads*
2 Round Nosed Scrapers – *shaping inside and outside*

To hold their edge the tools must be hardened and tempered. The method used has been outlined by John Sainsbury in *Woodworking Crafts,* October 1982 issue. This is an easy way to gain professional results.

Manufacturers may yet recognise the growing need for smaller tools and design some for the woodturner. In the meantime they can be bought direct from myself. (For leaflet, send s.a.e. to Michael J. Baker, 6 Valletort Park, Brixham, S. Devon.) The skew chisel and parting tool should be ground exactly as the standard article and sharpened on the ground levels. The scraping chisels are ground at 30°. I used these tools all day long at the last Woodworker Show. All that was necessary was to grind them occasionally, sharpen them thoroughly each day, and from time to time during demonstrations touch them up with the rubberised abrasive slip.

The main points are that the tools must be small, otherwise they obscure the work; they must be correctly handled, to give comfort and ease in use, without cramp; and the blades must be strong and initially sharp. (See Fig. 2).

TURNING A BUD VASE

A section of branch 2½″ long by 1″ diameter is mounted in the three-jaw chuck attached to the Minimat lathe. Rough turn to round using a ⅜″ gouge and plane with a skew chisel to a perfect surface. Leave the portion nearest to the chuck unturned. Mark out with pencil and use the parting tool. Turn the bowl then the stem before removing the running centre to use the tiny scraping chisel to bore out and shape the case stem. Most of this cutting and shaping can be done with the skew and a polished finish should be the aim. Touch up with fine paper, if necessary, and burnish with a small bundle of shavings or hessian. Polish and either part-off or leave the case attached to the basic stem. Vases in variety of shape and size will present little difficulty. (See sequence Fig. 3 to Fig. 8).

Fig. 3

Fig. 4

Fig. 5

Fig. 6

Fig. 7

Fig. 8

GOBLETS

(See sequence Fig. 9 to Fig. 14).
These can be turned using the same
basic technique as with bud vases

Fig. 9

Fig. 10

Fig. 11

Fig. 12

Fig. 13

Fig. 14

but the heavy turning – i.e. the
cutting of the bowl – should be
carried out before turning the stem,
when the material is still strong.
Complete the bowl, then shape the
outside, finishing the stem last.
Polish or oil after burnishing.

The bowl can be first bored out
then finished with a scraper.
Alternatively a tiny gauge can be
used to do the entire job.

An alternative method of holding is
also shown using the drill chuck.
Here a small spigot has been cut on
the underside to permit assembly.
(See Fig. 15).

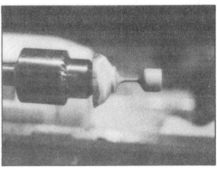

Fig. 15

Although the work shown has
been carried out on the miniature
lathe, the larger lathe will be quite
suitable. Use the highest speed the
lathe will allow. Tool rests may be a
problem since they will all tend to be
overlong. Make one from timber of
small section, screwed to a small
length of mild steel or angle iron.

Do not make excessive use of
abrasive paper since this will tend to
destroy sharp lines and burn over
the corners.

Have fun and see how small you
can get!

*(The next issue will contain an
article describing how you can make
your own tools for miniature turning.)*

CREATIVE USE OF THE ROUTER

The versatile router is invaluable, not only for hidden machining work, but also for adding interest to the appearance of a project

For those about to embark on an ambitious woodworking project, my message is clear . . . beg, borrow or preferably acquire a good router.

A good router is one with adequate power (above ½hp), plunge action and a price tag above £60. Perhaps I should not knock the cheapest of the range. One has to start somewhere and the raw amateur of today can be the router craftsman of tomorrow. It is just that the cheapest routers cannot include the robustness and quality of workmanship worthy of a project of which one expects to be justly proud.

The router is regularly employed to do basic structural work – i.e.

Fig. A2 Whilst interchange of cutters can produce original shapes, the standard ovolo will give a variety of effects at different depths.

machining work which is hidden from view, such as dowelling and housing. In this article, however, we will show you how the router can be used creatively to give warmth to a project and add interest to its lines.

USE OF SIDE FENCE

(See Fig. A). When moulding a straight edge of timber, the adjustable side fence is the natural choice for guiding the router. By adjusting the fence laterally, and varying the depth of cut, a variety of shapes can be formed from one single cutter. See Figs. A1 and A2. (See also sketch of ovolo cutter in Trend 7 group).

Conversely, attractive 'picture frame' type moulds can be obtained by running a series of cuts in parallel, fitting different cutters and superimposing them on each other (see Fig. B).

Fig. A Side fence has been fitted with an extension strip to give a longer bearing surface. A further insurance against running off course, at end of workpiece, is an 'overcut' board which should butt up tight against end of workpiece.

USEFUL TIPS

When using the side fence for edging work, affix a strip of thin plywood to the inside face of the fence so as to elongate the fence.

Fig. A1

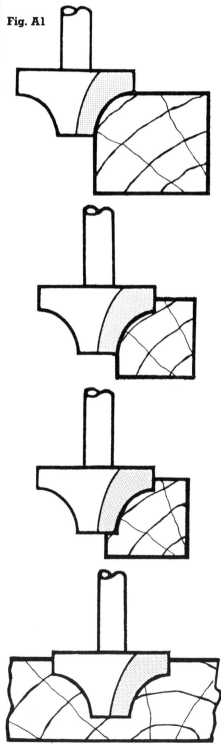

Fig. C1 The shield in 1¼″ mahogany was rough bandsawed and edges squared, smoothed and bevelled. Router with my anti-tipping block was passed around the workpiece anti-clockwise.

Fig. B A fine example of corner moulding where a number of passes have been made with three different cutters.

This will obviate the common problem of the router running off course as it reaches the end of the board.

A further insurance against this possibility is the introduction of an 'overcut' board (see Fig A). This has a dual purpose: apart from ensuring the router travels on a parallel path, the 'overcut' board prevents the router chipping out as it leaves the workpiece.

Fig. B2 Cutters used for the compound moulding on board edge.

Cutter 3/50 square groove	Cutter 7/2 outer ovolo mould	Cutter 84/42 'double' cove

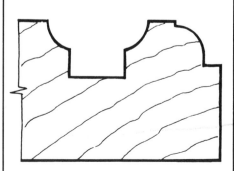

Fig B1 Cross section of wood showing more clearly the mould shapes produced by three passes of the router.

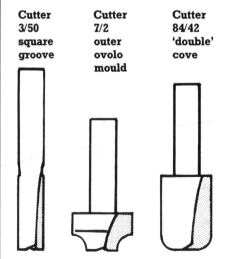

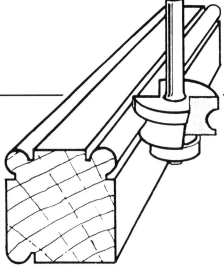

FREEHAND

Providing the original edge is smooth, guidance can be obtained direct from the cutter, using self-guided cutters. These have roller bearings mounted on their bases. (See sketch C, showing a bevel cutter 46/35 with bearing guide).

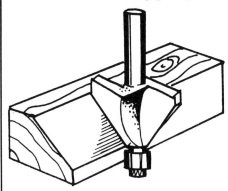

Fig. C A Ref. 46/35 Trend Self-Guide Cutter followed the square edge and produced a 35° bevel.

For a shaped workpiece, such as the shield illustrated at C2, this cutter is an ideal means of creating a bevel.

Fig. C3 illustrates a new introduction – a corner bead cutter with a self-guide facility.

Fig. C2 A finished shield which can be cut to shape, individually by band-sawing or in batches, using a template. The router does the edging work to perfection.

Fig. C3 Corner edging without a fence.

Cutters with guide pins rather than bearings are not recommended for professional wood finishes as they are inclined to mark the edges.

CORNER EDGING WITHOUT A FENCE

Freehand edging using self-guiding cutters precludes the need for a side fence.

The beading cutter Ref. 9/71 forms a neat radiused corner. Apart from its use to radius chair legs, attractive beading strips can be cut to embellish furniture.

CORNER BEADING

(See Fig. D). With a little imagination, even heating pipes can be attractively encased. If a decorative bead is cut on the edges of the box structure, the encasement can blend in with the furniture. The area within the box can be filled with polythene beads to retain the heat,

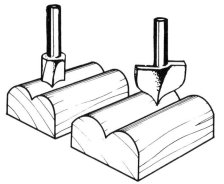

Fig. D1 Cutter Ref. 19/20.

Fig. D Boxed-in pipework can be given an attractive appearance if a decorative bead is applied to the corner edges.

Fig. E1 Same panel with template removed, showing the attractive effect of the groove cut with an 18/51 Classic panel cutter.

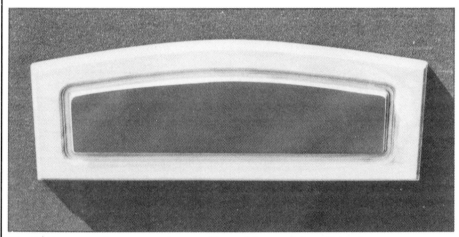

Fig. E Example of classic style panelling with template still in place.

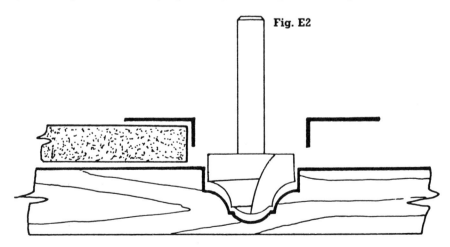

Fig. E2

obvious choice. But if cuts of irregular shapes are involved then templates are needed.

Since imperfections in the template will reflect in the finished work, care must be taken in making it. Preferably cut the template from 1/4″ thick hard plastic or dense plywood/hardboard.

Having chosen an appropriate panel cutter and guide bush, it is advisable to make some test runs on scrap wood.

Stick the template down with double-sided tape of a type that is removable – i.e. tape that will roll off with thumb after work completed.

Set router for shallow cutting – irrespective of generous power factor in router – for several reasons. Firstly, it is always easier to keep router on course when light cutting. Secondly, any burn marks can be skimmed off in final passes.

Should you decide to feed the router in an anti-clockwise direction, be sure to maintain constant side pressure to left, so router bush always engages the template.

To ensure against any possibility of tipping, 'pads' of same thickness as template can be stuck with D.S.T. at intervals around the working area so as to support the router base along its path. (An alternative is an anti-tipping block which affixes to router base – see Fig. C1).

and the top surface can be utilised for displaying decorative plate, silverware, etc. The cutter used for this finish was a Ref. 19/20 which has a 5/16″ radius. (A fence was used for guidance).

PANELLING USING A TEMPLATE

(See Fig. E). If panelling is exactly square or circular, straight edge guides and beam trammels are the

Fig. F

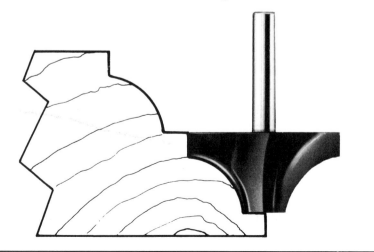

Fig. F1 Using the beam trammel with an ovolo cutter (Trend Ref. 7/7). A second cut at a greater depth offers a mould normally associated with a spindle moulder . . . a 'double' ovolo.

BEAM TRAMMEL

(See Fig. F). Circular work can be carried out with a beam trammel, using standard cutters. By adjusting the radius and interchanging cutters, numerous possibilities are opened up.

Fig. F4

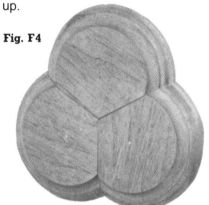

Even small circular patterns can be routed with a little ingenuity. An example of beam trammel work is shown at Fig. F4. My project was a candlestick base. A small home-made trammel (see Fig. F3) was fitted to the router base. This consisted of a sub-base with an adjustable slide to vary the radius. I chose Darvic plastic because it was on hand but any hard plastic or plywood would have been satisfactory. The router was set to first cut out three circular discs, using a ¼″ straight cutter followed by two circular cuts at different radii. (See Figs. F4 and F5).

Fig. F5

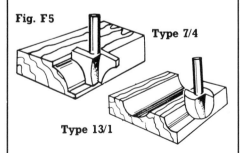

Type 7/4

Type 13/1

PROPOSED CANDLESTICK BASE

Three identical mahogany discs were cut using a mini-trammel, with two

Fig. F3 For small radii under 4″ the standard beam trammel is oversize. This home-made mini-trammel overcame this problem. The fine side adjuster was fitted to a slide on the router base to bring the fulcrum in and out.

moulds introduced: first ovolo Type 7/4, then radius cutter Type 13/1 on the top edge.

It shows how the router can be used for work normally only undertaken with a lathe.

PLANTING A DECORATIVE EDGE

(See Fig. G1). One attractive idea for decorative work is to rout a beading strip to one's own design by making a special jig. (See Fig. G).

The material is fed within the jig along a controlled path. The router is applied at 90° to form a series of stop grooves. The workpiece is reversed and cuts made from the opposite side.

To ensure the pattern is exact, with slots equivalent, a dovetail peg is slid into each preceding slot. It is not hammered into place. A sub-base, made from plastic or plywood, has length adjusting slots and a stop at one end. The base slides between two guides and ensures exact matching grooves. (See Figs. G and G2).

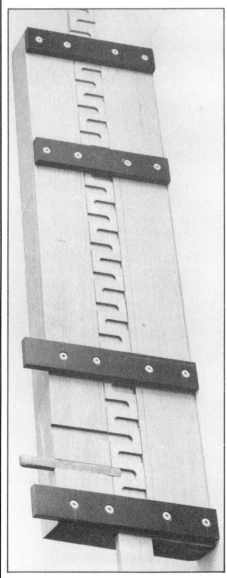

Fig. G

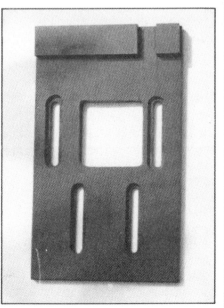

Fig. G2 The sub-base allows adjustment when screwed to the router base. The stop has an opening to allow the locator peg to enter.

Fig. G1 A finished length of bead made from a series of stop grooves cut from opposing sides.

TOY CAR DESIGN

From Newfoundland, a rather splendid toy limousine

The original model. Made from English brown oak, Canadian maple and American walnut. Finished in tung oil.

Most of us have an appreciation and even love for the motor vehicles of yesteryear, and to see a collection of these early forms of transportation is a pleasurable experience. Anyone who has been fortunate enough to visit the National Motor Museum at Beaulieu, for example, will know the joy of seeing machines that demonstrate the superb engineering and crafts-manship of that early period.

The toy or model car described in this article is an expression of those early vehicles. We are all familiar with the chunky wooden toy, and it is the intention of this design to go a few steps further. The objective, to get away from the elementary and endeavour to capture the very essence of the vintage motor car. The designer likes to think, and some may argue, that this miniature car falls somewhere between the simple toy and the scale model.

Depending on how one approaches a project of this kind, the result might well be a miniature car that is quite realistic. On the other hand, by using exotic and special woods, beautifully and properly finished, the outcome could be an object that will exhibit good workmanship and all the qualities of well chosen woods.

Having completed the project, the builder may wish to interpret other designs, both old and new. May its successful completion trigger such activity.

MACHINERY AND TOOLS

It is assumed the builder will possess a workshop more or less complete with basic machinery and hand tools.

Along with the table and band saw, a disc sander is considered an essential requirement. A woodturning lathe can certainly be put to use, but the simple needs of the design could be handled by an electric power drill set-up as a small lathe. This tool would be used to make such things as the wheels and headlamps.

A drill press has an important part to play. Some precision drilling has to be carried out and the machine will also be needed to accommodate drum sanders.

The plans reproduced here are half-size. When working from full-size plans, carbon paper can be used where necessary to transfer the designs to the wood, thus preserving the drawings.

Having studied the drawings and the material requirements, prepare stock to the various thicknesses. Hardwood is the material recommended, but the builder must make his own choice. The original model illustrated and described in this article was made from English brown oak, Canadian maple and American walnut.

CHASSIS

The chassis (A) forms the foundation and to make this will be the first step. Sand and finish to its proper shape together with the axle blocks

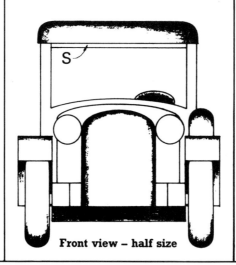

Front view – half size

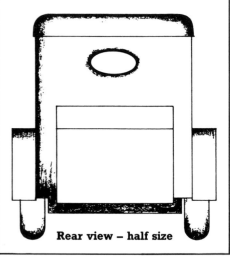

Rear view – half size

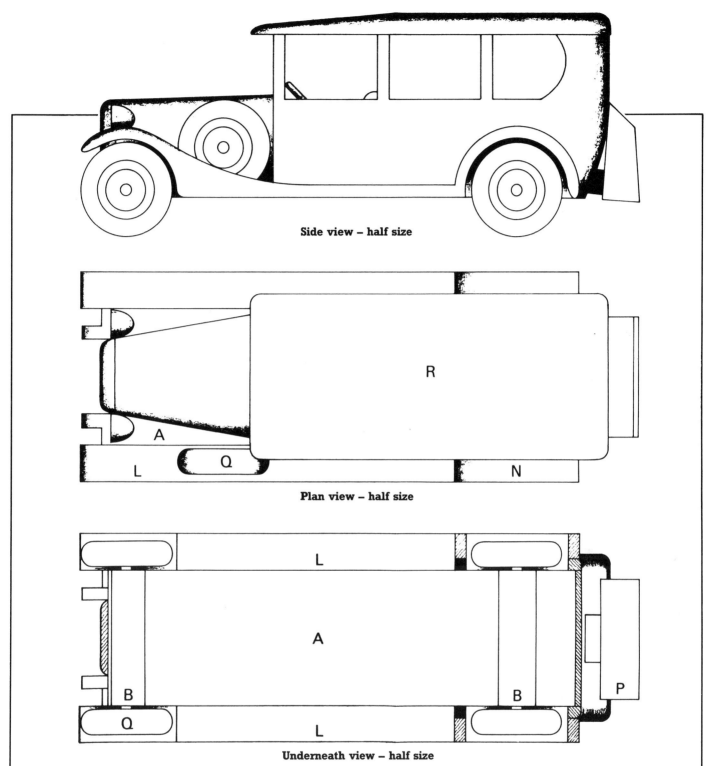

Side view – half size

Plan view – half size

Underneath view – half size

(B). Before drilling the holes for the axles in 'A', glue and clamp the axle blocks to the chassis.

The hood or bonnet (D) and radiator (C) should be made next. Before tapering 'D' block it would be best to first drill the ¼″ diameter holes that will accommodate the headlamps. The drilling is done while the hood is still a rectangular block. Final shaping and finishing of the two components 'D and C' is best done

after the two have been fitted and glued together.

Make the seats (G and H), the dash (E), the cab divider (I), and the car back (J). The car back can be left square at this stage, but cut and shape the rear window and carve away the interior as shown on the drawing. The final shaping of the back (J) can take place after the car sides (M) have been glued into place.

FITTING PARTS TO CHASSIS

All the following parts, the hood, dash, cab divider and car back can now be fitted to the chassis. Before gluing, make sure all the pieces are square and sanded smooth. For their precise location check against the profile of the car side (M). During the assembly the hood will provide support for the dash, and the assembled front and back seats will

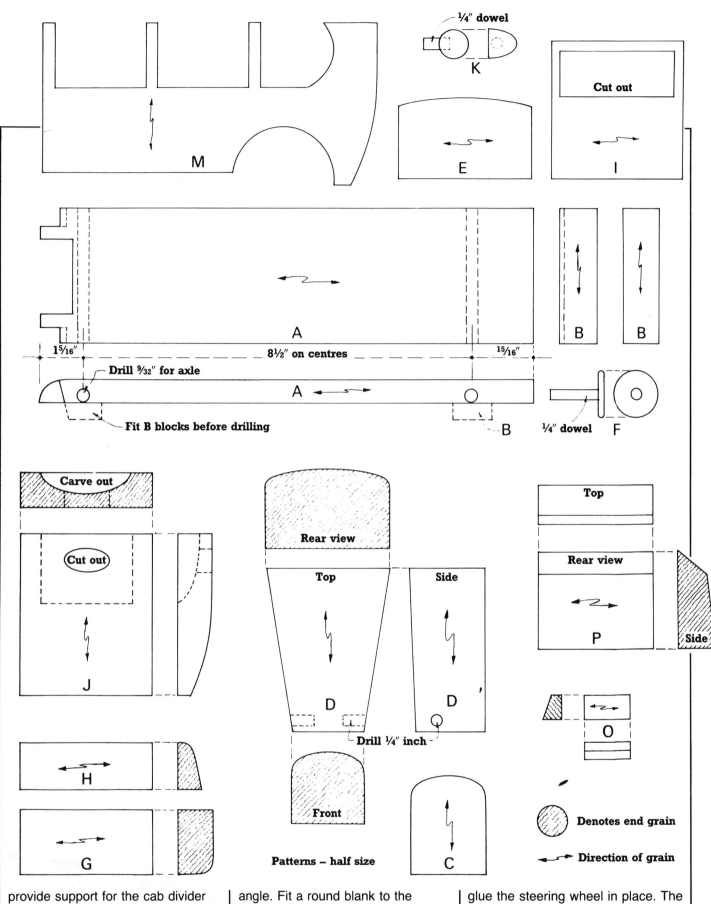

¼″ dowel

K

Cut out

M

E

I

A

8½″ on centres

1⁵⁄₁₆″   ¹⁵⁄₁₆″

Drill ⁹⁄₃₂″ for axle

A   B   B

A   B

Fit B blocks before drilling

¼″ dowel   F

Carve out

Cut out

J

Rear view

Top   Side

D   D

Drill ¼″ inch

Front

C

Top

Rear view

P   Side

O

Denotes end grain

Direction of grain

Patterns – half size

provide support for the cab divider and the car back.

The steering wheel and headlamps can now be made. To locate the wheel on the dash drill a ¼″ diameter hole at the appropriate

angle. Fit a round blank to the steering column (¼″ dowel), and shape and finish the wheel after the glue has set. The finishing work can be done on the electric power drill set-up as described earlier. Fit and

glue the steering wheel in place. The headlamps can be made on the same machine. Drill all holes before shaping. With the lamps made they also can be fitted and glued into position.

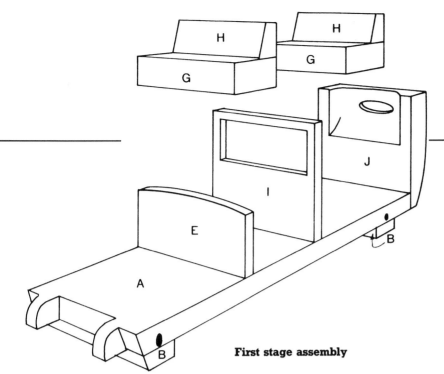

First stage assembly

SIDES

The car sides (M) are next. Cut out and finish to the profile outlined on the drawing. The bandsaw and flat files are the recommended tools here. Make sure the roof supports line up with the now assembled cab divider (I), and that the cut-out for the rear wheel (wheel well), is properly centered over the axle-hole in the chassis. With the car sides glued into position, the back can now be rounded-off and finished according to the outline and contours shown on the elevations.

WHEELS

To make the wheels use a precision hole-cutter. This will cut suitable blanks and drill the axle holes at the same time. For turning, spin the blanks on a ¼" x 2" round-head machine bolt. Tighten the blank onto the bolt with a nut and fit into the drill chuck of your mini-lathe. Turn the wheels and finish to the proper shape.

For the spare wheel that sits forward of the cab, simply cut-away the lower part and contour to fit the curve of the front-wing. Glue in place during the final stage of assembly.

As with most of the other parts for this car, the outline of the wings or mudguards and running boards can be transferred from full-size versions of the drawings to the wood by

means of carbon paper. Cut out these parts (L and N) with a band-saw and finish using the disc and drum sanders. Before glueing these parts into position, a final rounding-off by hand-sanding will remove the sharp edges where required.

Make the roof (R) and the trunk or boot (P), also the trunk spacer (O). Shape and finish these components but do not assemble until the finishing materials have been applied to the car body and various other parts.

FINISHING

Mask off the top surfaces of the car where the roof will sit and also the areas where the trunk will be fitted. Prior to applying finishes to the assembled car and other parts yet to be assembled, sand and smooth thoroughly.

The original model was finished in tung oil, an easily used material that brings out the character and beauty of the wood. Some may wish to use paints. If the car is to be used by children, make quite sure the materials to be used are non-toxic.

With all the parts of the car finished inside and out to the satisfaction of the builder, assemble the roof and the wheels onto the car body, together with the trunk. With a final polish and a good push, this car will be able to travel anywhere.

Note: full-size drawings for this car design can be obtained by sending $5.00 US to: Dawson Designs, P.O. Box 5624, St. John's, Nfld, Canada, A1C 5W8. Price includes postage and handling.

PART	DESCRIPTION	L	W	T	MATERIAL	QTY
A	Chassis	10¾"	2⅞"	½"	Hardwood	1
B	Axle blocks	2⅞"	13/16"	5/16"	Hardwood	2
C	Radiator	2⅛"	1⅝"	5/16"	Hardwood	1
D	Hood	3⁷⁄₁₆"	2¾"	1⅝"	Hardwood	1
E	Dash	2⅞"	1¾"	¼"	Hardwood	1
F	Steering Wheel	1" dia.	—	⅛"	Hardwood	1
G	Seat	2⅞"	1⅜"	¾"	Hardwood	2
H	Seat back	2⅞"	1"	½"	Hardwood	2
I	Interior divider	2⅞"	3"	¼"	Hardwood	1
J	Car back	2⅞"	3½"	¾"	Hardwood	1
K	Headlights	⅝" dia.	—	¾"	Hardwood	2
L	F. wings and running boards	8¼"	1⅝"	¾"	Hardwood	2
M	Car sides	7⅜"	3½"	¼"	Hardwood	2
N	Rear wings	2⅞"	1⅝"	½"	Hardwood	2
O	Trunk spacer block	1"	½"	⅜"	Hardwood	1
P	Trunk	2⁹⁄₁₆"	2¹⁄₁₆"	⅞"	Hardwood	1
Q	Wheels	2" dia.	—	9/16"	Hardwood	5
R	Roof	7⅞"	3½"	⁷⁄₁₆"	Hardwood	1
S	Top frame – windshield	2⅞"	¼"	³⁄₃₂"	Hardwood	1

CUTTING LIST

SUNDRIES: ¼" dowel for axles, steering column and headlights. 4 ¼" washers.

A WOODEN FIREPLACE SURROUND

This Adam style design could be adapted to fit your fireplace.

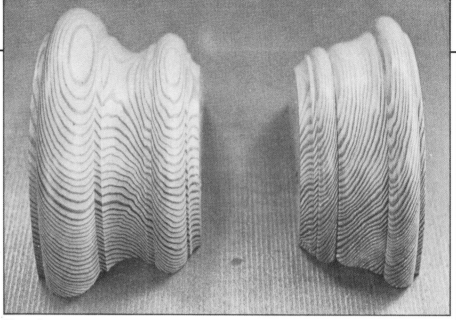

Photo 2

Some 20 years ago, while building my bungalow "Ellen Vale" – so named from the valley we overlook – I installed in the lounge a rather plain but elegant Italian marble fireplace.

Recently, it occurred to me that the addition of an Adam style surround would enhance the appearance of the fireplace and bring it back into fashion. Since the fireplace is quite large, a ready-made surround was out of the question. So I decided to construct the surround myself and to photograph the various stages for the benefit of other woodworkers who may wish to have a go themselves.

With a fairly clear idea in mind of how I wished the surround to look, I began by making a few drawings of the mouldings etc that would be needed.

Photo 1

Photo 1 shows such a drawing for the half columns, base and plinth. The two half columns were made as one whole column; so was the base and capital. Having determined the sizes I would require, the base, column and capital pieces were glued together with a thin piece of card between the piece, i.e. in the joints. This was to enable me to "split" the sections into halves when turning was complete.

Photo 2 shows a base and a capital after being turned and split. I

use the term split lightly. In fact, they part quite easily with a wood chisel driven gently into the card joint. I drilled the column blank ⁵/₁₆" diameter and about 2″ deep at each end and turned it on these centres. (The idea was to use the drilled holes for setting up the column for the fluting operation.)

FLUTING JIG

To flute the columns I made a simple jig, photos 3 and 4. One end of the jig can be seen in close-up in photo 4. The other end was similar and allowed the column to rotate on the ⁵/₁₆" diameter fitted steel spindles in the holes previously drilled.

I then cut a template from a thin piece of card the same diameter as the turned column, and divided the

Photo 3

template equally into the number of flutes I would require. (A similar template can be seen in photo 4.)

Photo 4

The template was then glued to one end of the column so that each division would line up with an index mark on the jig end as the column was rotated. (See pencil pointing photo 4.) Two pieces of lath were tacked to the jig, one each end, to give a predetermined length for the flutes, i.e. as stops for the router.

The fence was now fitted to the router and the cutter positioned so

Photo 6

that the centre of the cutter coincided exactly with the index mark. I used Trend cutter ref. No. 12/7 (see diagram A), setting the depth stop as required. With the first template division mark lined up with the index mark, a "holding screw" was inserted through the jig end and into the column end. This keeps the column steady and secure whilst routing.

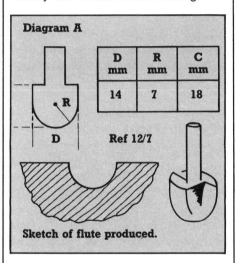

Diagram A

	D mm	R mm	C mm
	14	7	18

Ref 12/7

Sketch of flute produced.

CUTTING THE FLUTES

The first flute was now cut. The sequence *'remove the holding screw, re-position the column for the next flute, replace the holding screw and so on'* was then followed until all the

flutes were completed. A little thought is needed, when positioning the template on to the column end, to ensure the flutes show equally when the half columns are complete.

Photo 5 shows the base, column and capital split and ready for assembly. (Note the holes previously referred to and the film of thin card still adhering to the pieces.) Photo 6 shows the pair of half columns complete. At this stage they had been given a light cut on the surface

planer which removed the remaining card traces and trued everything up.

JAMBS

The body of the surround is made mainly from ¾" birch plywood, and I decided to make the jambs next. Photo 7 shows the basic start including the groundwork for the plinth the half columns would sit on. Photo 7a gives an internal view of this same component with triangular blocks glued in for added strength and rigidity.

Photo 7

MOULDINGS

Photo 8 shows the mouldings I made for the column plinths. The groundwork needed to be thickened up to take these mouldings and this

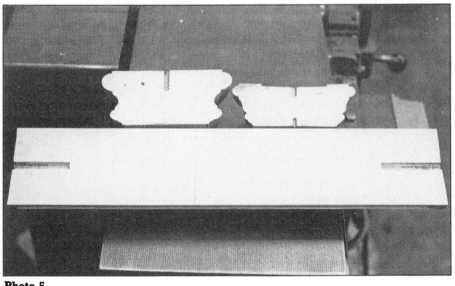

Photo 5

Photo 7a

can be seen in photo 9. I used ¾″ and ¼″ ply (I did not have any 1″) with all mating surfaces glued and pinned. In this same photograph one can see the mouldings fitted and the half column in place. I also needed to profile this member to fit around the marble hearth.

Photo 8

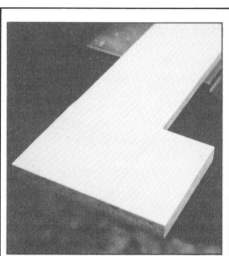

Photo 9

Photo 10

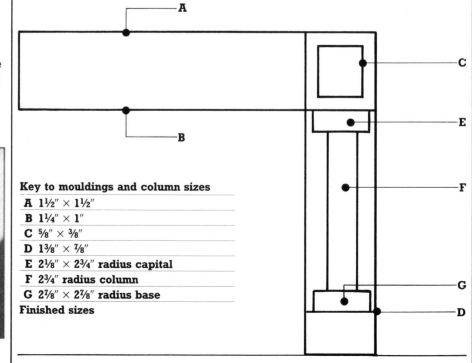

Photo 11

TOP SECTION

The top section was next, again ¾″ ply pinned and glued together. Photo 10 shows the first stage of this component. Note blocks glued to inside. These I inserted wherever I could. They consist of no more than ply offcuts. For the top shelf I glued two pieces of ¾″ ply together mainly to get the thickness I wanted and to receive the mouldings I had planned for. See photos 11 and 12.

Key to mouldings and column sizes

A 1½″ × 1½″
B 1¼″ × 1″
C ⅝″ × ⅜″
D 1⅜″ × ⅞″
E 2⅛″ × 2¾″ **radius capital**
F 2¾″ **radius column**
G 2⅞″ × 2⅞″ **radius base**
Finished sizes

Photo 12

The mouldings for the top shelf are shown in photo 13. For some unknown reason I overlooked getting a close-up shot of the mouldings I made for the bottom edge of this component, though they can be seen fitted elsewhere.

REMOVABLE

I wished to make the whole thing easily removable and did not want any fixings to show. Whilst the jambs are fixed with simple metal brackets

Photo 13

Photo 14

Photo 15

Photo 16

housed internally, I decided to make keyhole fixing plates for the top section. See photos 14 and 15. It is now a simple job to remove the surround completely when decorating needs to be done. Note also in these photographs the use of triangular glue blocks.

The next operation was for me the most interesting and I could begin to see things taking shape. The project was now beginning to look like a fireplace surround. Photos 16, 17 and 18 show the mouldings fixed; again all mating surfaces glued and pinned. The larger moulding I made on the spindle moulder, making my own cutters from old planer blades.

Photo 17

Photo 18

Photo 20

Photo 19

The astragal mouldings to form the panels were made with the router and Trend Cutter ref. no. 18/51. (See diagram B.)

As the surround was to be a sprayed white finish I did not see the point in spending hours carving the decorations. These are moulded and are very good in detail; the grain of the "timber" can be seen quite easily. They are obtainable in various wood colours from Valform, Lansdown Industrial Estate, Cheltenham, Glos., GL5 8PL.

Diagram B

D mm	d mm	C mm	R mm
19·0	6.4	12.7	3.2

Ref 18/51

Sketch of mould produced

Photo 21

Photo 22

my friend, and the loan of his equipment, I am quite pleased with the results. I chose a white cellulose base finish, somewhere between matt and eggshell which was obtained together with a suitable primer from Trimite Limited, Arundel Road, Uxbridge, Middlesex, UB8 2SD.

Photo 23 shows the surround in its final position and awaiting spraying, and photo 24 is the completely finished surround.

DECORATIONS

The whole group I chose can be seen in photo 19. What I did find with these pieces was that the back surface was not at all flat. This I considered to be essential or they would not bed down neatly and would cause problems with gluing. However, I overcame this minor problem very simply by rubbing them on a sheet of glasspaper drawpinned to a flat surface. Groups of the decorations can be seen fixed in photos 20, 21 and 22.

FINISHING

A most essential part to a good finish is filling and stopping. All nail holes, open grain or any other imperfections need to be treated in great detail, or rest assured they will show very clearly when finishing, or in my case spraying, takes place.

I used Metalux from J. Brown Co. Ltd., Dewsbury. It is a two-part filler and sets very quickly. The problem I found was it very soon clogged the glasspaper, though I overcame this to a large extent by removing most of the surplus with a sharp cabinet scraper.

Spraying time arrived and I draped polythene sheets in the garage to form my own "spray booth", *not forgetting to remove the car first.*

I had not done any of this work before, though with the guidance of

Photo 23

Photo 24

You will gain a lot of satisfaction from completing this project successfully

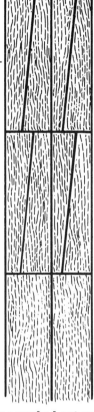

Fig. 3 Staves marked out on board.

Long before the days of washing machines it was quite usual for clothes to be washed in circular tubs known as keelers. They were made from a number of tapered pieces of wood, usually oak, called staves which were securely held together by wrought iron hoops (Figs. 1 and 2).

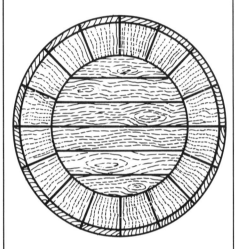

Fig. 1 Plan of Keeler.

Shrub tubs are constructed in a similar manner to keelers but because they do not have to be watertight they are not quite so difficult to make.

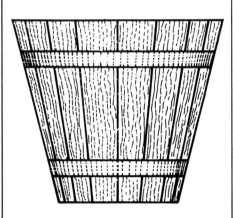

Fig. 2 Elevation.

The bottom of the tub is made from a number of narrow boards accurately jointed and fitted into a channel cut into the staves. If a watertight keeler is required it is essential for the chamfer of the

bottom to be a good fit in this channel.

The number and width of the staves will determine the size of the keeler. If we wanted it to be 2' (612mm) diameter at the top tapering

Fig. 4 24 staves drawn in circle with radiating lines from centre to ascertain bevel angle.

to 1'3" (380mm) at the bottom and 1'6" (457mm) deep we should require 24 staves. The staves would be 3" (76mm) wide at the top and taper to 1⅞" (48mm) at the bottom.

EDGE ANGLE

From a board 6' (1836mm) long, 11" (280mm) wide and 1" (25mm) thick the 24 staves are marked out as shown in Fig. 3. Having cut out all the staves it is now necessary to plane the edges to the correct angle so that when they are assembled they will butt closely together and not leak. The most straightforward method of finding this angle is to set out the number of staves in the circle and draw radiating lines from the centre (Fig. 4). According to the number of staves in the keeler so will the angle vary and it is consequently essential to have the right number of staves in the drawing. For a 24-stave keeler the bevel angle is 82½° as shown in Fig. 5. *Although absolute precision regarding the width of the individual staves does not have to be*

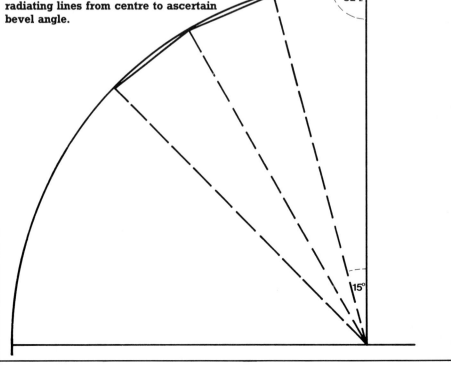

adhered to the edge angle must be exact. (With this number of staves, a simple planing jig is worth constructing. – Ed.)

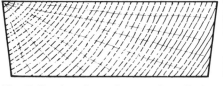

Fig. 5 Section through stave bevelled at 82½°.

BOTTOM

Once the staves are tapered and their meeting edges bevelled their ends must be squared off. Squaring off is done from the centre line, not the edge, so that the angle between each bevelled edge and the lower end of the stave is exactly the same (Fig. 6). From this squared off end a gauge is used to mark off the groove which will accommodate the bottom. A cooper would use a croze to cut this groove into the assembled tub but we shall saw it out on the narrow or inside face of the stave. The groove needs to be about ⅜″ (10mm) wide and the bottom should fit the groove as shown in Fig. 7 and not as shown in Fig. 8.

If our keeler is intended to hold water it will help if two short dowels are put in the edges of each stave as in Fig. 9. The dowel holes are drilled at an exact angle of 90° to the edge of the stave and the dowels are cut slightly shorter than the combined length of the holes. If this precaution is overlooked and the dowels 'bottom' the staves will never come together.

For a shrub tub which is not intended to be watertight the dowels can be omitted.

The bottom, which is made from accurately jointed narrow boards, should be dowelled together whether the tub is to hold water or not. To preserve, as far as is possible, the bottom in a flat condition, the boards

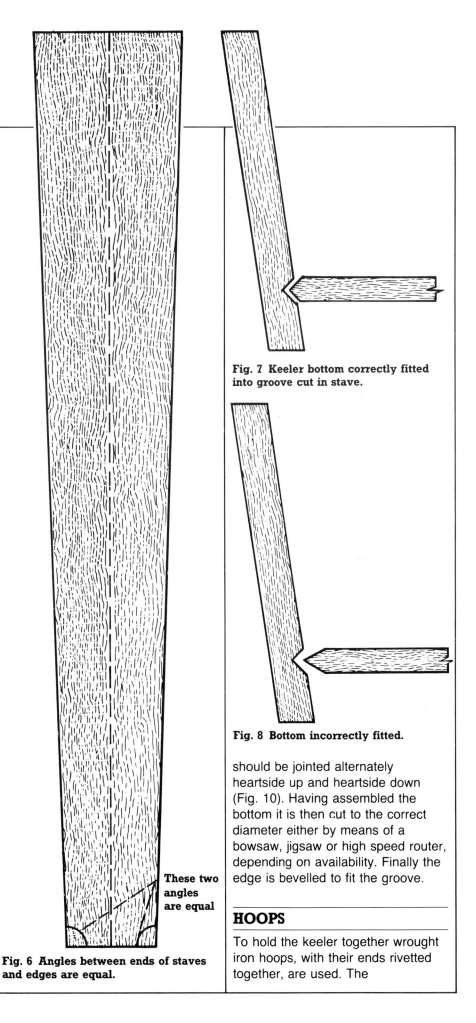

These two angles are equal

Fig. 6 Angles between ends of staves and edges are equal.

Fig. 7 Keeler bottom correctly fitted into groove cut in stave.

Fig. 8 Bottom incorrectly fitted.

should be jointed alternately heartside up and heartside down (Fig. 10). Having assembled the bottom it is then cut to the correct diameter either by means of a bowsaw, jigsaw or high speed router, depending on availability. Finally the edge is bevelled to fit the groove.

HOOPS

To hold the keeler together wrought iron hoops, with their ends rivetted together, are used. The

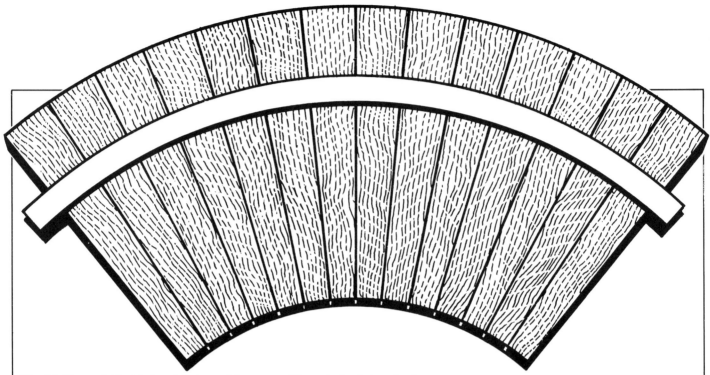

Fig. 11 Staves laid side by side to enable curve of hoop to be determined.

circumference of the tub is measured at the position where the hoops are to be positioned and sufficient overlap for the rivet allowed before the hoop iron is cut to length. The iron now has to be curved to enable the hoop to fit the tapered sides of the keeler. The staves are laid out side by side on a flat surface as in Fig. 11. The iron strip is laid on a really solid base (I have a short length of railway line) and one edge is hammered along its entire length. After a few blows the curvature is checked by laying the iron strip on top of the laid out staves. When the curve of the strip matches the curve of the staves the ends of the strip are drilled and rivetted. Two hoops will be needed; the upper hoop will of course be that bit longer than the lower one.

ASSEMBLY

It will probably be less difficult to assemble the keeler if it is placed upside down. Put four staves on one side of the bottom with the bevelled edge engaged in the groove. Place four more staves, similarly engaged opposite them. More staves are added until about half of them are in position when the smaller hoop is gently slipped in place. The remaining staves are put in place and the hoop is ready for driving home. For this task, a cooper's driver is the correct tool to use. It is like a cold chisel except that it has a groove in place of a cutting edge. The groove is placed on the edge of the hoop which is then hammered evenly all the way round. A block of hardwood will act quite well in place of a driver.

The second hoop can now be put in position and driven home to complete the keeler.

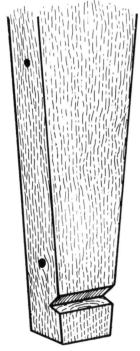

Fig. 9 Channeled stave bored for dowels.

Fig. 10 Bottom boards alternate heartside up and down.

CUTTING LIST						
PART	DESCRIPTION	L	W	T	MATERIAL	QTY
1	Staves[1]	18″	3″	1″	Oak	24
2	Bottom boards	15″	2½″	1″	Oak	6

NOTES: 1. See Fig. 3 for method of cutting out 24 staves from one board 6′0″ x 11″ x 1″.
SUNDRIES: 2 iron strips to make 2 hoops, dowels (optional).

THE DOVETAIL JOINT

*Well-made dovetail joints are a mark of craftsmanship. They improve
the construction and enhance the appearance of furniture*

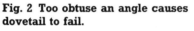
Short grain

If properly made, the dovetail joint is mechanically strong and cannot come apart except from the direction in which it was put together. The joint consists of wedge-shaped pins which fit into similarly shaped sockets.

BOX DOVETAIL

As its name suggests, this joint is used at the corners of boxes and its correct form is shown in Fig. 1(a). Its incorrect form is shown in Fig. 1(b).

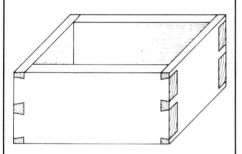

Fig. 1(a) Correctly formed Box Dovetail.

The difference is a matter of appearance. In 1(a) the pins are cut on the end pieces and the sockets cut on the front and back, with the result that less end grain is shown at the front. In 1(b) the joint is cut the other way round and a great deal of end grain is displayed.

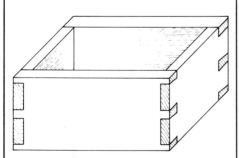

Fig. 1(b) Incorrectly Dovetailed Box.

Provided the joint is properly marked out and carefully cut the box dovetail is not difficult to make. There have been many arguments as to the correct method of setting out: whether the pins should be set

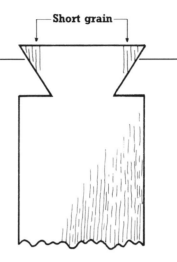

Fig. 2 Too obtuse an angle causes dovetail to fail.

out first or the sockets. The beginner may find it easier to cut the sockets first but both methods will be described. Whatever the method it is first necessary to decide on the angle of slope of the pins. Too obtuse an angle must be avoided because the short grain of the dovetail is easily broken when pulled and the joint will fail (Fig. 2). If there is insufficient angle the joint will have no holding power. A compromise can be reached by giving the tails a slope of 1 in 6 for softwood or 1 in 8 for hardwood.

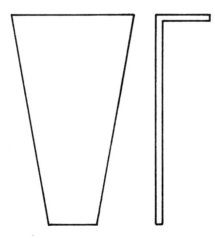

Fig. 3 Dovetail template. Front and side elevations.

Marking out is simplified if a dovetail template is made from sheet metal to the desired slope (Fig. 3). If many dovetails are to be cut it will probably be worthwhile buying a

template which has provision for fitting blades with slopes of 1 in 6 or 1 in 8. It is also possible to set the required slope on a sliding bevel and use this to mark out the tails. For maximum strength and good appearance the pins should be as light as possible and not spaced too far apart.

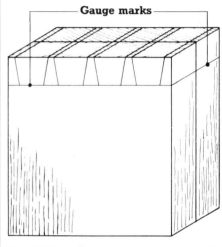
Gauge marks

Fig. 4 Sloping lines of sockets marked out.

'SOCKETS FIRST' METHOD

The pieces are planed true and the ends accurately shot on the shooting board. The front and back pieces are placed face to face in their final positions and tacked together with fine panel pins. The marking gauge is set to the thickness of one of the sides and the ends of the two pieces are gauged.

Half of the width of a socket is then marked off at the two ends of the gauge line and the intervening space is divided into as many equal parts plus one as there are to be whole sockets. From each dividing line, half the width of a socket is marked on both sides. Using either the template or the sliding bevel the sloping lines are marked (Fig. 4). Finally lines are squared over the ends.

When sawing the sockets, it helps if the pinned front and back pieces

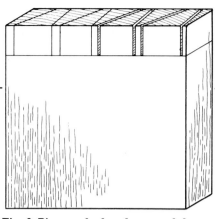

are gripped in the vice at such an angle that the saw can be held upright while the right hand halves of the sockets are sawn. Having made all the right hand cuts the two pieces are slanted in the vice at the opposite angle while the remaining halves of the sockets are sawn. When both ends have been marked and sawn the pins are withdrawn and the pieces separated in

Fig. 6 Pins marked and squared down. Pins on right sawn down to gauge line.

readiness for marking the pins on the side pieces.

Grip one of the side pieces upright in the vice with the outerside facing you. The front is placed on this piece at right angles with the inside facing downwards and the edges precisely level. By inserting the point of the saw in the kerf the pins can be marked on the end grain. Identification marks are pencilled on both pieces before separating. From the marked lines on the ends the pins are squared down to the shoulder lines (Fig. 6).

The sockets between the tails are cut away with a small bevel edged chisel. If the sockets are wide as in Fig. 7, much of the waste can be

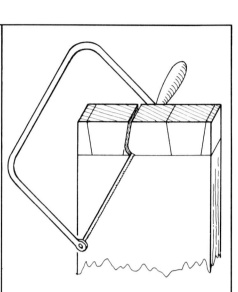

Fig. 7 Wide socket – waste sawn out with Coping Saw.

sawn out with a coping saw. Saw almost down to the line and pare away the remainder with a bevel edged chisel. The waste between the pins on the side pieces is also largely removed with the coping saw and finished off with the chisel. The joint can now be assembled.

One of the ends is held upright in the vice and the pins glued. Check

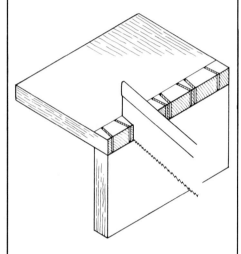

Fig. 5 Saw in kerf of sockets marking pins on end grain.

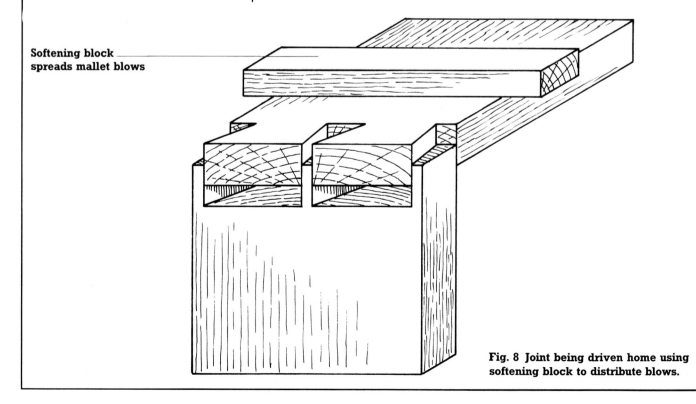

Softening block
spreads mallet blows

Fig. 8 Joint being driven home using softening block to distribute blows.

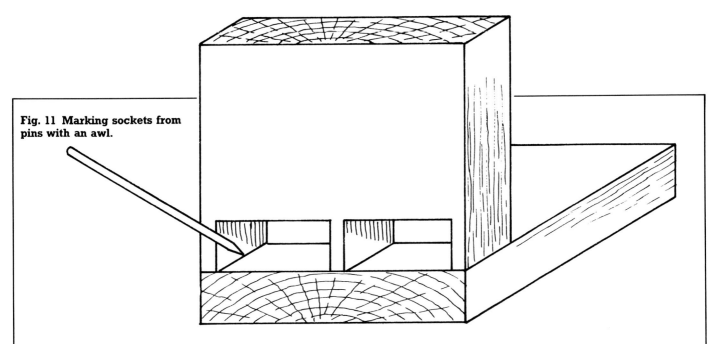

Fig. 11 Marking sockets from pins with an awl.

the identifying marks and place the front (or back as appropriate) in position. With a mallet, gently tap this piece to engage the pins. Then with a piece of waste wood placed across the top to act as a softening block and to spread the blows, drive the joint home (Fig. 8).

'PINS FIRST' METHOD

This method will probably prove easier for the inexperienced although it takes a little longer.

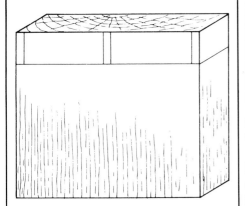

Fig. 9 Pins spaced out with dividers and lines squared down.

As before, all the pieces are planed true and the ends shot on the shooting board. The marking gauge is set to the thickness of the front (or back) and a shoulder line is gauged on the side pieces. On the shoulder line and on the outer face is

measured off at each end half the thickness of the thinnest side of the pin. Between these marks, step out with dividers as many parts plus one as there are to be whole pins. On each side of these divisions mark off half the thickness of the pin (Fig. 9).

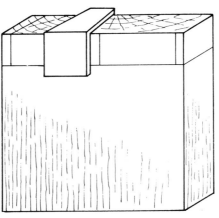

Fig. 10 Marking ends of pins with template.

From these marks lines are squared down to the shoulder line. The work is gripped upright in the vice and the ends of the pins are marked with the template or sliding bevel (Fig. 10). It is advisable to square down the lines on the other face. With a dovetail saw on the waste side of the lines the pins are sawn down to the shoulder lines. The bulk of the waste between the pins is sawn out with a coping saw and the remainder chiselled away.

The sockets are marked from the pins by laying the piece for the sockets flat on the bench and placing the pins vertically on it (Fig. 11). Using a sharply pointed awl, the shape of the pins is marked on the piece to be socketed. Identifying marks are pencilled on the two pieces. Lines are squared across the ends, the sockets sawn and the waste chiselled out.

LAPPED DOVETAIL

This joint is used to join drawer fronts to their sides because end grain is not shown at the front but only at the sides (Fig. 12). The drawer front is thicker than the sides to allow the length and width of the pins to equal the thickness of the sides.

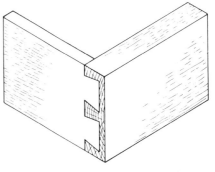

Fig. 12 Drawer front Lap-dovetailed.

The marking gauge is set to the thickness of the sides and a shoulder line A (Fig. 13) is scribed all round at

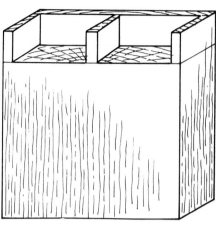

Fig. 15 Finished drawer front with pins cut out.

the end of the front, except of course for the outer face. In first class work, where a gauge mark across the top edge of a drawer front is unacceptable, a pencil line can be squared across. A well sharpened H pencil will be hard enough and the mark be easily erased after the joints have been cut. Holding the stock of the gauge against the inner face of the drawer front, another line B is gauged along the edge.

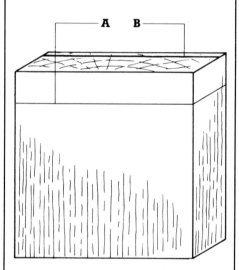

Fig. 13 Scribing shoulder and edge lines on drawer front.

The pins are set out by marking half the thickness of the pin from each end of the front on the shoulder line A. With a pair of dividers step out equally as many spaces plus one as there are to be whole pins. Half

the thickness of the pins is marked on either side of these marks and lines are squared down to the ends (Fig. 14).

Using either a template or a sliding bevel the dovetails are marked on the edge. With the dovetail saw held at the required angle cuts are made slightly outside the marked lines down to both gauge lines. Removal of the waste is by means of a bevel edged chisel.

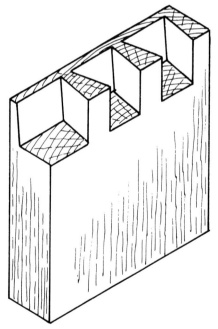

Fig. 16 Sloping cuts prevent joint coming together properly.

Fig. 15 shows the finished drawer front with the pins cut out. It is essential when cutting out the pins to keep the chisel upright and not allow the cuts to slope outwards (Fig. 16) otherwise the joint will not fit together properly. The sockets in the drawer

sides are marked from the front by placing the end grain of the front towards the end of the side in the correct position for assembly and marking with an awl (Fig. 17).

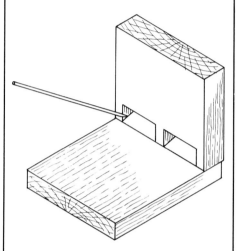

Fig. 17 Marking sockets from pins with an awl.

Alternatively the sockets on the drawer sides can be cut first and from these the pins on the front can be marked (Fig. 18). The front is held upright in the vice and the side supported over it at a right angle, with its end level with the gauge line on the edge. The pins are marked with an awl, the marks squared down on the inner face and the pins cut in the usual way.

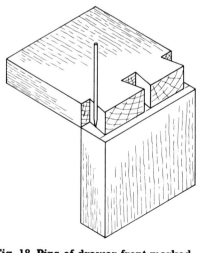

Fig. 18 Pins of drawer front marked from sockets.

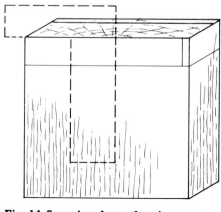

Fig. 14 Squaring down the pins.

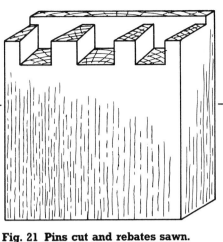

Fig. 21 **Pins cut and rebates sawn.**

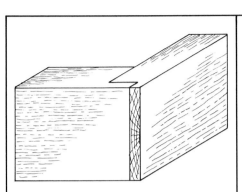

Fig. 19 External appearance of Double Lap-dovetail.

DOUBLE LAP DOVETAIL

This joint has a lap on both pieces which hides the dovetails and shows the minimum of end grain (Fig. 19). If pins are to be set out on a drawer front the marking gauge is set to the thickness of the side and a line is scribed on the inside and top and bottom of the ends. The gauge is then set to one third the thickness and a second line marked parallel to the others (Fig. 20).

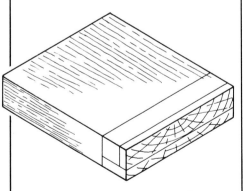

Fig. 20 Drawer front scribed with marking gauge for Double Lap-dovetail.

The pins are set out with the dividers on the shoulder line, squared to the edge and the dovetails marked on the end with the template as far as the outer lines. In this joint, where neither pins nor sockets are visible, it is usual to make the pins and sockets equal in size.

With the dovetail saw, the pins are sawn on the slant and the waste

chiselled away. The saw then cuts down the outer gauge lines and, when the cuts meet, the joint will appear as in Fig. 21.

To set out the sockets on the sides, set the gauge to two thirds the thickness and mark a shoulder line at the end and on the side edges. Place the stock of the gauge against the inner face of the side and mark a line on the end edge. The sockets are now scribed from the pins with an awl in a similar manner to that shown in Fig. 17. The marked lines are squared over as far as the gauge line. Having sawn down the lines, the waste is chiselled out. Fig. 22 shows the completed sockets. Sometimes, to improve the appearance of this joint, the corner is rounded over.

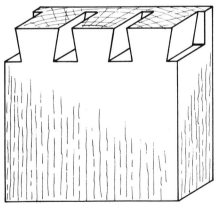

Fig. 22 Completed sockets of Double Lap-dovetail.

BOX DOVETAIL WITH EDGE MITRE

The joint depicted in Fig. 23 has a neat appearance at the corner and is mainly used where a moulding is worked on the edge. The dovetail

nearest to the mitre is cut square instead of the usual dovetail angle.

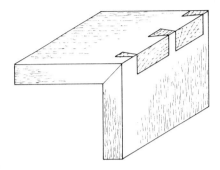

Fig. 23 Box dovetail with edge mitre.

BOX DOVETAIL WITH REBATED EDGE

The dovetail is set in from the rebated edge and a small square is formed to fill in the end of the rebate (Fig. 24).

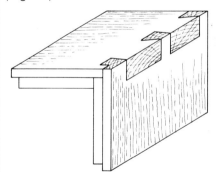

Fig. 24 Box dovetail with rebated edges.

CARCASE LAPPED DOVETAIL

To overcome any likelihood of the sides warping and twisting outwards small dovetails are cut at the ends (Fig. 25).

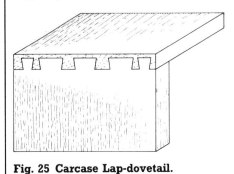

Fig. 25 Carcase Lap-dovetail.

For those of you possessing a green thumb and who would like to display some of your plants indoors, this tiered plant stand may meet your fancy

Fig.1

The stand is designed to keep all the plants close together yet facilitate easy watering and simultaneously provide adequate sunlight. Fig. 1 illustrates this with an assortment of African Violets. There are two semi-circular shelves on which to arrange your plants as desired. Each of the two shelves is constructed with a different radius enabling the sun's rays to reach each plant.

Unit support is provided by three legs which connect at the top of the stand to form an apex. Reinforcement is added by attaching each shelf to each of the three legs. A top finishes off the stand and conceals the connection where the legs join at the apex.

I have selected eastern white pine (pinus strobus) for its construction; however, any wood species can be used to blend with the decor of one's home. Eastern white pine is very abundant here in the northeastern part of the United States and is one of my favourite furniture woods. It is creamy white in colour and very soft textured because of its low density (.25) making machining or handtooling extremely easy and fast. Another advantage of the white pine is its ability to take a wide variety of stains if artificial colour is desired.

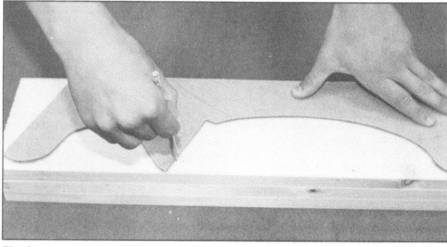

Fig. 2

THE LEGS

To begin the construction of the stand, the legs must be designed. When selecting a design, I took into consideration some important factors.

Support/Strength: The legs are to support the two semi-circular shelves. Therefore, notched flats are provided on each leg. The size of the flats will assist in determining the width of each shelf. In addition, the top of each leg is cut special in order to facilitate the attachment of the top.

Stock Selection: Three-quarter thickness provides ample strength.

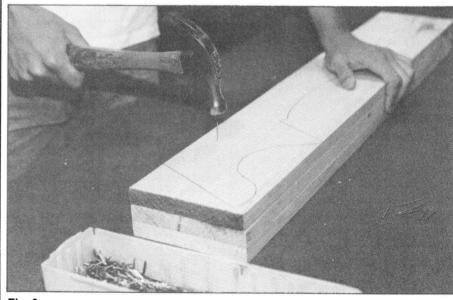

Fig. 3

Grain Direction: When selecting the wood for each leg, it is important to have the grain direction running with the length of the leg. Also avoid spike, large, or black knots when using eastern white pine in order to have maximum strength.

Design: I have provided some irregular contours into the shape of the legs in an effort to enhance the overall appearance of the unit.

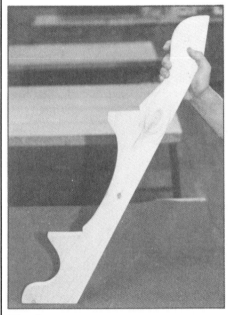

Fig. 4

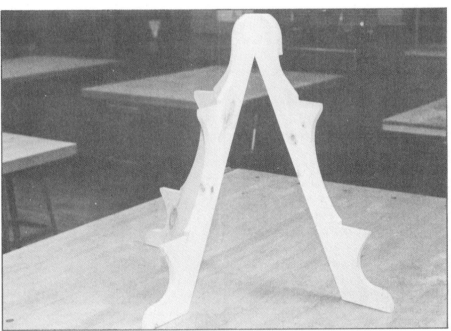

Fig. 5

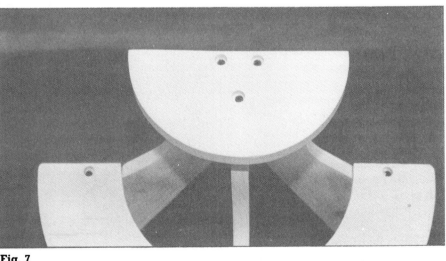

Fig. 6

Using kraft paper or poster board, draw the chosen shape. Then cut the leg shape out. This becomes your template. If you plan to utilize the stand in the future, cut your template out of ⅛″ hardboard or a similar thin material. Now trace the leg shape onto rough stock using the template (Fig. 2). Don't forget to run the grain with the leg length!

If you feel added grain strength is needed, simply glue several wood strips edge to edge to form the desired leg width. I believe you will find that with this size plant stand additional grain reinforcement is not necessary.

Next, brad all three legs together (Fig. 3) and shape on a bandsaw or scroll saw. After shaping, do not

Fig. 7

remove the brads until you have rough sanded the contours.

Finally, separate the legs and fill the brad holes with a mixture of fine sanding dust and polyvinyl glue. Finish sand the surfaces, contours and slightly round the edges with 120 grit abrasive paper. Fig. 4 illustrates the finished leg.

THE LEG BRACE

All the legs are fastened at the apex from the back side by utilizing a small piece of ¾" pine, which braces the unit forming a tripod. The shape of the brace is not critical since it will not be noticed from the back. Place two legs side by side on a flat surface butting the tops together. This will give you the exact surface area the leg brace will cover. Proceed to layout, shape and rough sand the brace piece.

From the back face of the brace counter bore two ½" holes ³⁄₁₆" deep for attaching the front leg. Then counter bore two holes for each of the side legs (Fig. 5). Now drill each counter bore with a ¹⁄₁₆" pilot hole. Rough sand the surfaces and edges. Lay out the side legs (next to each other) on a flat surface. Using No. 6, 1¼" wood screws, fasten the brace to the legs. Standing the side legs upright, fasten the front leg to the unit (Fig. 6). The reason for assembling at this time is to assist in better determining the two shelf radii and provide time to fit the shelves and make any necessary adjustments.

Note: Also at this time, check the unit for alignment.

THE TOP

The top is a semi-circular piece of ¾" pine. Once the piece is laid out, shape and sand accordingly. Counter bore three holes, one for each leg, drill pilots and fasten with No. 6, 1½" wood screws (Fig. 7).

Fig. 8

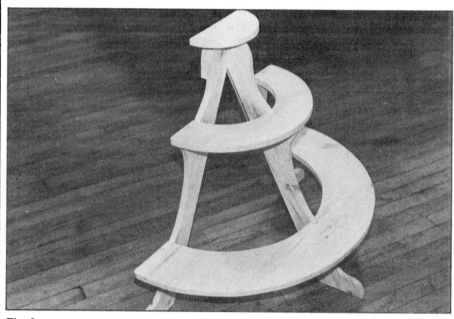

Fig. 9

Fig. 10

THE SHELVES

Now for the last component of the stand, the shelves. First determine the inside radius needed for each shelf and add the shelf width dimension to obtain the outside radius of each shelf. With these radii, lay out the shelves on kraft paper, poster board, or as I have done, directly on the rough blank. The easiest method of doing this is with trammel points attached to a thin wood strip (Fig. 8).

Next determine the size board needed to make up each shelf. Select ¾″ pine stock, avoiding knots or any defects which would weaken the shelves, and glue edge-to-edge. The rough blank sizes are provided in the bill of materials.

Using the made-up template, trace the shapes onto the pine blanks.

Shape the shelves on the band or scroll saw and rough sand each shelf. Place each in position on the legs and make any necessary adjustments.

Be exact in making certain both shelves fit snugly to each leg by notching each shelf to the front leg.

Lay out the locations for attaching the shelves to the legs which are directly over each leg flat. In other words, each shelf is fastened to each of the three legs. Do this by counter boring twice for each shelf-leg attachment. Before assembling, finish sand both shelves and slightly round the outside edge of each. Fasten the shelves to the flats with No. 6, 1½″ wood screws. A larger gauge screw is not necessary since the shelf load will be direct (Fig. 9).

FINAL FINISHING

Cut enough ½″ pine plugs for all the counter bores (Fig. 10), and glue them into place being certain to match the plug grain with the board. If the plug seems slightly loose in the counter bore, soak it in water for

Fig. 11

thirty seconds or so, wipe dry and glue in place. Allow the plugs to dry overnight, and then level each plug with a good sharp ¾″ wood chisel holding the bevel up. Lightly sand each plug making sure each is level with the primary component.

The stand is now complete and ready for a protective finish. Since moisture will be a constant companion to the stand, it is important to seal and use some type of water resistant finish. Fig. 11 displays the stand after finishing.

The following process was used:
1. Rough Sanding – 120 grit abrasive.
2. Final Sanding – 180 grit abrasive.
3. Oil Walnut Stain – One coat wiped on.
4. Sealer Coat – Polyurethane reduced 75/25 Sprayed on.
5. Finish Coats – Two polyurethane Sprayed on.
6. Wax Coat – Liquid wax wiped on Buffed.

CUTTING LIST						
PART	DESCRIPTION	L	W	T	MATERIAL	QTY
1	Leg	31″	7″	¾″	Eastern white pine	3
2	Leg brace	6″	4″	¾″	Eastern white pine	1
3	Upper shelf	22″	14″	¾″	Eastern white pine	1
4	Lower shelf	35″	21″	¾″	Eastern white pine	1
5	Top	9″	4½″	¾″	Eastern white pine	1

NOTES: 1. Unless they are arranged so as to limit the amount of short grain, the use of solid boards for the shelves could lead to problems. Possibly a manufactureed board, correctly lipped, would be more suitable. 2. The use of wax where moisture is present is perhaps questionable. 3. Lack of the portable machinery listed should not deter you from having a go.

SUNDRIES: Polyvinyl resin glue, abrasive papers (120 and 180 grit), wood screws (No. 8 – 1½″, No. 6 – 1¼″, No. 6 – 1½″).

EQUIPMENT: Makita ⅜″ variable speed drill, Powermatic 24″ planer, Boise-Crane spindle sander, Powermatic 14″ bandsaw, Powermatic 7½″ drillpress, Powermatic combination sander, Rockwell 12″ tilting arbor saw, Rockwell 8″ jointer, Makita straight-line sander.

TOOLS: 1/16″ (3mm) twist drill, ½″ (13mm) machine bit, ½″ (13mm) plug cutter, trammel points, 24″ framing square, standard head driver bit.

BUILDING A SPAN-ROOF GREENHOUSE

A portable design made in six sections – two roof frames, two sides and two ends

Gardeners can often be heard debating which is the most suitable type of greenhouse, the metal or the wooden variety. One of the factors which makes the wooden house so popular is that it can be built to whatever size the gardener requires whereas the metal greenhouse must be the manufacturer's stock size.

Size is of course very important. Availability of space, building costs and the uses to which the greenhouse will be put have all to be considered. The span-roof greenhouse shown in Figs. 1 and 2 is approximately 10'0" (3050mm) long, 7'0" (2135mm) wide, 7'6" (2285mm) high to the ridge with an eaves height of 5'6" (1675mm).

The precise dimensions will depend on the sections of timber employed and the sizes of the panes of glass.

Standard size sheets of glass 24" x 12" (610mm x 305mm) are shown

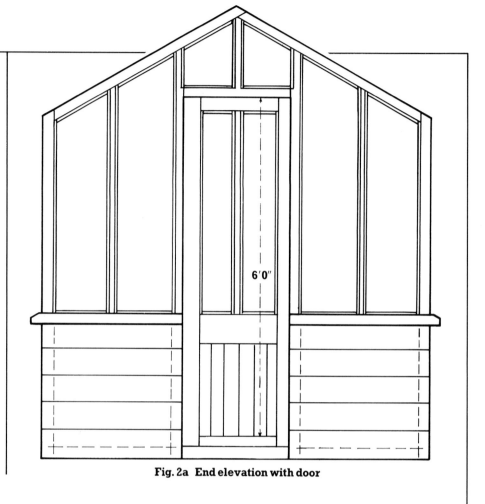

Fig. 2a End elevation with door

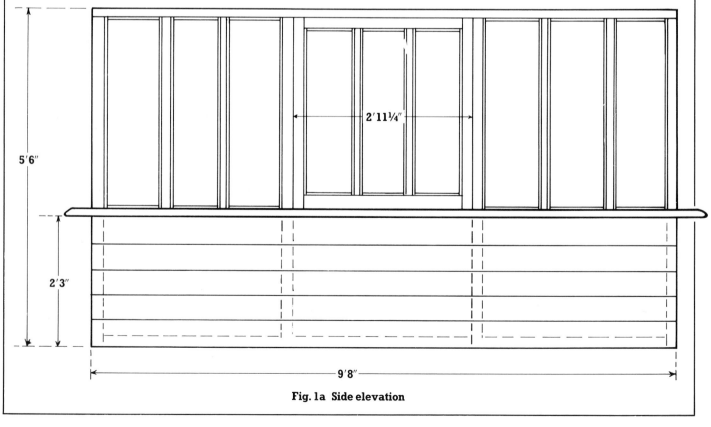

Fig. 1a Side elevation

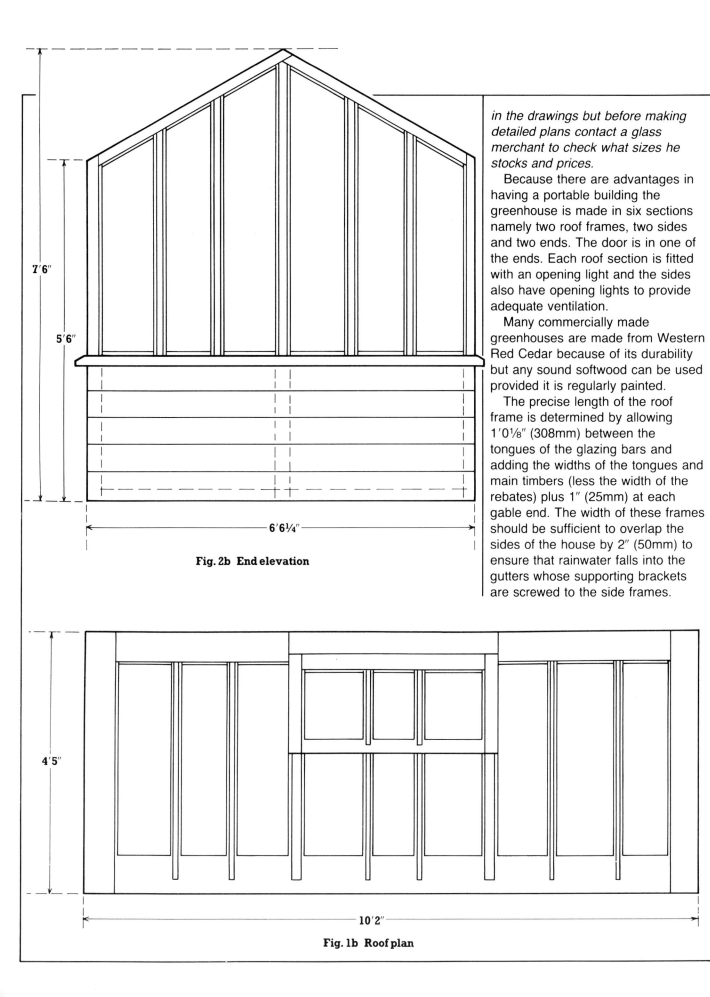

7'6"

5'6"

6'6¼"

Fig. 2b End elevation

4'5"

10'2"

Fig. 1b Roof plan

in the drawings but before making detailed plans contact a glass merchant to check what sizes he stocks and prices.

Because there are advantages in having a portable building the greenhouse is made in six sections namely two roof frames, two sides and two ends. The door is in one of the ends. Each roof section is fitted with an opening light and the sides also have opening lights to provide adequate ventilation.

Many commercially made greenhouses are made from Western Red Cedar because of its durability but any sound softwood can be used provided it is regularly painted.

The precise length of the roof frame is determined by allowing 1'0⅛" (308mm) between the tongues of the glazing bars and adding the widths of the tongues and main timbers (less the width of the rebates) plus 1" (25mm) at each gable end. The width of these frames should be sufficient to overlap the sides of the house by 2" (50mm) to ensure that rainwater falls into the gutters whose supporting brackets are screwed to the side frames.

THE SIDES

The sides butt against and are bolted to the inner faces of the gable ends and in consequence the length of the sides is reduced by 4″ (100mm) which is the combined thickness of the two ends. The glazing bars are positioned so that they follow the lines of the bars in the roof frames.

Open mortise and tenon joints are used at the corners of the side frames and are secured by draw-boring. The head and main uprights of the frames are rebated to the same dimensions as the rebates in the glazing bars. The rebates of the main uprights, if worked by hand, are stopped level with the sills. If prepared stuff, which has already been rebated, is used then some of the framework tenons will of necessity have a short shoulder (Fig. 3). The glazing bars have a similar short shoulder where they are

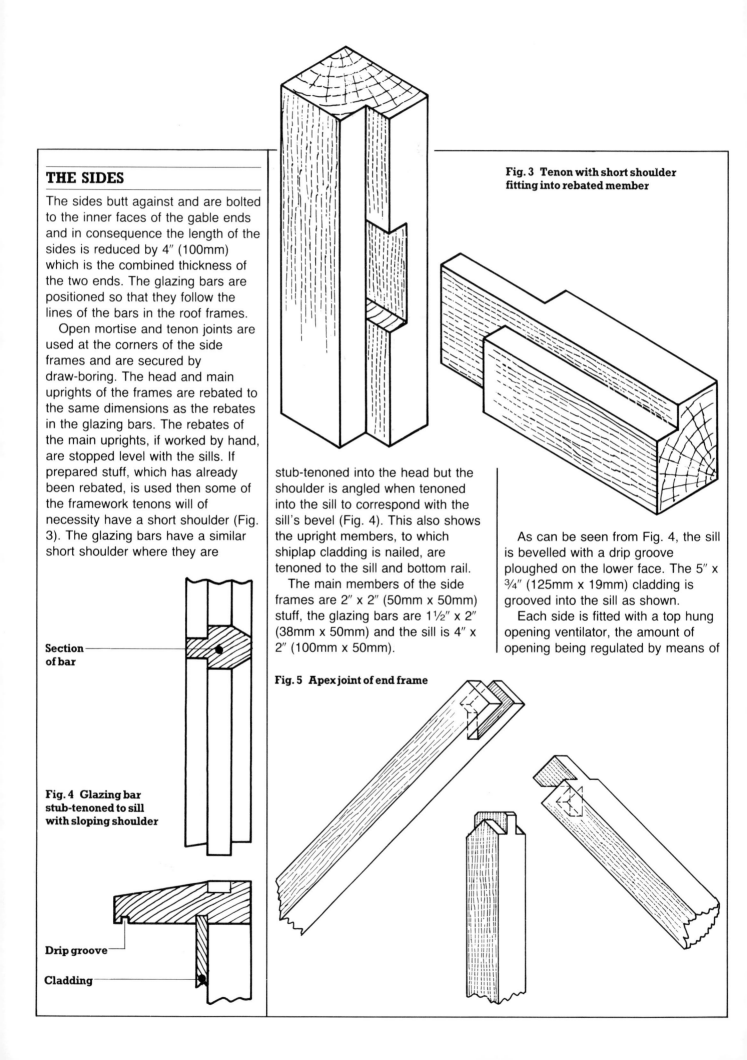

Fig. 3 Tenon with short shoulder fitting into rebated member

Section of bar

Fig. 4 Glazing bar stub-tenoned to sill with sloping shoulder

Drip groove

Cladding

Fig. 5 Apex joint of end frame

stub-tenoned into the head but the shoulder is angled when tenoned into the sill to correspond with the sill's bevel (Fig. 4). This also shows the upright members, to which shiplap cladding is nailed, are tenoned to the sill and bottom rail.

The main members of the side frames are 2″ x 2″ (50mm x 50mm) stuff, the glazing bars are 1½″ x 2″ (38mm x 50mm) and the sill is 4″ x 2″ (100mm x 50mm).

As can be seen from Fig. 4, the sill is bevelled with a drip groove ploughed on the lower face. The 5″ x ¾″ (125mm x 19mm) cladding is grooved into the sill as shown.

Each side is fitted with a top hung opening ventilator, the amount of opening being regulated by means of

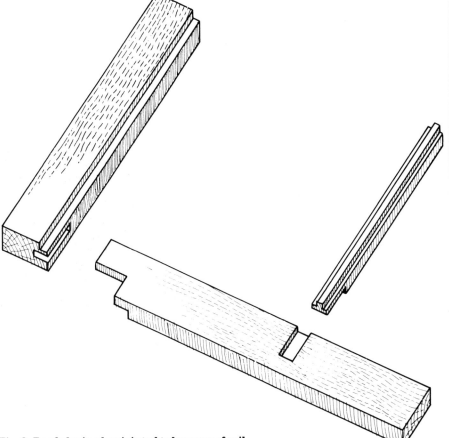

Fig. 7 Hingeing of roof ventilators

Ridge cap
Transom
Ridge piece

a casement stay. Construction is similar to that of the side frames, the corners being mortised and tenoned with the glazing bars stub-tenoned into the top and bottom rails. For ease of opening it is advisable to allow ⅛″ (3mm) clearance all round.

THE ENDS

The two ends are made from 2″ x 2″ (50mm x 50mm) framing and although the external measurements are identical, provision for a 6′0″ x 2′0″ (1830mm x 610mm) door is made in one of the ends.

Draw-bored mortise and tenon joints are used at the base and the eaves. The apex joint is shown at Fig. 5. The glazing bars are stub-tenoned into the head rails and the sill. If a plain sill (Fig. 6a) is used it will be necessary to cut 1″ x ½″ (25mm x 12mm) fillets to fit between the glazing bars to form putty rebates for the lower edges of the glass. If a rebated sill (Fig. 6b) is used there will be no need for such fillets.

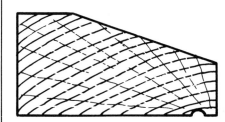

Fig. 6a Plain sill

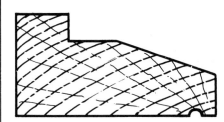

Fig. 6b Rebated sill

The end frame containing the door has two 2″ x 2″ (50mm x 50mm) door posts tenoned into the bottom and head rails. A door head rail of similar section is tenoned into the two posts. The edges of the posts

and head rail are rebated ½″ (12mm) where necessary for the glass. The sill is tenoned into the door posts and also into the corner posts where the bevelled front edge of the sill is carried over the posts sufficiently to allow the ends to be mitred to fit the ends of the sills on the side frame. Door stops are nailed around the door framing.

THE ROOF

The two roof sections comprise top rails of 4″ x 2″ (100mm x 50mm) haunch mortised and tenoned into two end rails of similar section. The bottom rails of 5″ x 1″ (125mm x

25mm) are similarly haunch mortised. All these joints are wedged. Barefaced tenons are cut on the bottom rails and the mortises for these tenons are cut slightly below the rebates. This ensures that after glazing there will be a space between the glass and bottom rail which will allow any moisture on the underside of the glass to drain away and not rot the rail.

Side and cross ventilator rails of 2″ x 2″ (50mm x 50mm) are placed at the ridge of the roof, corresponding in position with the side ventilators. The roof ventilators are made to lie on top of these rails as shown in Fig. 7.

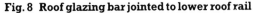

Fig. 8 Roof glazing bar jointed to lower roof rail

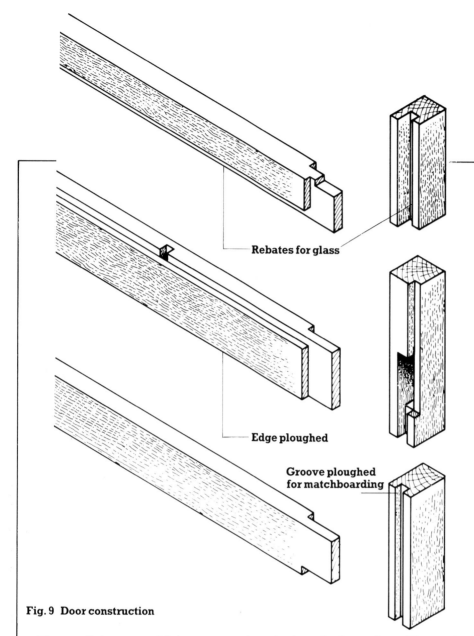

Fig. 9 Door construction

The ventilators are of lighter construction than the side vents. The top rail and stiles are of 2″ x 1½″ (50mm x 38mm) stuff and the lower rail of 3″ x ¾″ (75mm x 19mm). The mortises for the bottom rail tenons are set below the rebates, as in the roof frames, to allow condensation to drain away.

Transoms for the top ventilators are fitted to the side ventilator rails and the top edge of the transom is bevelled similarly to the top edge of the roof frames so as to fit snugly against the 5″ x 1″ (125mm x 25mm) ridge board. The underside of the ridge board is notched where it fits over the apex of the end frames (Fig. 10). The top rails of the roof are bored and screwed to the ridge board. A capping rail of 3″ x 1″ (75mm x 25mm) is nailed to the ridge board (Fig. 7) and has the top face bevelled and drip grooves

worked on the lower face. The roof glazing bars are fitted into the lower roof rail as shown in Fig. 8.

THE DOOR

The door (Fig. 11) is 6′0″ (1830mm) x 2′0″ (610mm) x 1½″ (38mm) thick.

The two stiles are made from 3″ x 1½″ (75mm x 38mm) stuff, the top rail from 3″ x 1½″ (75mm x 38mm), the lock rail from 6″ x 1½″ (150mm x 38mm) and the bottom rail from 6″ x 1″ (150mm x 25mm). The top rail is haunch mortised and wedged into the stiles, the lock rail mortised, tenoned and wedged while barefaced tenons are cut on the bottom rail. This is set back to allow the match boarding to be nailed over the rail and allow rain water to run clear. The door is rebated where necessary for the glass and, if two panes of glass are preferred instead of one, an upright glazing bar can be stub-tenoned between the top and lock rails. The lower edge of the lock rail and the inner edges of the stiles below the lock rail are ploughed to accept rebates worked on the top and side edges of the matchboarding.

ASSEMBLY

Having prepared a level site some assistance will be required to hold one of the side frames upright while one of the ends is bolted to it. The other side and remaining end are bolted together and the structure is checked to ensure it is square. The notched ridge piece (Fig. 10) is nailed to the apex of the gable ends and it is a good plan to remove the

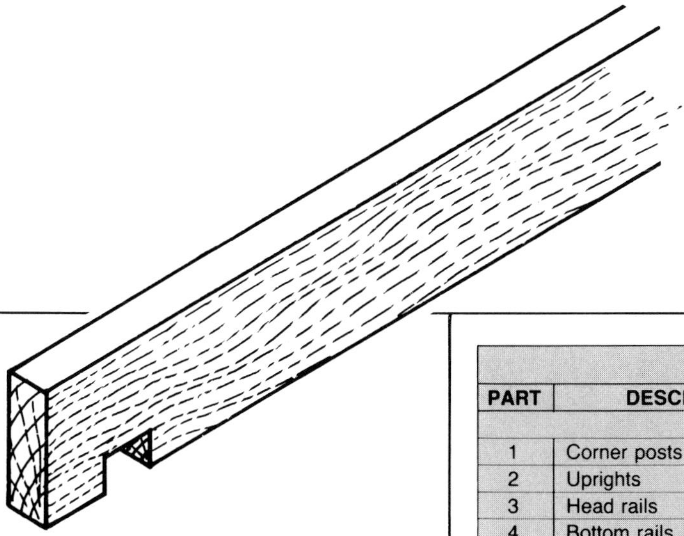

Fig. 10 Ridge board notched to fit over apex of end frame

apex so that the notch of the ridge sits snugly on this flat surface.

A roof section is placed in position and screwed to the ridge and gable ends. The second roof section is similarly screwed in place. The capping can now be nailed to the ridge. The shiplap cladding is nailed in place, the door, fitted with a rim lock is hung, and all is ready for finishing and glazing.

FINISHING

Greenhouses made from Western Red Cedar are resistant to rot and are usually treated with a special preservative which not only preserves the wood but also maintains its colour.

If pine has been used it is a good plan to apply a clear preservative both inside and out and allow it sufficient time to dry before brushing on a coat of priming paint. Glazing can be carried out when the primer is dry.

The roof is glazed first starting at the eaves and working towards the ridge. Allow about 1″ (25mm) overlap and bed the glass in linseed oil putty and secure with glazing brads. Top putty is not required on greenhouses and can be a disadvantage because any cracks which might form could hold rainwater and cause rot. The sides, ends and door can now be glazed and here again an overlap of 1″ (25mm) is advised. Two coats of white paint now follow, taking care to brush the paint just over the edge of the glass to form a watertight seal.

The shiplap cladding would look well painted green.

CUTTING LIST						
PART	DESCRIPTION	L	W	T	MATERIAL	QTY
SIDES						
1	Corner posts	5'6″	2″	2″	Softwood	4
2	Uprights	5'6″	2″	2″	Softwood	4
3	Head rails	9'8″	2″	2″	Softwood	2
4	Bottom rails	9'8″	2″	2″	Softwood	2
5	Sills	10'4″	4″	2″	Softwood	2
6	Glazing bars	3'5″	2″	1½″	Softwood	8
SIDE VENTS						
7	Rails	2'11¼″	2″	2″	Softwood	4
8	Stiles	2'11″	2″	2″	Softwood	4
9	Glazing bars	2'9″	2″	1½″	Softwood	4
10	Shiplap	10'	6″	¾″	Softwood	10
END						
11	Corner posts	5'8″	2″	2″	Softwood	2
12	Centre upright	7'6″	2″	2″	Softwood	1
13	Head rails	4'2″	2″	2″	Softwood	2
14	Bottom rail	6'6¼″	2″	2″	Softwood	1
15	Sill	6'10¼″	4″	2″	Softwood	1
16	Glazing bars	4'6″	2″	1½″	Softwood	2
17	Glazing bars	3'10″	2″	1½″	Softwood	2
18	Shiplap	6'6¼″	6″	¾″	Softwood	5
DOOR END						
19	Corner posts	5'8″	2″	2″	Softwood	2
20	Door posts	7'0″	2″	2″	Softwood	2
21	Door head rail	2'4″	2″	2″	Softwood	1
22	Bottom rail	6'6¼″	2″	2″	Softwood	1
23	Head rails	4'2″	2″	2″	Softwood	2
24	Sills	2'5⅛″	4″	2″	Softwood	2
25	Glazing bars	3'10″	2″	1½″	Softwood	2
26	Glazing bar	1'6″	2″	1½″	Softwood	1
27	Shiplap	2'3⅛″	6″	¾″	Softwood	10
28	Door stops	6'0″	¾″	½″	Softwood	2
29	Door stop	2'0″	¾″	½″	Softwood	1
DOOR						
30	Stiles	6'0″	3″	1⅛″	Softwood	2
31	Top rail	2'0″	3″	1⅛″	Softwood	1
32	Lock rail	2'0″	6″	1⅛″	Softwood	1
33	Bottom rail	2'0″	5½″	¾″	Softwood	1
34	Matchboards	2'0″	4″	¾″	Softwood	6
35	Glazing bar	3'10″	2″	1½″	Softwood	1
ROOF						
36	Top rails	10'2″	4″	2″	Softwood	2
37	Stiles	4'5″	4″	2″	Softwood	4
38	Bottom rails	10'2″	5″	1″	Softwood	2
39	Side vent rails	4'3″	2″	2″	Softwood	4
40	Cross vent rails	3'5″	2″	2″	Softwood	2
41	Transoms	2'11¼″	4″	1½″	Softwood	2
42	Glazing bars	4'1″	2″	1½″	Softwood	8
43	Glazing bars	2'4″	2″	1½″	Softwood	4
ROOF VENTS						
44	Top rails	2'11¼″	2″	1½″	Softwood	2
45	Stiles	1'9″	2″	1½″	Softwood	4
46	Bottom rails	2'11¼″	3″	¾″	Softwood	2
47	Glazing bars	1'7″	1½″	1½″	Softwood	4
48	Ridge board	10'6″	5″	1″	Softwood	1
49	Capping piece	10'6″	3″	1″	Softwood	1

SUNDRIES: 4 casement stays, 4 pairs 2½″ steel butts with screws, 1 rim lock and furniture, 1 pair 3″ steel butts and screws, 8 coach bolts 5″ x ⅜″ with washers, glass, putty, glazing brads, wood preservative and paint.

MODELLING PLANS FOR JEW'S COTTAGE

Detailed step-by-step plans for making a doll's house with a difference

The ¹⁄₄₈ scale model of Jew's Cottage is based on the original fisherman's cottage at Polperro in Cornwall and owned by the National Trust.

It is believed to have been built in 1697 for a local banker. Situated on the harbour, it is extensively painted and photographed. Visitors will know it as one of Polperro's most well known landmarks.

The original building was built in the old style with rough Cornish stone. The high gloss, immaculate finish of today's 'machine age' joinery is missing, giving the building an 'antique' look.

The measurements have been reduced from feet and inches and, therefore, no attempt has been made to convert into metric measurements. All diagrams are the exact size required and have been produced on ¹⁄₁₀th inch squared paper. No measurements are shown but can be obtained by using a good quality rule to measure directly from the diagrams.

Dotted lines are for guidance only and indicate where other diagrams fit into the whole.

The Doll's House size can be obtained by multiplying all measurements by four and following the notes given for each diagram.

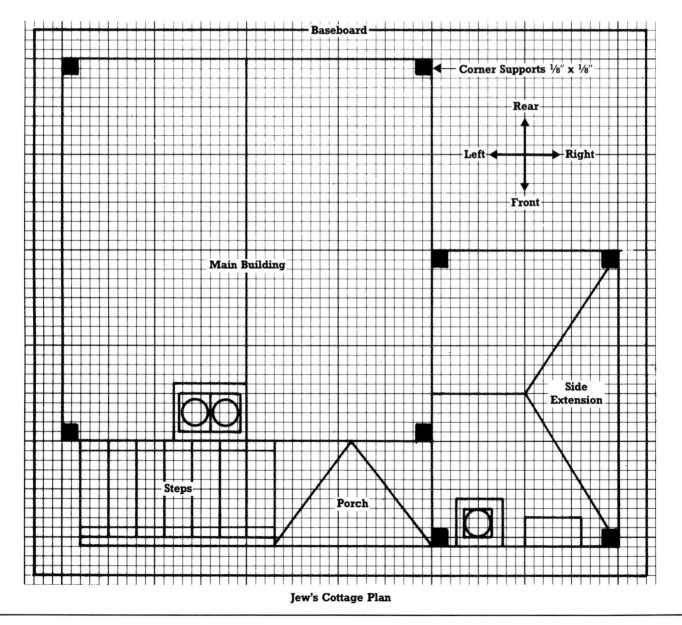

Baseboard

Corner Supports ⅛″ x ⅛″

Rear

Left — Right

Front

Main Building

Side Extension

Steps

Porch

Jew's Cottage Plan

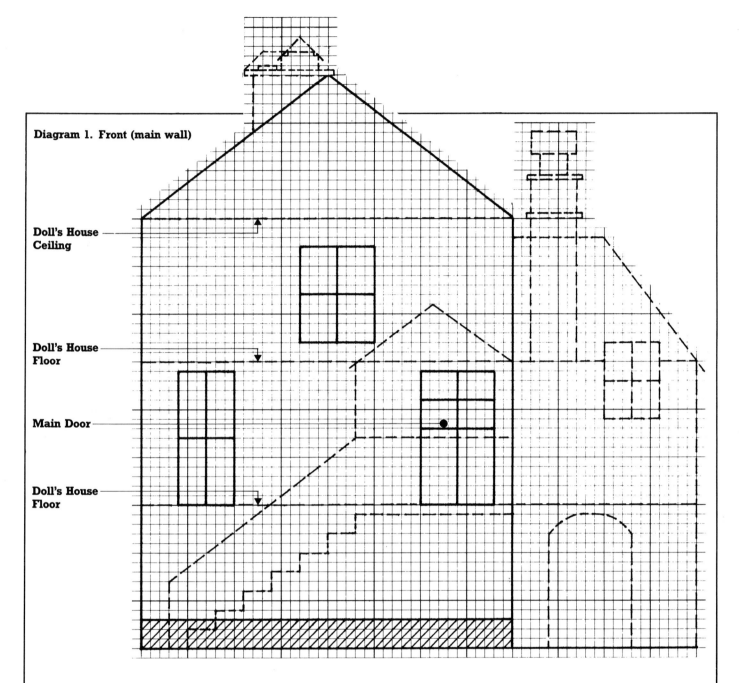

Diagram 1. Front (main wall)

Doll's House Ceiling

Doll's House Floor

Main Door

Doll's House Floor

MATERIALS AND TOOLS

The whole model is made from common ⅛″ hardboard, except for the chimneys, steps and corner supports. The latter are lengths of ⅛″ x ⅛″ wood. (Available from most model shops.)

Also needed are white emulsion, black paint, paper printed to look like cobbled stone and woodchip wall paper to give the appearance of rough, Cornish stone for outside walls. Also (for the windows) black cartridge paper and self-adhesive white labels.

The usual DIY tools should include a good 12″ steel rule, a very sharp Stanley knife, fret saw, set square, various grades of sandpaper and some good carpenter's glue.

Doll's House note: 6mm ply, ½″ chipboard and hardboard will be required. (The chipboard to give depth to the walls for the inset windows.)

Please see special notes for the construction of the windows and doors.

PREPARATION

1. At all stages, great care should be taken to ensure that the pieces are carefully cut to size and that they are vertically and horizontally square.

2. The diagrams are the actual size on ¹⁄₁₀″ squared paper, so no measurements are given.

3. The cottage consists of four key parts which will be dealt with in turn:
a. The main building.
b. The side extension.
c. The front (covering the porch and steps).
d. The extras, such as windows, doors, steps and chimneys.

4. Most corner joints of the walls are mitred, glued, filled and sandpapered before the woodchip paper is pasted onto the outer walls. The windows should be carefully positioned before the whole is glued up and white emulsioned.

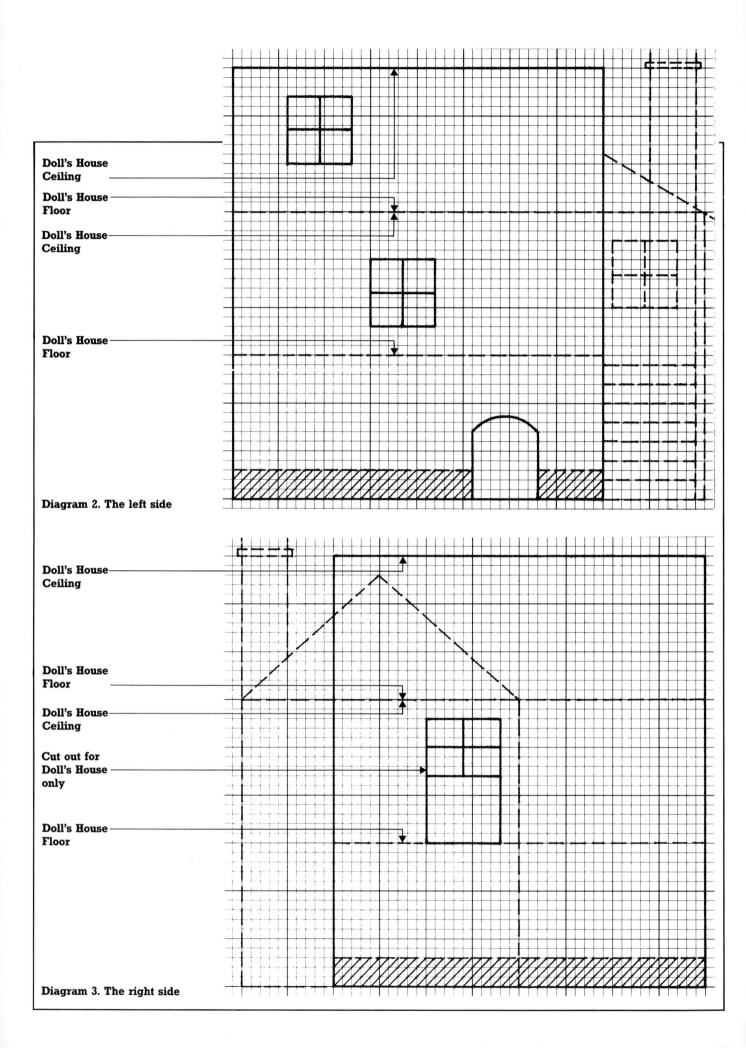

Doll's House
Ceiling

Doll's House
Floor

Doll's House
Ceiling

Doll's House
Floor

Diagram 2. The left side

Doll's House
Ceiling

Doll's House
Floor

Doll's House
Ceiling

Cut out for
Doll's House
only

Doll's House
Floor

Diagram 3. The right side

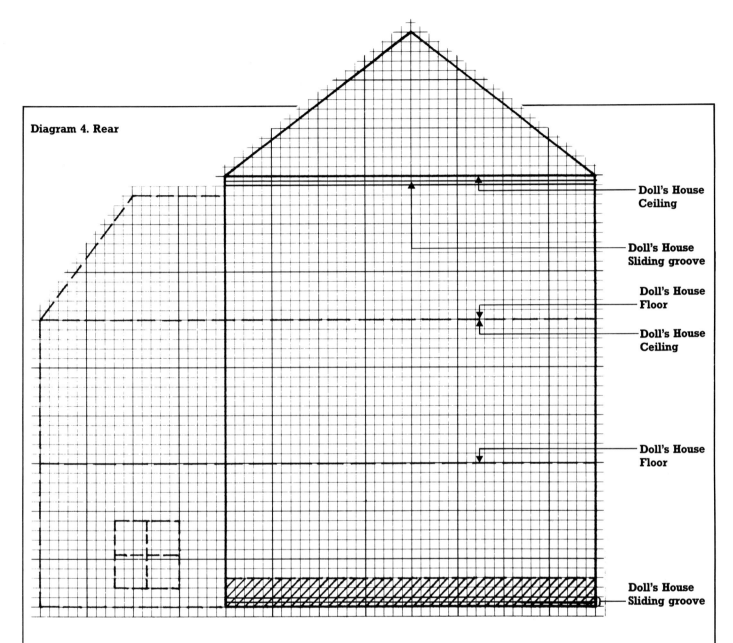

Diagram 4. Rear

Doll's House Ceiling

Doll's House Sliding groove

Doll's House Floor

Doll's House Ceiling

Doll's House Floor

Doll's House Sliding groove

5. The main (and side extension) unit can be held in position with strong elastic bands until the glue is set. (Make sure that all is square.)

6. Doll's House note: the corners should be *pinned* and glued – WITHOUT mitreing.

Use the ½″ thickness on walls in which there are windows, to give the impression of the deep inset. The other walls can be 6mm ply.

CONSTRUCTION

a. The main building

Notes: Windows and doors should be cut out carefully for later treatment.

Mitre left and right hand edges.

Doll's House note: Diagram 4 only, the loft above the ceiling is glued and fixed – the lower three-floors part is in sliding grooves for easy access to the rooms.

The roof consists of two pieces of hardboard, measuring *exactly* 2⁷/₁₀″ x 4³/₁₀″. This size will allow an overhang at the ends and sides.

The edges at the apex are chamferred to make a good gluing contact. In addition, a ½″ strip of strong self-adhesive tape is applied to add to the strength of this main roof and all others in due course.

b. The side extension

This is in four parts to form a box with mitred edges for gluing, plus the roof.

Only part of the window as shown in Diagram 5 is cut from the top edge because the upper part of the window is cut out from the roof to make a very deep set window.

The apex at the top forms a support for the extension roof. (See Diagram 6.)

The roof over the extension can be seen as dotted in Diagrams 1, 5, 6 and 7.

An additional ⅛″ should be allowed for the overhang at the eaves – see Diagram 9.

Chamfer the pieces that are touching and the whole is glued and rested on the upper angle of diagram 6. Also tape touching edges.

The three sizes required are shown in Diagram 9.

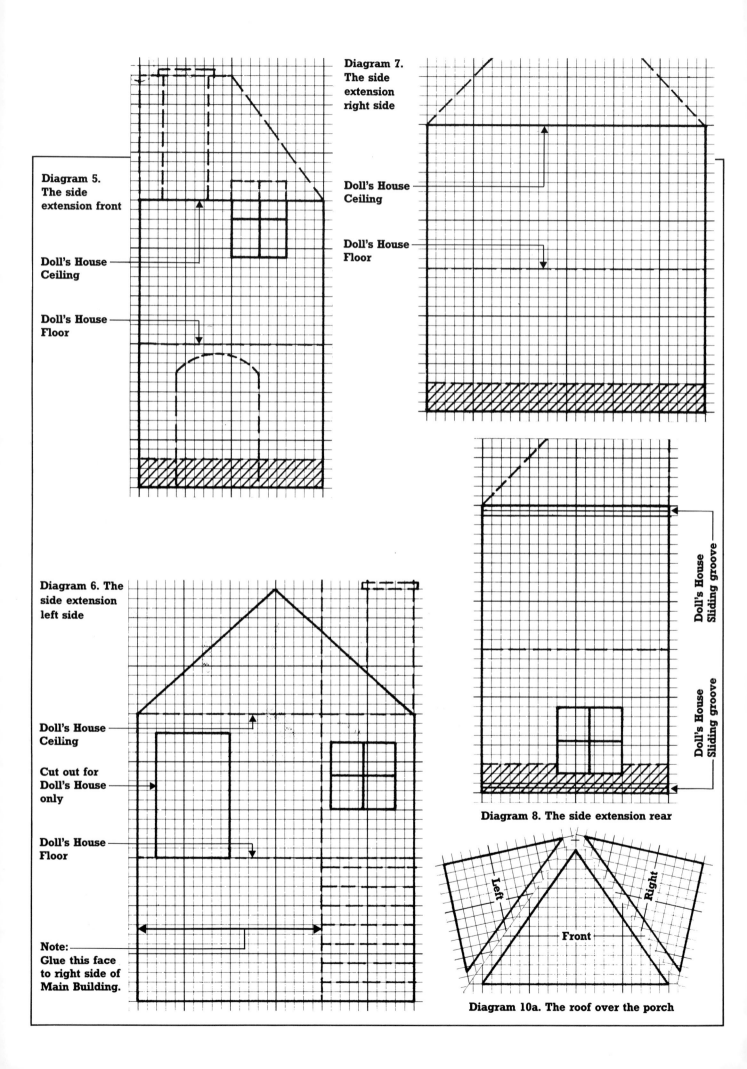

Diagram 7. The side extension right side

Doll's House Ceiling

Doll's House Floor

Diagram 5. The side extension front

Doll's House Ceiling

Doll's House Floor

Diagram 6. The side extension left side

Doll's House Ceiling

Cut out for Doll's House only

Doll's House Floor

**Note:
Glue this face
to right side of
Main Building.**

Doll's House Sliding groove

Doll's House Sliding groove

Diagram 8. The side extension rear

Left

Right

Front

Diagram 10a. The roof over the porch

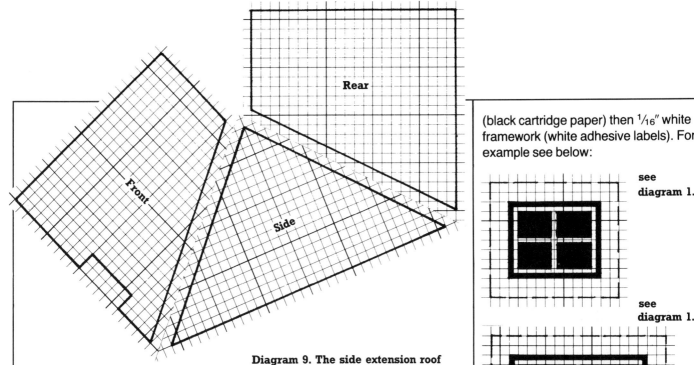

Diagram 9. The side extension roof

(black cartridge paper) then $^1/_{16}''$ white framework (white adhesive labels). For example see below:

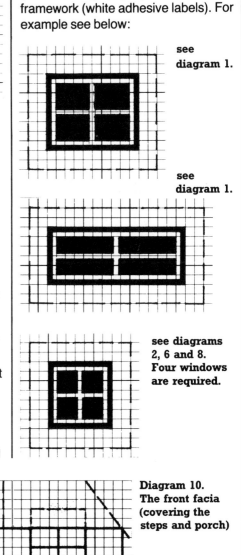

see diagram 1.

see diagram 1.

see diagrams 2, 6 and 8. Four windows are required.

Use $^1/_2''$ strip of strong self-adhesive tape to support the glued edges where parts of the roof touch. (See Diagrams 9 and 10(a)).

An additional $^1/_8''$ has been allowed for the overhang at the eaves.

Chamfer the pieces that are touching for better gluing.

The left (steps) edge is supported by a $^1/_8'' \times ^1/_8''$ piece of wood that also stabilises the main window of Diagram 10 by gluing to the front wall, Diagram 1.

c. The front facia (covering the steps and porch.)

Only part of the right hand window (Diagram 10) is cut from the top edge because the upper part of the window is cut from the roof, together with the part cut as shown in Diagram 5, to accept a very deep-set window.

d. The extras

The windows: the diagrams show the exact size of each aperture. These are filled by $^1/_{16}''$ black surround

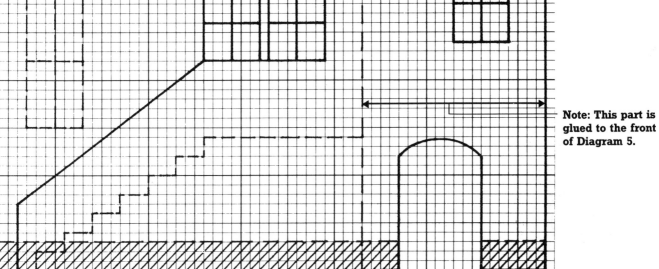

Diagram 10. The front facia (covering the steps and porch)

Note: This part is glued to the front of Diagram 5.

The porch window in Diagram 10. and the deep inset window seen in Diagrams 5. and 10. require special treatment.

Diagram 10. (porch). The top and left hand supports are formed by 1/8" x 1/8" wood, firmly glued to the hardboard. The window is then formed as the others. For example:

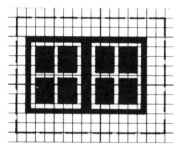

The dotted overlap on all these window diagrams is for gluing at the back of the aperture.

The deepset window. (see Diagrams 5. and 10.) Ensure that the apertures in the three parts match up – if not, open up so that they do. Using 1/16" wood sheet (or similar), construct a four sided, open box with outside measurements the same as the aperture and 3/8" deep.

Glue window, as for others. ⟶

The whole of the box is blackened. ⟶

3/8" deep ⟶

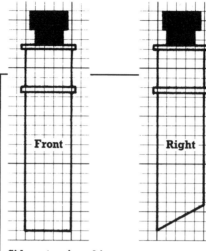

Front　　　　**Right**

Side extension chimney

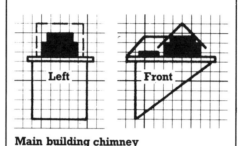

Left　　　　**Front**

Main building chimney

Note that the box is glued into the aperture with the lower part flush with the outer wall. The roof (cobbled paper) overlaps the top of the box.

Doll's House note: the windows are made in a similar way with 2mm glass or cellophane sheet, with black painted 1/8" x 1/16" wood glued to form the framework and 1/16" x 1/16" wood, painted white, to form the sashes.

The base: cut to size as shown on the plan, with cobbled paper (eventually) covering that which shows.

The chimneys: the angles at the base should ensure that they are vertical when glued onto the roof.

The doors: the following diagrams illustrate the three doors required, which can all be seen in the photograph of the finished model.

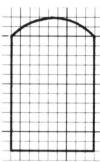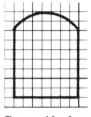

Green side door see Diagram 2.

Green door see Diagram 10.

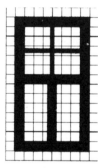

Main door constructed in the same manner as the windows in black and white, see Diagram 1.

The steps: the block may be made solid, or a quantity of wood can be saved where dotted lines are shown.

The front is glued to the back of the facia (see Diagram 10.)

The right is glued to the left side of the side extension (see Diagram 6.)

The steps are covered with cobbled-stone paper, with black strip edges.

The steps leading to the main door.

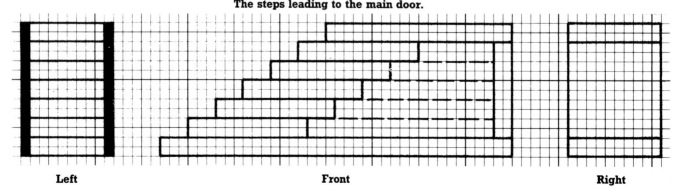

Left　　　　　**Front**　　　　　**Right**

CREATIVE USE OF THE ROUTER

By the author of the book 'Techniques of Routing'

Forethought in designing jigs and fixtures, can bear fruit with some remarkable results.

PEG FRAME JIG

Using a home-made 'peg frame', cross hatching grooves can be cut with a minimum of setting-up time and maximum confidence that parallelity will be maintained.

MESHWORK PATTERNS

With this jig, a series of grooves can be cut equidistant, and by reversing and grooving across the grain on the back of the board, most attractive patterns emerge, see photo 2.

The jig illustrated was made from ⅜″ thick Tufnol, a hard dense plastic but could easily be constructed from plywood. Dowel pegs, carefully spaced and inserted at 90°, form the basis of the jig. The frame, which is constructed from four components, is collapsible, and adjustable in size to accept different size workpieces.

The system for using the jig is based on cutting a series of parallel grooves, with guide fence locating on the dowel pegs at either end – see photo 1. Cuts are made across the grain first, then along the grain on the reverse side.

By varying the size and shape of cutters used in the router, totally original patterns are made. For this exercise, a radiused cutter, 16mm diam. was used – photo 3.

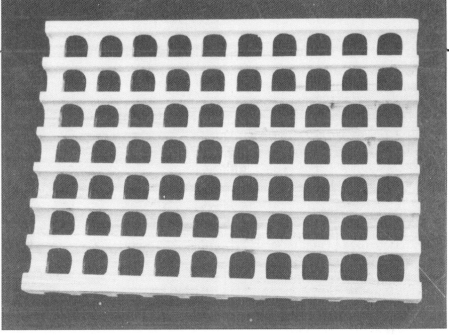

Photo 2 An example of an attractive mesh pattern produced on the peg frame. Radiused grooves were cut on both sides at 90° to each other.

DECORATIVE EDGE STRIPS

Apart from mesh type patterns, if slivers of material are cut across the board, attractive edge strips can be obtained. By cutting longitudinally, a clever means of producing mouldings emerge. By substituting a radius cutter for an ovolo, or classic style cutter, some astonishing effects can be obtained, many being totally original.

Trend Ref 13/1

Photo 3 The 13/1 Radiused cutter was used to produce the meshwork pattern.

A cutter chart and guide for router cutters such as these is available free of charge from Trend Cutting Tools, Unit N, Penfold Works, Imperial Way, Watford, Herts WD2 4YF – Ed.

Photo 1 The adjustable peg frame jig for cutting parallel grooves and shapes.

NEST OF TABLES

These space-saving mini-tables will make a welcome addition to your home – or a splendid present for someone you esteem.

The finished nest of tables.

In these days of snack meals whilst watching television a nest of tables can prove to be a useful asset to almost every living room. They can provide a resting place for those spillable items which cannot be balanced on one's knee and yet take up little space when not in use.

TABLE NO. 1

The smallest of the three tables is the most conventional in construction. It consists simply of four rails, four legs and a top and it has been found best to make this one first and work upwards in size.

JOINTS

These are simple haunched mortice and tenon joints and for this size of timber I suggest using a $5/16''$ mortice chisel. Setting out is best started with the legs cramped together side by side and the legs cramped together in pairs. This way the main measurements are made only once, thus reducing opportunities for error and saving time. The various members are subsequently separated and lines squared round with a very sharp hard pencil.

Shoulder lines for the tenons are marked with a knife.

At this stage I advocate numbering the joints 1 to 8 in order to eliminate confusion in fitting and gluing up.

GAUGING

The tips of the pins of the mortice gauge are first set to the exact width of the chisel and the stock is then adjusted to centralise the pins on the edge of the rails. All gauging is then carried out from the outer face (i.e. the numbered face) of all rails and legs.

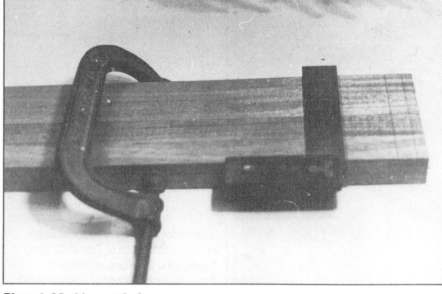

Photo. 1 Marking out the legs.

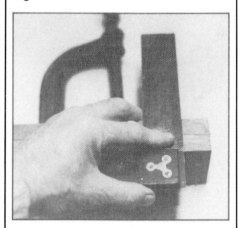

Photo. 2 Marking out the rails in pairs.

Photo. 3 Numbering the joints.

Photo. 4 Setting the mortice guage.

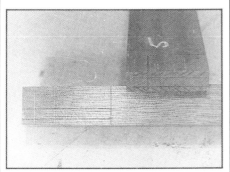

Photo. 5 The joints marked out.

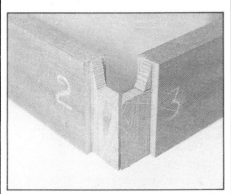

Photo. 6 The ends of the tenons mitred and secret haunches cut.

Photo. 7 The finished joints ready for gluing.

CUTTING THE JOINTS

This should present no problems to the average craftsman but it should be borne in mind when fitting the joints that the ends of the tenons must be mitred where they meet inside the mortices.

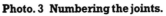

Tip 1

Tip 1. When cutting stopped mortices, a piece of masking tape round the blade of the chisel makes an effective depth gauge.

Tip 2

Tip 2. When sawing tenons, a vee cut chiselled on the waste side of the shoulder line helps to guide the saw to make an accurate cut.

TAPER THE LEGS

To taper or not to taper is a matter for personal taste. The tables shown have the legs tapered from about 1½" below the joints to 1" square at the bottom. This is achieved by planing the inside of the legs before gluing up.

GLUING UP

This is carried out in two separate stages. First the two side frames are glued and cramped and checked that they are:

Photo. 8 Testing the side frames for squareness.

Square – if the legs are tapered the square must be used to check

Photo. 9 Measuring the diagonals to test for squareness.

from the outside of the legs to the rails.

Parallel – by measuring the overall width top and bottom.

Flat – by sighting across the legs.

When these have set, the long rails are glued in and the above checks are repeated for the front and back. A fourth check is necessary at this stage for the squareness of the top. The best method is to make sure the diagonals are equal.

CLEANING UP

The use of a finely set smoothing plane will probably be necessary to ensure the faces of the legs and rails are flush followed by rubbing down with two or three grades of glasspaper. The "horns" are cut off flush with the tops of the rails and the side rails will have to be recessed 1/16″ (1.6mm) to accommodate expansion plates. These can easily be fabricated from aluminium, brass or mild steel. Suggested dimensions are given in the cutting list. Each plate will require 3 holes, two countersunk to attach to the top of the rail and the third to accept a No. 6 1/2″ round head screw which in turn secures the top to the rails. The plates attached to the long rails will require a slot to allow for the movement of the top. *Note: the slots are at right angles to the grain.* Modified mirror plates could also be

used instead and where necessary the hole could be elongated, i.e. the hole that is not countersunk!

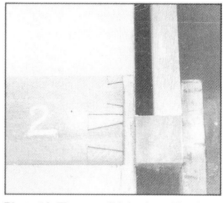

Photo. 10 The top rail joint for tables 2 and 3 marked out and with waste marked.

TABLES 2 AND 3

The two larger tables are slightly different in construction in that they have only three mortice and tenoned rails. The fourth *(front)* rail is dovetailed. It is best to leave the jointing of this rail until the side frames have been glued and the back rail fitted but not glued. The long and short shoulders of the dovetails can then be calculated accurately and the tails cut. The sockets are scribed on to the tops of the side frames after the horns are cut off. Lines can then be squared down to the thickness of the front rail and the joints cut, fitted and glued.

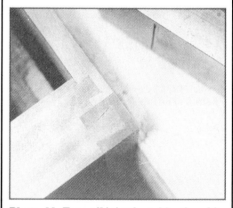

Photo. 11 Top rail joint for tables 2 and 3 cut and fitted.

Photo. 12 'L' shaped runners to support the smaller tables.

RUNNERS

The L shaped runners which support the smaller tables are most easily made by cutting a rebate on the edge of a 1⅛″ thick board and ripping off afterwards. They are then cut away to fit in between the front and back legs and glued and screwed to the side rails.

Photo. 13a 'L' shaped runners cut and fixed in position.

Photo. 13b 'L' shaped runners as seen from below.

After the tops are fixed with suitable screws the legs may need a final adjustment to give about ⅛″ ground clearance to each of the two smaller tables when stacked.

FINISHING

This is a matter of personal taste. I usually favour a waxed finish which reaveals the natural grain of the

Photo. 14 The finished nest of tables stacked.

timber at its best. However, in view of the fact that these tables are likely to be subjected to hot dishes and spills, two coats of satin polyurethane, with a light rub down between coats and a final burnishing with wax polish, is probably the best treatment.

PART	DESCRIPTION	L	W	T	MATERIAL	QTY
\multicolumn{7}{CUTTING LIST}						
			TABLE No. 1			
1	Legs	18½″	1⅜″	1⅜″	Sapele	4
2	Short rails	8½″	2¾″	¾″	Sapele	2
3	Long rails	13¾″	2¾″	¾″	Sapele	2
4	Top	15¼″	10″	⅝″	Sapele	1
			TABLE No. 2			
5	Legs	20″	1⅜″	1⅜″	Sapele	4
6	Side rails	9¾″	2¾″	¾″	Sapele	2
7	Back rail	17½″	2¾″	¾″	Sapele	1
8	Front rail	17½″	2½″	½″	Sapele	1
9	Top	19″	11¼″	⅝″	Sapele	1
			TABLE No. 3			
10	Legs	21½″	1⅜″	1⅜″	Sapele	4
11	Side rails	11″	2¾″	¾″	Sapele	2
12	Back rail	21¼″	2¾″	¾″	Sapele	1
13	Front rail	21¼″	2½″	½″	Sapele	1
14	Top	22¾″	12½″	⅝″	Sapele	1
15	Runners (to cut 4)	11″	6″	1⅛″	Sapele	1
16	Expansion plates	1½″	1″	1/16″	Aluminium, brass or mild steel	18

Items 2, 3, 6, 7, 11 & 12 allow 1⅛″ tenons
Items 1, 5 & 10 leg lengths allow ½″ horns which will be cut off

NOVELTY GRINDER

A toy for all ages, young and old alike! Simply work the mechanical arm back and forth watching and feeling the glides smoothly track. "A fascinating gadget." The grinder is rather inexpensive to make since the construction is simple and the materials needed are minimal. Give it a try, it tends to entertain everyone.

The completed novelty grinder

MAKING THE BASE BLOCK

1. I have chosen white ash, but straight grain hardwood (timber) will suffice. A stock thickness of one inch (25mm) would be ideal. If the stock is thicker, simply plane down to approximately one inch.

2. Lay out the base block on the stock using a try square. Be careful to maintain a square block throughout construction to insure proper location of the dovetail tracks later in the construction process. Figure 1.

Figure 1

3. With a sharp hand rip saw cut the block to width. Proceed to cut the block to length using a sharp hand crosscut saw. Note: When sawing, always saw to the outside of the lines. The reason for this is to insure that you don't lose your reference lines, mainly thickness, width and length.

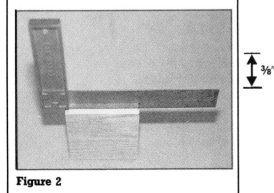

Figure 2

4. Using a smoothing plane, true one surface maintaining level as you plane.

5. Proceed to true both edges maintaining level and square. Figures 2, 3. Check to be sure you are four inches wide throughout.

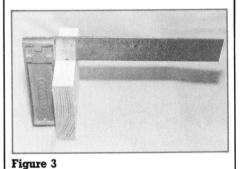

Figure 3

BASE BLOCK Full Size

4″

4″

3/8″

1/2″

1″

1⅞″   1⅞″

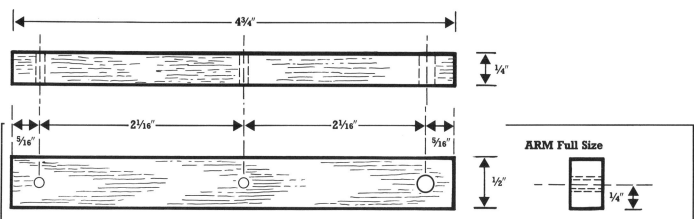

ARM Full Size

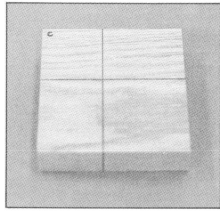

Figure 4

6. Using a block plane, true both end grains keeping level and square.

7. We are now ready to cut our dovetail grooves. From one corner measure in 1¾″ (44mm) each way and make a mark. With your try square draw two lines. These lines are the reference lines for cutting the grooves. Figure 4.

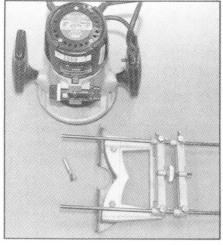

Figure 5

8. For cutting the grooves we will utilize a portable router, ½″ dovetail router bit and a router guide. Figure 5. Place the bit into the collet (chuck)

and set the cutting depth to ⅜″ (10mm). Insert the guide into the router. Then proceed to align the guide by setting the wing of the router bit with the reference lines established in Step 6. Lock the guide in place. Route both dovetail grooves and round all sides with a file, lightly sand inside the grooves. Figure 6. The base block is now complete.

Figure 6

If you don't have a portable router, cut your dovetail grooves with your dovetail saw and chisel the grooves bottom level. *This is critical to insure smooth tracking of the glides.*

MAKING THE ARM

1. Taking a scrap piece from the original stock, lay out the arm placing the length with the grain. Figure 7.

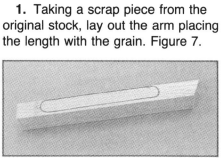

Figure 7

2. Cut the arm to size using the same sawing procedure you used on the base. You now have a ½″ × 4¾″ (13mm × 120mm) component).

3. Using the dovetail saw, cut the wood to a thickness of ⁵⁄₁₆″ (8mm).

Figure 8

The arm is now cut to its basic size. Proceed to final shape with the smoothing plane and wood file, including the rounding of both arm ends.

4. Locate the shank holes for the wood screws and drill two ⅛″ (3mm) diameter holes. Then locate the hole for the knob and proceed to drill the appropriate diameter needed. Figure 8. The arm is now completed.

MAKING THE GLIDES

1. Using the remaining wood, cut one piece to a rough size of: ½″ T × 1″ W × 3½″ L (13mm T × 25mm W × 88mm L).

2. Draw a centre line down the length of the piece dividing the width in half. Lay out the top width of the glide, ³⁄₁₆″ (5mm), and the bottom width of the glide. ½″ (13mm), on the end of the stock. Do this on the opposite end. You now are ready to cut your glide angles. Figure 9. In the figure, the glide portion is darkened in for the purpose of illustration.

Figure 9

GLIDE Full Size

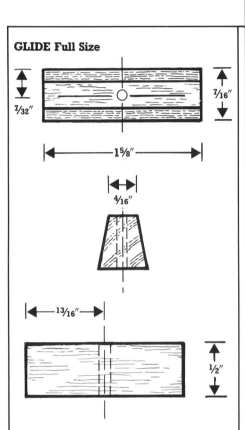

3. With the dovetail saw, proceed to cut the angles.

4. Continue to final shape the glides to dimension with the smoothing plane and wood file. Cut two glides to final length using the dovetail saw. Now using the hand drill, drill a ¹⁄₁₆″ (1.5mm) pilot hole in the centre of each glide. Figure 10. You now have the completed glides.

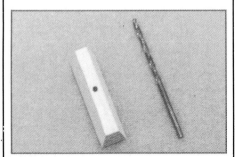

Figure 10

FINAL SURFACE PREPARATION

Using a fine piece of glasspaper, light sand all the components. Lightly scuff all sharp corners and edges.

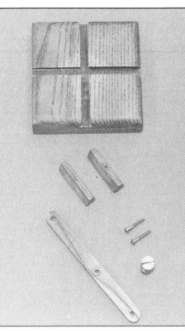

Figure 11

NOTE: Be extremely careful not to over sand the glide sides (angled surfaces) and the dovetail grooves. The glides should fit loosely in the grooves and move back and forth freely.

APPLYING THE FINISH

Liberally apply boiled linseed oil to all the grinder components. Allow the oil to soak in for several hours and *lightly* sand with fine glass paper. Apply a second coat and wipe dry. Allow 24 hours drying time before assembly of the grinder and before applying any wax to the grooves or glides.

FINAL ASSEMBLY

1. Apply wax to the glide sides and bottoms; groove sides and bottoms and wipe off.

2. Attach the *end* of the arm to one of the two glides with a wood screw, barely snug the two together.

Figure 12. Then insert the glide in a groove.

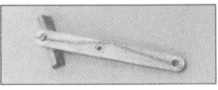

Figure 12

3. Use the same procedure and attach the second glide. Once again barely snugging the two together.

4. Attach the knob to the arm and tighten securely.

The novelty grinder is now completed. Figure 13.

Figure 13

TESTING OF PROPER MOVEMENT

If properly constructed, the arm should move the glides smoothly back and forth. If the movement is difficult, back off the glide screws just slightly until the movement is ideal.

CUTTING LIST

PART	DESCRIPTION	L	W	T	MATERIAL	QTY
1	Base block	4″	4″	1″	Hardwood	1
2	Arm	4¾″	½″	¼″	Hardwood	1
3	Glides	1⅝″	½″	⁷⁄₁₆″	Hardwood	2

SUNDRIES: 2 brass round head screws No. 5 – ¾″, 1 brass knob ⁷⁄₁₆″ diameter ½″ high with fastener (approximate size), boiled linseed oil for finishing.

EQUIPMENT: Router, straight edge, 12″ try square, crosscut handsaw, rip handsaw, block plane, smoothing plane, cabinet scraper, dovetail saw, screwdriver, hand drill, wood file, ½″ dovetail router bit, glass paper, wax, ⅛″ and ¹⁄₁₆″ twist drills.

THE USE OF THE CABINET SCRAPER

Used and sharpened correctly, the cabinet scraper is an extremely useful finishing tool.

It is often found difficult to produce a good finish on some stripy or wild grained hardwoods and even the sharpest and most finely set smoothing plane will tear the grain, leaving a great deal of work to be done with glasspaper.

A very small outlay, and a little patient practice in the use of a cabinet scraper, will save a lot of hard work and probably some harsh words.

A scraper removes a fine shaving by means of a burr on its edge which is produced as follows:

Photo 1

Photo 1. Holding the scraper perfectly upright, square the edge on an oilstone.

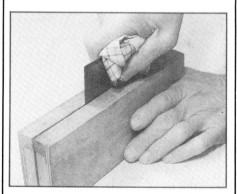

Photo 2

Photo 2. If it is found difficult to keep the scraper vertical, or if the stone is worn hollow, the method shown in photo 2 may be found preferable as the edge of the stone is more likely to be straight and the box holds the scraper vertical.

Photo 3

Photo 3. Using a small screwdriver or a large bradawl as a 'ticketer' (burnisher), place the scraper flat on the bench, moisten the ticketer in the mouth and draw it flat and firmly along each edge once or twice and on both sides.

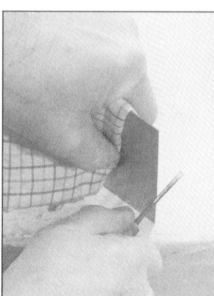

Photo 4

Photo 4. Holding the scraper upright, moisten the ticketer again and draw it firmly and sharply up the edge two or three times; at first at 90° but on subsequent strokes swinging round to 85 or 80°. Repeat this on all four long edges.

Photos 5, 6, 7 and 8 show the method of holding and using the scraper.

When all four edges become dull they can be restored several times by repeating steps 3 and 4 before it is necessary to resort to the oilstone again.

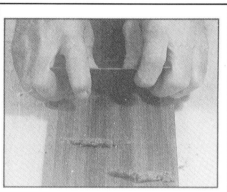

Photo 5

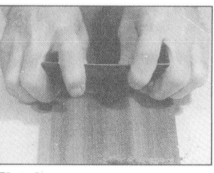

Photo 6

Photo 7

Photo 8

A much enlarged cross section of the scraper could be illustrated as above.

TEA CARRIER

A sound design for a piece that will last a lifetime.

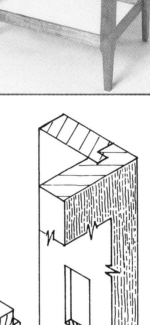

As an alternative to a tea trolley, this medium-sized piece enables one to carry adequate afternoon tea or morning coffee requirements. The trolley type of conveyance works well on a smooth floor but 'snags' often are met between kitchen and lounge or garden.

An open-leg type of construction admirably lends itself to this project.

Method used to secure trays to legs:

let dovetails project ⅛″ to fit into mortise which positions trays. Fit two screws at each corner from inside tray.

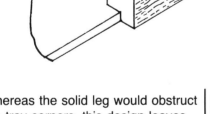

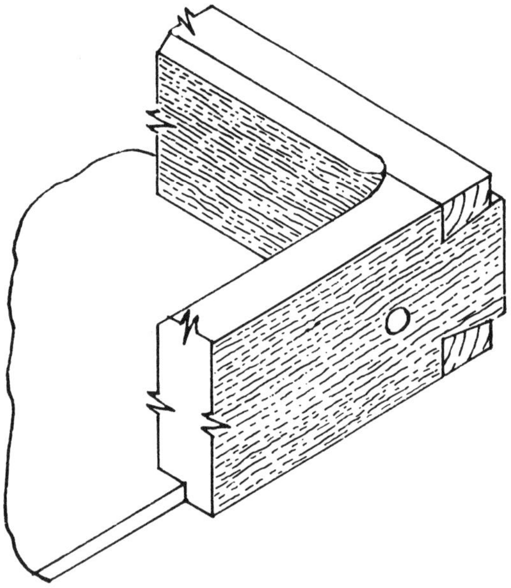

blade and the depth set at ¼″. Work the grooves on the wider pieces.

If desired, the plough can also be used to cut the tongues on the narrower pieces, but allow a *very slight* increase between the fence and the blade. This should leave a thicker tongue which can be eased to make a push-in, not forced, fit when the parts are assembled.

Clean up all surfaces away from the tongues and proceed to glue up as indicated under NOTES on the drawing.

DOVETAILS

The common dovetail is used for the tray corners, but lengthen the dovetails ⅛″ to fit into the mortises shown in the picture view on the drawing. This locking device takes all the weight on the shelves.

When the carrier is put together the dovetail joints are not seen. Therefore, when cutting the rebates for the tray bottoms, there will be no need to stop the rebates on the tray ends.

Cut the mortises which receive the dovetail spurs on the correct inside faces of each leg. Clean up all the tray sides, inside and out, and work the chamfers on the top inside corners of the tray sides. These may now be glued together and checked for squareness.

Whereas the solid leg would obstruct the tray corners, this design leaves clear every square inch of surface.

If one can obtain, maybe by special order, the ⅛″ plastic laminate, both the clean surface and the weight problem are improved. A 6mm plywood with a plastic veneer overlay could provide a reasonable surface. A good class fine grained cabinet wood is recommended for the framework.

Begin by making a Cutting List.

With a sharp ¼″ plough iron, set the plough fence ¼″ away from the

CUTTING LIST

PART	DESCRIPTION	L	W	T	MATERIAL	QTY
1	Legs	24½″	1¾″	½″	Cabinet wood	4
2	Legs[1]	24½″	1½″	½″	Cabinet wood	4
3	Tray sides	34″	1¾″	½″	Cabinet wood	4
4	Handles	15½″	3¼″	⅝″	Cabinet wood	2
5	Trays[2]	19½″	11½″	6mm	Plywood	2

NOTES: 1. Plane all pieces to the given widths; an extra ¼″ has been allowed on part 2 for the tongue. 2. It is recommended to add a plastic veneer overlay over the 6mm plywood, or alternatively use ⅛″ plastic laminate instead.

SUNDRIES: 16 screws for tray corners.

EQUIPMENT: Boxwood folding rule, Steel rule, Trysquare, Marking gauge, Mortise gauge, Crosscut Hand saw, Tenon saw, Coping saw, Jack plane, Smoothing plane, Rabbet plane, Plough plane, Spokeshave, Hand drill, Twist drills, Screwdriver, ½″ and ⅜″ Firmer chisels, ½″ B.E. chisel, Cabinet scraper.

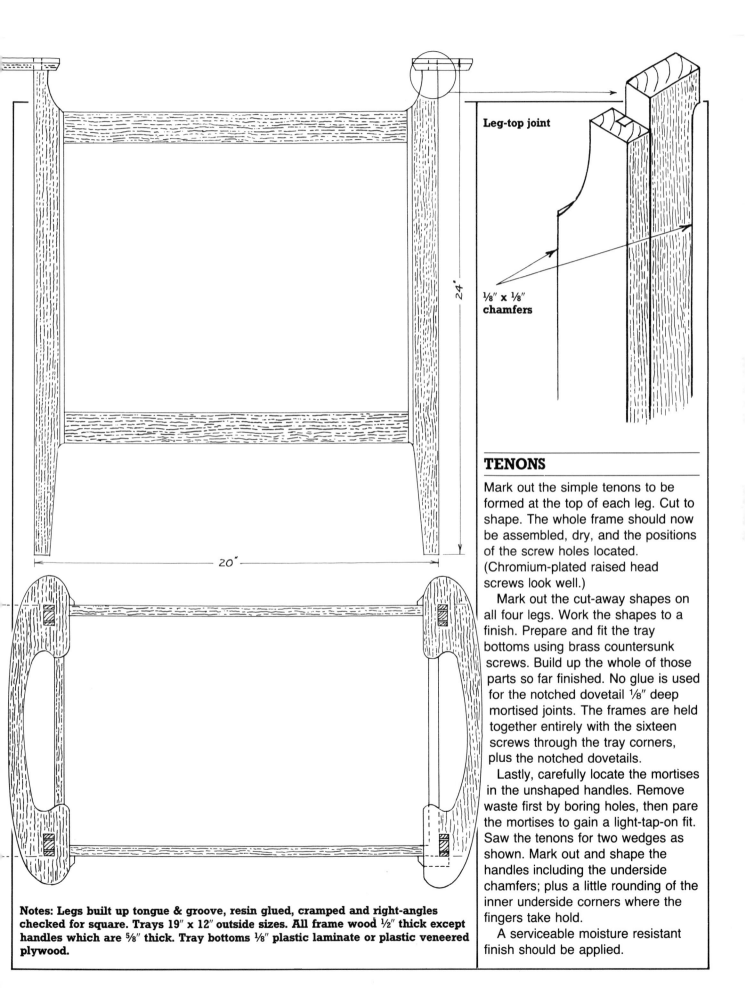

Leg-top joint

⅛″ x ⅛″ **chamfers**

24″

20″

TENONS

Mark out the simple tenons to be formed at the top of each leg. Cut to shape. The whole frame should now be assembled, dry, and the positions of the screw holes located. (Chromium-plated raised head screws look well.)

Mark out the cut-away shapes on all four legs. Work the shapes to a finish. Prepare and fit the tray bottoms using brass countersunk screws. Build up the whole of those parts so far finished. No glue is used for the notched dovetail ⅛″ deep mortised joints. The frames are held together entirely with the sixteen screws through the tray corners, plus the notched dovetails.

Lastly, carefully locate the mortises in the unshaped handles. Remove waste first by boring holes, then pare the mortises to gain a light-tap-on fit. Saw the tenons for two wedges as shown. Mark out and shape the handles including the underside chamfers; plus a little rounding of the inner underside corners where the fingers take hold.

A serviceable moisture resistant finish should be applied.

Notes: Legs built up tongue & groove, resin glued, cramped and right-angles checked for square. Trays 19″ x 12″ outside sizes. All frame wood ½″ thick except handles which are ⅝″ thick. Tray bottoms ⅛″ plastic laminate or plastic veneered plywood.

A design without angular corners. The rounded ends give a pleasant smooth finish and the table will accommodate four people comfortably.

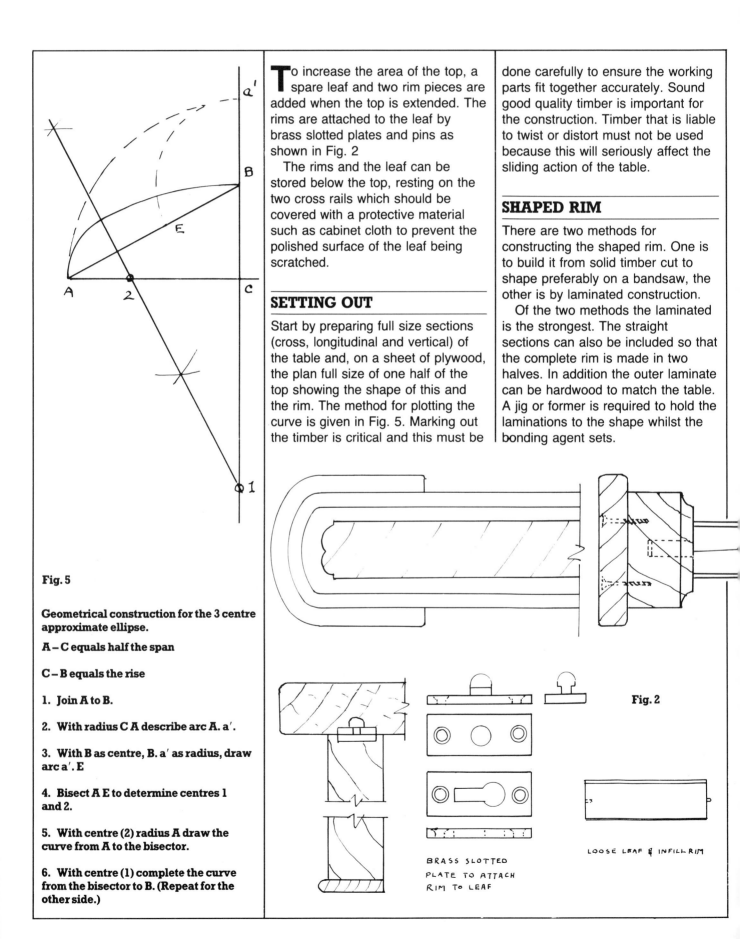

To increase the area of the top, a spare leaf and two rim pieces are added when the top is extended. The rims are attached to the leaf by brass slotted plates and pins as shown in Fig. 2

The rims and the leaf can be stored below the top, resting on the two cross rails which should be covered with a protective material such as cabinet cloth to prevent the polished surface of the leaf being scratched.

SETTING OUT

Start by preparing full size sections (cross, longitudinal and vertical) of the table and, on a sheet of plywood, the plan full size of one half of the top showing the shape of this and the rim. The method for plotting the curve is given in Fig. 5. Marking out the timber is critical and this must be done carefully to ensure the working parts fit together accurately. Sound good quality timber is important for the construction. Timber that is liable to twist or distort must not be used because this will seriously affect the sliding action of the table.

SHAPED RIM

There are two methods for constructing the shaped rim. One is to build it from solid timber cut to shape preferably on a bandsaw, the other is by laminated construction.

Of the two methods the laminated is the strongest. The straight sections can also be included so that the complete rim is made in two halves. In addition the outer laminate can be hardwood to match the table. A jig or former is required to hold the laminations to the shape whilst the bonding agent sets.

Fig. 5

Geometrical construction for the 3 centre approximate ellipse.

A – C equals half the span

C – B equals the rise

1. Join A to B.

2. With radius C A describe arc A. a′.

3. With B as centre, B. a′ as radius, draw arc a′. E

4. Bisect A E to determine centres 1 and 2.

5. With centre (2) radius A draw the curve from A to the bisector.

6. With centre (1) complete the curve from the bisector to B. (Repeat for the other side.)

BRASS SLOTTED
PLATE TO ATTACH
RIM TO LEAF

LOOSE LEAF & INFILL RIM

Fig. 2

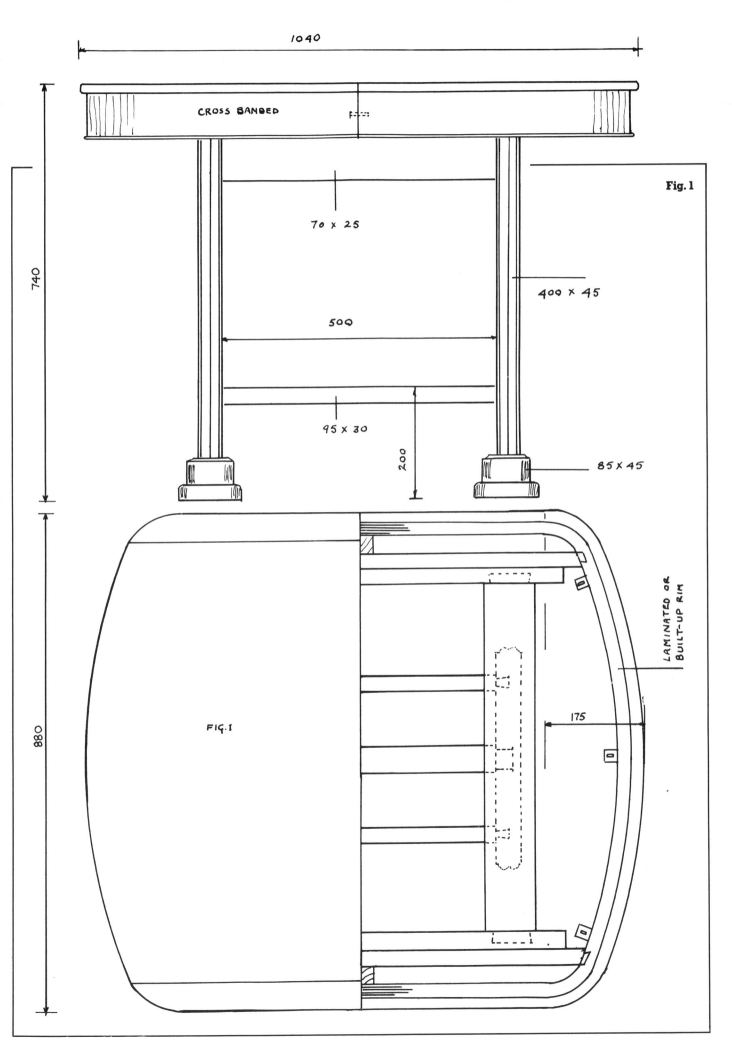

1040

740

CROSS BANDED

Fig. 1

70 x 25

400 x 45

500

95 x 30

200

85 x 45

880

FIG.1

LAMINATED OR BUILT-UP RIM

175

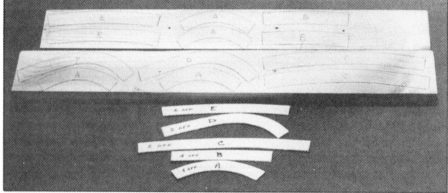

1. **Built-up rim. Templates are necessary to mark the shapes on the material. The shapes can be cut with a bow saw but a band saw is essential to give a neat square cut with minimum of waste.**

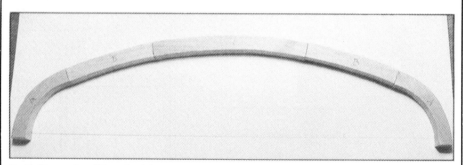

2. **Built-up rim. After the joints have been fitted, glue the first layer to a piece of paper on which the outline has been marked. When the adhesive has set, the remaining pieces can be added.**

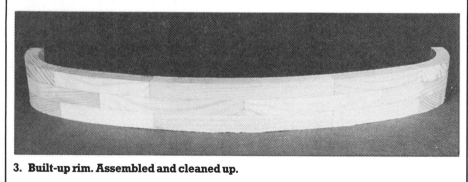

3. **Built-up rim. Assembled and cleaned up.**

An advantage with the built-up method is that no jigs are necessary; the rim is assembled on the plan set out. When the jointing of the segments has been satisfactorily completed they can be bonded together. A board placed on top of the rim with heavy weights will provide sufficient pressure to ensure good joints are made. The curved part of the rim should be cleaned up and finished to size before joining to it the straight sections of the rim with dowels.

VENEERING

The rim is finished by hand veneering on both sides. To prevent the segments showing through the veneer, as much time as possible should be allowed before veneering. Check the surfaces of the rim to make sure no movement has taken place since the initial finishing and adjust if necessary. Two veneers should be used on the outside, the outer one can be cross-banded.

ALTERNATIVE

An alternative to the shaped table top frame is shown in Fig. 4. This can be used if preferred. A mitred tongued joint is shown at the intersection of the side and end rims with a glue block in the internal angle. The top can still have a very small curvature and lightly rounded corners.

LEGS

The legs are made from solid timber moulded on both edges. These are tenoned into the base and the top cross rail. Screwed to the base at each end are feet which assist if the floor should be uneven. The legs are framed together with top and bottom rails. The lower rail is tenoned and the top rails are dovetailed as shown in the details Fig. 3.

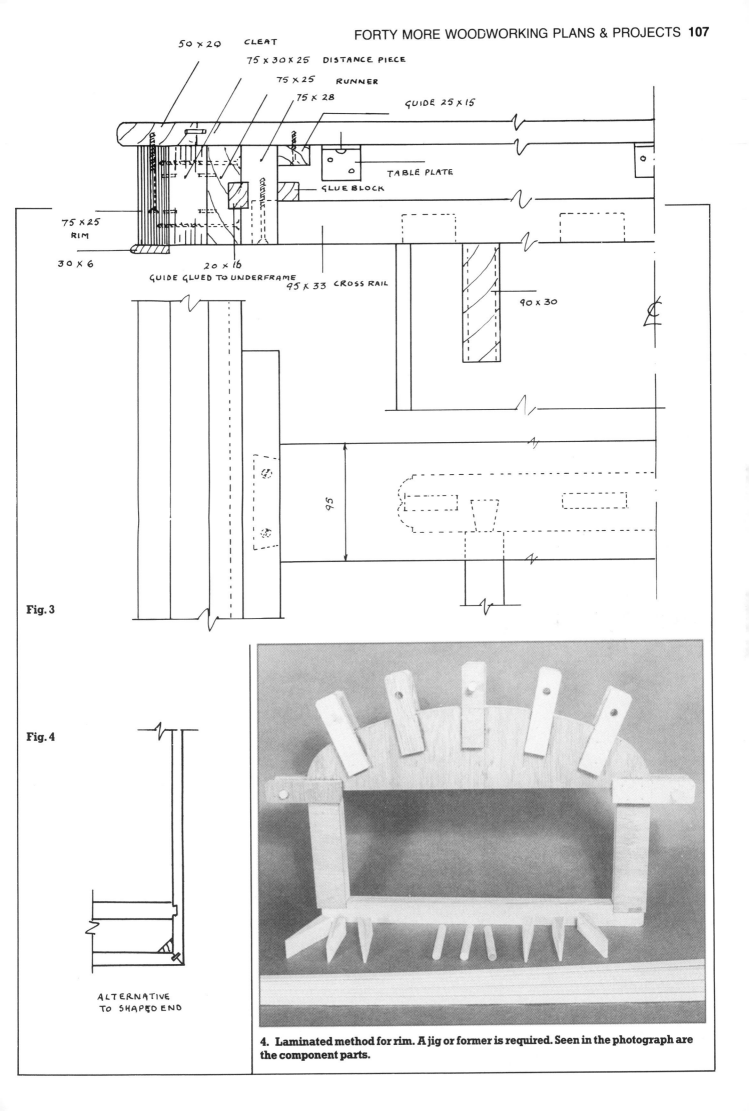

50 × 20   CLEAT

75 × 30 × 25   DISTANCE PIECE

75 × 25   RUNNER

75 × 28

GUIDE 25 × 15

TABLE PLATE

GLUE BLOCK

75 × 25
RIM

30 × 6

20 × 16

GUIDE GLUED TO UNDERFRAME

95 × 33   CROSS RAIL

90 × 30

95

Fig. 3

Fig. 4

ALTERNATIVE
TO SHAPED END

4. Laminated method for rim. A jig or former is required. Seen in the photograph are the component parts.

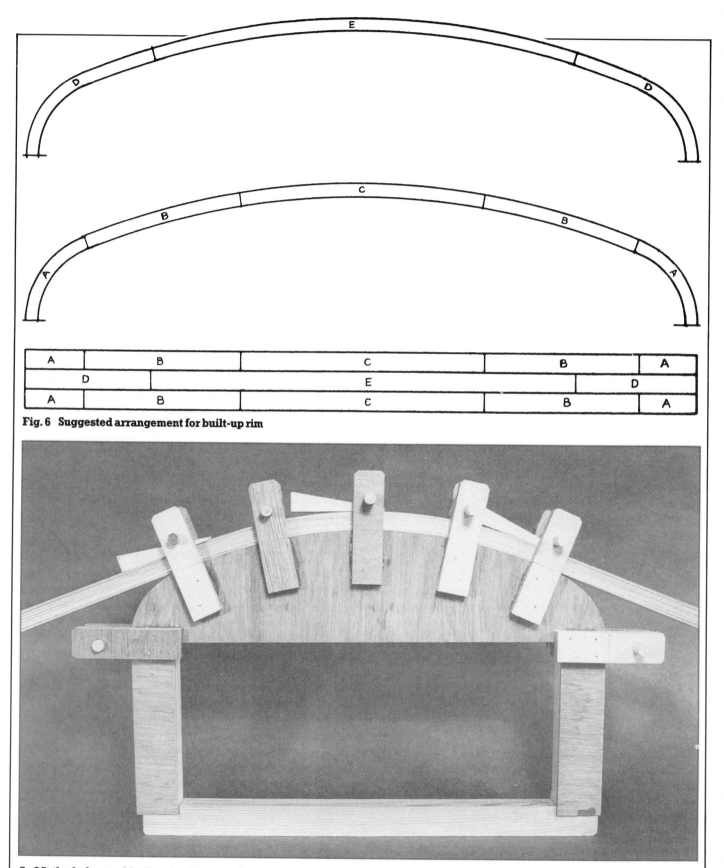

A	B	C	B	A
D		E		D
A	B	C	B	A

Fig. 6 Suggested arrangement for built-up rim

5. **Method of assembly. Laminations are placed between the spokes, the pins pushed through the holes, then the wedges driven in to compress the laminae. Paper must be used between the face of the jig and the work to prevent these being stuck together.**

The two long runners which complete the underframe are connected to the cross rails with lap dovetails, glued and screwed. Seasoned quarter sawn English Beech is a suitable timber for the underframe and rim construction. This timber has a smooth hard wearing surface ideal for the purpose.

RUNNERS

The frames that are attached to the top consist of the rim and grooved runners. The runners are dovetail housed to the rim at one end and

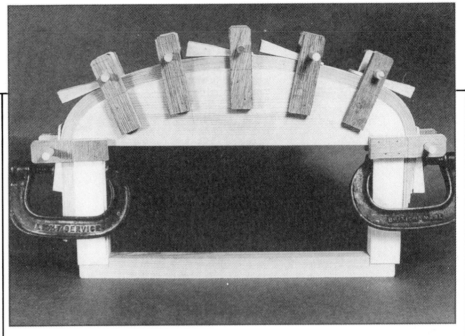

6. Rim assembled dry. The ends of the laminae needed treatment with hot water to soften the fibres before bending, leave to cool and dry before assembling with a suitable adhesive such as a resin and a hardener applied separately.

PART	DESCRIPTION	L	W	T	MATERIAL	QTY
\multicolumn{7}{c}{**CUTTING LIST**}
1	Top	820	530	20	Hardwood	2
2	Cleat	450	50	20	Hardwood	4
3	Distance piece	75	30	25	Hardwood	4
4	Runners	450	75	25	Hardwood	4
5	Guide	300	25	15	Hardwood	4
6	Rim bead (to temp)	450	30	6	Hardwood	4
7	Rim bead (to temp)	250	30	6	Hardwood	2
8	Rim bead (straight)	380	30	6	Hardwood	4
9	Leaf	820	460	20	Hardwood	1
10	Cleat	460	50	20	Hardwood	2
11	Rim	460	75	25	Hardwood	2
12	Rim bead (for leaf)	460	30	6	Hardwood	2
\multicolumn{7}{c}{UNDERFRAME}
13	Runner	760	75	28	Hardwood	2
14	Guide	760	20	16	Hardwood	2
15	Cross rail	680	95	33	Hardwood	2
16	Top rail	550	90	30	Hardwood	2
17	Bottom rail	550	95	30	Hardwood	1
18	Legs	650	400	45	Hardwood	2
19	Base	460	85	45	Hardwood	2
20	Feet	120	110	25	Hardwood	4
\multicolumn{7}{c}{RIM (built-up)}
21	To temp (A)	150	25	25	Hardwood	8
22	To temp (B)	240	25	25	Hardwood	8
23	To temp (C)	430	25	25	Hardwood	4
24	To temp (D)	230	25	25	Hardwood	4
25	To temp (E)	550	25	25	Hardwood	2
26	Straight (F)	400	75	25	Hardwood	4
\multicolumn{7}{c}{RIM (laminated)}
27	Laminae	1.800	80	3	Hardwood	16

SUNDRIES: 6 table plates, screws, dowel rod, 4 brass slotted plates, adhesive.

fixed at the other end with a 30 x 25 block dowelled, screwed and glued. The distance piece is required to position the grooved runner so that it is set at the correct place, relative to the underframe of the table, to provide a close running fit. Stops are screwed to the runners to control the distance the tops are extended, sufficient space being allowed to remove the spare leaf from its stowage position and to place it in the space between the top. Dowels are used to locate and keep it in place.

TOP

The top of the table is shown made from quarter sawn timber with cleats grooved, tongued and glued. Sound well seasoned timber must be used with a suitable moisture content. Alternatively the cleats can be omitted leaving the end grain exposed and carefully finished. The timber specification must be as stated above.

A paraffin wax candle applied to the runners will reduce friction and make them slide freely.

A full French polish adds to the appearance and brings out the beauty of the grain.

An eye-catching home for some of your prized pieces.

Photo 1 Rebating and moulding: router set up with the table to operate as a spindle machine. This method provides perfect control over the full length of the workpiece. Router cutter for ovolo No. 7D 1 (Trend).

Photo 2 Mitre cutting moulding, chisel angled to prevent 'nicking' the shoulder on the face side. (One hand removed for clearness.)

Photo 3 Assembling and gluing. (Note door is supported on bearers which have been checked for alignment.)

This corner cabinet is designed for display purposes and as a free-standing unit. Made in an appropriate hardwood, it looks particularly attractive because of the angle the front presents to a room.

If the main part of the cabinet is to fit close to the wall then the plinth will have to be reduced where there are existing skirting boards. When the cabinet is to be placed in a particular corner it is advisable to check the angle between the wall surfaces before setting out the workshop rod.

CONSTRUCTION

Fig. 1 shows the elevation, vertical section and the plan. Set out full size a vertical section and the plan. In this way the angles for the rails, shapes of the shelves, corner pieces etc. can be obtained. Commence with the carcase by preparing the front corner pieces to their section, cut these and finish them neatly to length in readiness for dovetailing. The top rail, and the front section of the bottom, can now be carefully marked out directly from the plan. (See Fig. 2 for details.) Cut these to their shape and mark and cut the dovetails. The major part of the bottom is made from blockboard. This is tongued and glued to the bottom section to form the base of the cabinet.

The plywood backs can next be cut and finished to size. Rebate one piece at the back corner and drill the holes for the screws in preparation for assembly. Check that all parts of the carcase are correct for size and shape by placing them on the rod.

SHELVES

Before proceeding with the assembly, the shelf arrangement must be taken into consideration. Whilst shelf bearers can be fixed at a later stage, it is easier to mark their

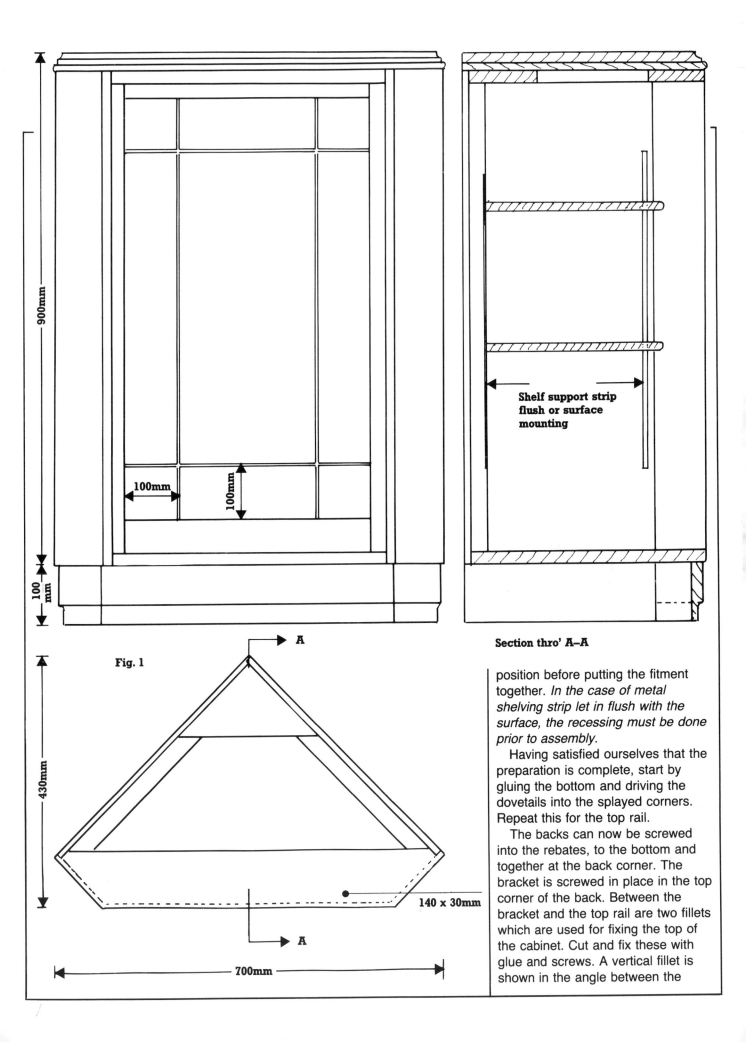

900mm

100mm

100mm

100 mm

Shelf support strip
flush or surface
mounting

Section thro' A–A

Fig. 1

430mm

A

A

140 x 30mm

700mm

position before putting the fitment
together. *In the case of metal
shelving strip let in flush with the
surface, the recessing must be done
prior to assembly.*

Having satisfied ourselves that the
preparation is complete, start by
gluing the bottom and driving the
dovetails into the splayed corners.
Repeat this for the top rail.

The backs can now be screwed
into the rebates, to the bottom and
together at the back corner. The
bracket is screwed in place in the top
corner of the back. Between the
bracket and the top rail are two fillets
which are used for fixing the top of
the cabinet. Cut and fix these with
glue and screws. A vertical fillet is
shown in the angle between the

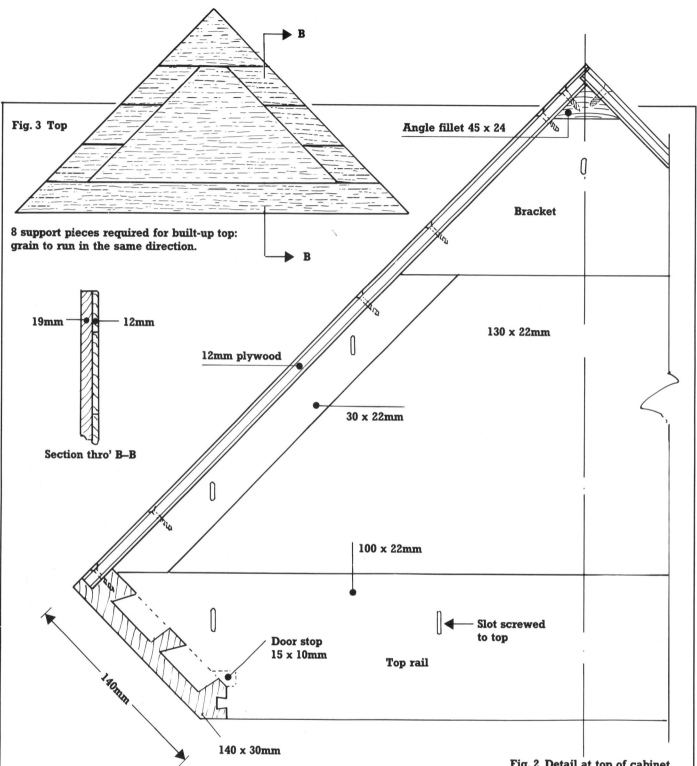

Fig. 3 Top

8 support pieces required for built-up top: grain to run in the same direction.

19mm — 12mm

Section thro' B–B

B

B

Angle fillet 45 x 24

Bracket

130 x 22mm

12mm plywood

30 x 22mm

100 x 22mm

Slot screwed to top

Top rail

Door stop 15 x 10mm

140mm

140 x 30mm

Fig. 2 Detail at top of cabinet

backs. This is recessed and carries the shelving support strip.

The top of the cabinet is built up with two thicknesses adhesed together as shown in Fig. 3. The underneath section is made from a number of pieces joined together, the grain running in the same direction as the top. This will then behave in a similar manner to a solid piece of timber.

PLINTH

Details for the plinth are shown in Fig. 4. The front and the two splayed ends should be worked in one length. First cut the ends square and rebate them. The moulding is then run on the face side. The length of the pieces are next marked from the rod. Cut the mitres and groove the ends for tongues. The joint at the

back corner of the plinth can be either dovetailed or rebated and screwed. Assemble the plinth dry and check with the rod before finally gluing together.

At this stage, the top can be completed, the front of the cabinet and the plinth prepared for the finish. It is an advantage to leave the parts separated for the polishing process so that the edges and ends are not

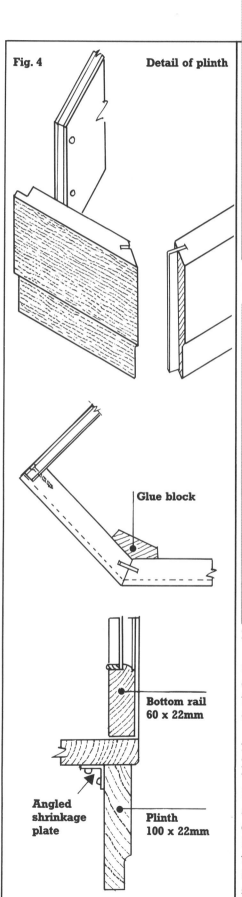

Fig. 4   **Detail of plinth**

Glue block

**Bottom rail
60 x 22mm**

**Angled
shrinkage
plate**   **Plinth
100 x 22mm**

Photo 4 Mitres are cut for the astragal moulding after assembly, followed by recessing for the bars.

Photo 5 Showing astragal moulding mitred and fitted before adhesing to bars.

restricted by projecting parts. A cleaner finish will be obtained and the difficulty of using the rubber in corners is avoided.

DOOR

The details for the door are given in Fig. 5. It has an ovolo moulding and a rebate worked on the solid. The construction follows normal practice, being mortise and tenon joints with the moulding mitred in the corners. A built-up glazing bar, with an astragal section to match the frame moulding,

is shown. Commence by making the frame which is then assembled. One method for marking the position of the bars is to cut and fit a piece of plywood neatly in to the rebate. On this the centre and the width of the bar is set out. The plywood is now replaced in the rebate and the lines transferred to the frame.

The mitres are cut using a standard mitre template; leave sufficient for final fitting. The recesses on the back of the door which receive the bar are the next operation. The bars are then cut and fitted. Place the vertical bars into the recesses and with a straight edge mark the position of the halving on the bars. This method is repeated for the horizontal bars. Cut the halvings and glue the bars in place.

The astragal moulding can now be mitred and fitted to the door. A very thin blade small tooth saw must be used if the mouldings are to be cut and fitted direct from the sawcut. Personally I prefer to use a shooting board for fitting.

A much cleaner result is procured at the intersection of the mitres if the moulding is 'bodied-up' in length before cutting. This leaves just the application of the final coat of French polish. A little extra care in handling is required.

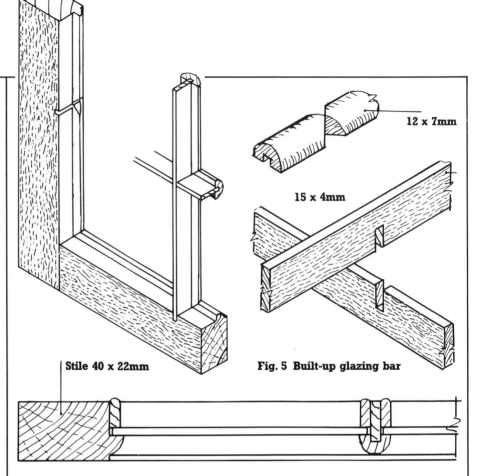

12 x 7mm

15 x 4mm

Stile 40 x 22mm

Fig. 5 Built-up glazing bar

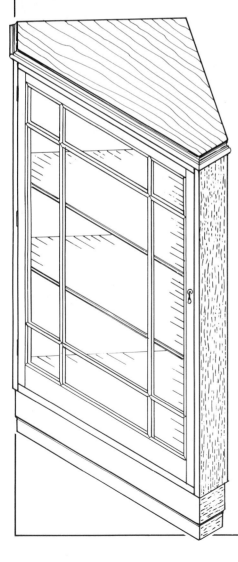

CUTTING LIST						
PART	DESCRIPTION	L	W	T	MATERIAL	QTY
1	Splayed corner	900	140	30	Hardwood	2
2	Top rail	740	100	22	Hardwood	1
3	Bottom section	740	100	22	Hardwood	1
4	Bottom	740	350	22	Blockboard	1
5	Back	900	560	12	Plywood	2
6	Bracket (top)	300	130	22	Redwood	1
7	Fillet (top)	330	30	22	Redwood	2
8	Angle fillet	900	45	24	Hardwood	1
9	Shelves	700	330	20	Hardwood	2
10	Top	750	450	19	Hardwood	1
11	Pieces for top[1]	*	*	12	Hardwood	*
PLINTH						
12	Front & ends	900	100	22	Hardwood	1
13	Back	500	100	12	Plywood	2
14	Glue blocks	100	22	22	Redwood	5
DOOR						
15	Stiles	870	40	22	Hardwood	2
16	Top rail	520	40	22	Hardwood	1
17	Bottom rail	520	55	22	Hardwood	1
18	Bar	780	12	22	Hardwood	2
19	Bar	480	12	22	Hardwood	2
20	Glazing beads	870	10	3.5	Hardwood	4
21	Glazing beads	540	10	3.5	Hardwood	4

SUNDRIES: 3 shelf support strips 550mm metal, screws, adhesive, shrinkage plates, glass. NOTE: [1]Please refer to Fig. 3.

CUTTING TENONS

A choice of ways to cut accurate tenon joints.

Any method available to ease the preparation and the basic construction of a project I consider should be welcomed and utilised. Personally, I find including a machine process makes the job more interesting. This may mean jigs are necessary to carry out routine operations. If so, consideration must be given to the quantity of work involved, the adaptability of the jig for future use or to whether the jig is essential even for a one-off operation.

Tenon joints are used in timber assemblies in a large variety of work; it is one of the arrangements to unite parts most frequently employed in construction. There are several ways tenons can be formed apart from the tenon machine used for quantity production in a factory.

  a Tenons cut by hand
  b Tenons cut on a circular saw
  c Tenons cut on a bandsaw

HAND CUT TENONS

For hand cut tenons, the saw required depends on the width of the section. For instance, the middle or bottom rail of a room door will need a half rip or hand saw to cut these large tenons, but for a glazing bar a small backed saw is more suitable and would be selected. Considerable skill and practice in sawing is necessary to cut tenons that fit correctly in the mortise without any adjustment being needed. To accomplish this the following points will help considerably.

1. Set the mortise gauge points to the actual chisel to be used (not to a rule).

2. Cut the tenon by sawing in the wastewood as close as possible to the gauge line, using the correct saw.

3. Use a sharp saw with the minimum of set.

Photo. 1 Hand cut tenon. First cut across the end, down approximately 6mm. (Do not start from a corner because this means two lines have to be followed simultaneously.)

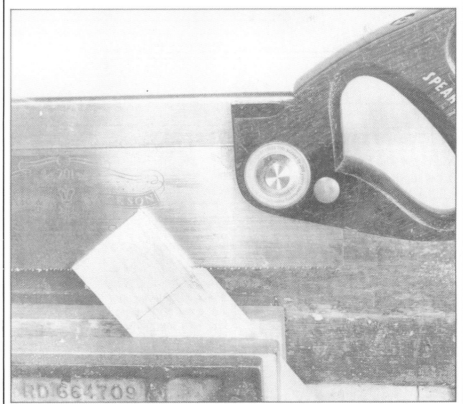

Photo 2 Turn rail in vice, place the saw in cut previously made and cut down the line visible to the shoulder line, reverse the rail in the vice and repeat for the other side. Finally set the rail upright in the vice and complete the sawing, let the saw run freely in cuts and finish to the shoulder line.

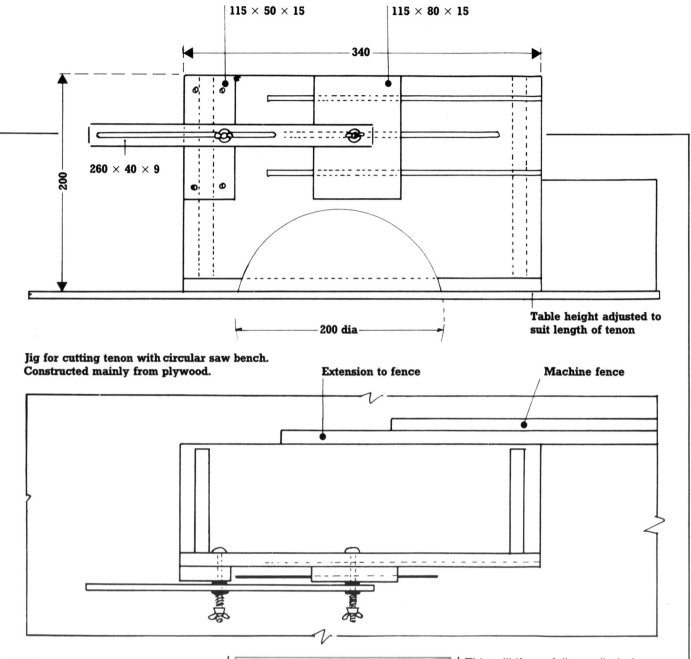

115 × 50 × 15   **115 × 80 × 15**

340

200

260 × 40 × 9

200 dia

Table height adjusted to
suit length of tenon

Jig for cutting tenon with circular saw bench.
Constructed mainly from plywood.

Extension to fence   Machine fence

CIRCULAR SAW METHOD

A circular saw machine can be used
to cut tenons, but this system can be

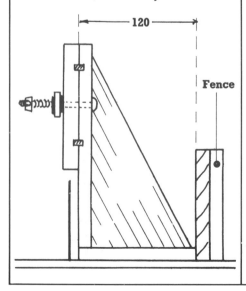

120

Fence

Photo. 3 Circular saw. Showing the first
cut, a mark is necessary on the table in
line with the teeth of the blade, this is
the stop line for the shoulder.

hazardous when the rail is raised
and is resting on a corner in the
position shown in the illustration.
When the circular saw is used for
this purpose then a jig should be
employed to hold the work securely.

This will if carefully applied give
reasonable safety. *(Before you reach
for your pen or telephone – Yes, this
is a most dangerous operation and
we do not advise this method.
However, for those without a*

Photo. 4 Firm control is required and
slow steady movement when the rail is
raised. There is a risk factor if this
method is used.

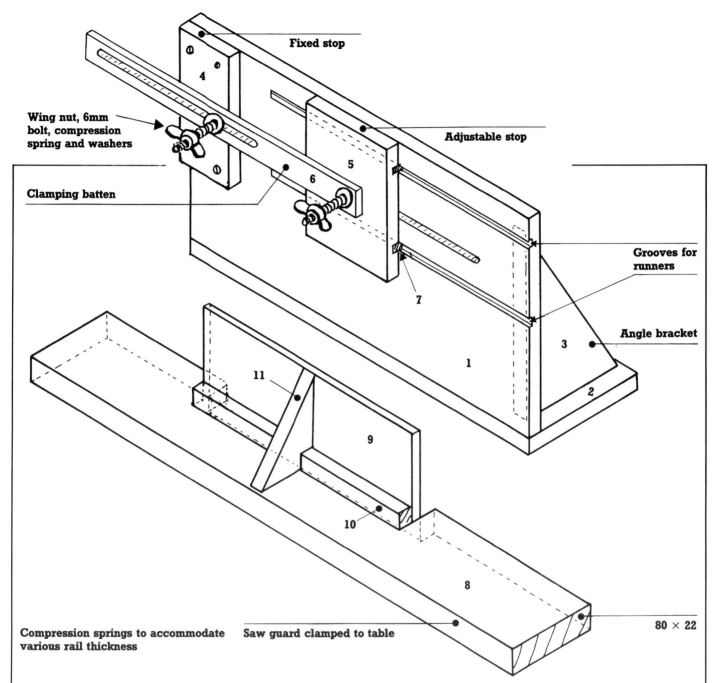

Fixed stop

Wing nut, 6mm
bolt, compression
spring and washers

Adjustable stop

Clamping batten

Grooves for
runners

Angle bracket

Compression springs to accommodate
various rail thickness

Saw guard clamped to table

80 × 22

bandsaw, which is the preferred
machine method, we must add, in all
fairness to the author, that he has
provided constructional details of a
safe and well proven jig. This type of
jig is traditional and commercially
available from some saw bench
manufacturers, although quite simple
to make yourself. – Ed.)

The jig shown in Fig. 1 is designed
to run against an extended fence on
a machine that can be adjusted to
vary the height of the blade. A guard
is also necessary to cover the
exposed saw.

The face side of the rail is placed
against the jig, one side of the tenon
is cut on each rail, the fence is then
adjusted for the second cut and the
process repeated. (The working
drawing for the jig is intended to be

used in conjunction with a 250mm
(8″) sawblade. If your sawbench
takes larger diameter sawblades,
then the drawing will require slight

modification. Some jigs are designed
to slide in the saw table groove,
which is even safer and more
accurate. – Ed.)

CUTTING LIST						
JIG						
PART	**DESCRIPTION**	**L**	**W**	**T**	**MATERIAL**	**QTY**
1	Back board	340	200	15	Plywood	1
2	Base	340	120	15	Plywood	1
3	Brackets	200	85	15	Plywood	2
4	Fixed stop	115	50	15	Plywood	1
5	Adjustable stop	115	80	15	Plywood	1
6	Clamp	260	40	9	Plywood	1
7	Runners	80	10	6	Hardwood	2
GUARD						
8	Base	500	80	22	Softwood	1
9	Guard	220	80	15	Plywood	1
10	Fillet	220	22	22	Softwood	1
11	Bracket	110	50	15	Plywood	1

Photo. 7 Tenons cut on bandsaw.

BANDSAW METHOD

This is the method I now use because it gives a quick and excellent result. It is easy to set up, the work is in contact with the table and the fence at all times and it is possible to take the work right to the shoulder line. Haunched and mitred tenons can also be cut perfectly. The essentials are a sharp blade and a deep fence set parallel to the blade and square to the table.

Whilst there is a risk factor in many things we do, and particularly in the use of woodcutting machinery, operations on a bandsaw, when carried out correctly, provide a high degree of safety. The blade running vertically has no effect on the work apart from the cutting action. Most other machines have a varying

amount of 'kick' when the work or the tool is applied at the start of the operation and provision must be made to control this, a condition that does not apply to a bandsaw.

Photo. 10 Bevel haunch.

Photo. 5 Band Saw. Checking blade and fence for accuracy.

Photo. 8 Cutting width of haunch.

Photo. 11 Mitre out to end of tenon.

Photo. 6 Cutting down tenon.

Photo. 9 Square haunch.

Photo. 12 Mitre cut with table inclined, suitable for wide tenon.

CHEST OF DRAWERS IN CHERRY

A project to satisfy high flyers and encourage others to raise their sights.

Fig. 2 Integral drawer runners and kickers.

English Cherry is the most versatile of all the fruitwoods. Its abundance and availability in larger sizes, and a greater variety of thicknesses and sections, makes it a most useful wood for the furniture maker.

Cherry is much under-rated and under-used, and seems to have been ignored by many woodworkers, but being "out of fashion" makes it currently available at an attractive price.

Machine planing and moulding requires care to avoid excessive tearing; patience at this stage will avoid scraper-burnt fingers later. Cherry is one of those "difficult" woods that cause woodworkers much frustration. One piece produces beautiful shavings from the smoothing plane, the next will not plane in any direction and the scraper has to be used. Another ailment that cherry suffers is dead knots which have become loose during conversion. These are best pushed out and repaired with a suitable cherry plug (end grain showing).

Cherry is a "fresh" wood, much suited to a bedroom setting. Time and patience taken in cleaning up will be more than rewarded in the finished product.

Fig. 1 End panel details and decoration.

This Chest of Drawers is both an attractive and extremely practical piece of furniture for the bedroom. It is traditionally styled, ageless and appealing to everyone, and of sensible proportions with a capacity able to solve the "crumpled shirt" problem.

CARCASE

The main structure of the chest is made entirely of cherry (although the inner framework of runners, kickers and guides could be got out of oak for extra resistance to wear). Basically, the carcase is made up of two framed and panelled ends,

joined together by the framework of the drawer rails, runners and kickers.

Each end consists of two corner posts and a top and bottom rail surrounding a flat panel. Corner posts are morticed to accommodate end rails and also the twin tenons of the drawer rails. Some small detail is applied to the inside of the panel framework (an ovolo or bead). (Fig. 1.) The $5/8$ thick panel is relieved at the back, to fit in a $5/16 \times 3/8$ deep groove.

Eight horizontal rails separate the ends. These are paired up and made into four frames to incorporate drawer runners and kickers. (Fig. 2.) The bottom pair of rails are kept thicker to give the piece a bit of stiffness and hopefully avoid any sagging over the length. All frame work is of mortice and tenon construction. Mortices for drawer divisions are also cut at this stage, divisions being 'sprung' in after assembly of the carcase.

BASE

The base has an ovolo mould worked along the top edge, and after being mitred at the corners is fixed by glue and screws (and the odd corner block) to the front and ends. The bracket shape can be bandsawn out before fitting or jigsawn

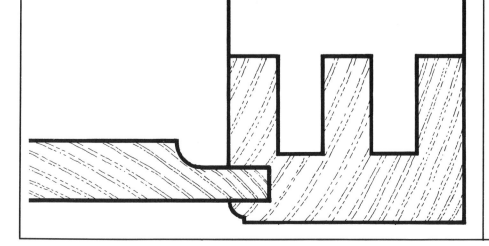

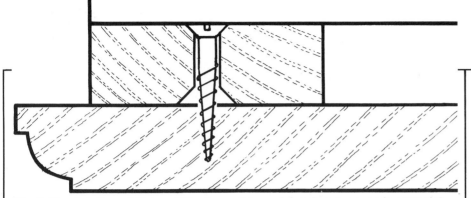

Fig. 3 Top details and fixing. Allowing solid wood freedom to move is essential.

afterwards. Either way the form requires very little cleaning up, other than a nice clean outline on the face.

WOOD

Wood selection requires the best stuff be set aside for top, drawer fronts and panels. The top obviously will be made up of two or more pieces. (You may be able, as I was, to get away with one piece panels, if you have the facility to plane and thickness them.) A good match of figure is a priority on the top. Good selection of boards, combined with a slightly hollowed edge joint, using PVA and held overnight with sash cramps, will result in a top that will remain stable and trouble free. An ovolo moulding softens the edges of the top and matches the base.

The top is fixed down by screwing through the top drawer rails and kickers, enlarging the clearance holes to allow for movement. Fig. 3. *(An old but useful technique which deserves to be more widely known.–Ed.)* The top overhangs the base by ¾" and 1" at the rear to overcome any skirting.

Drawer guides are accurately fixed behind divisions and at ends. This is also the time to make sure all inside bits are free from glue blobs and other obstructions. Removal of sharp edges will also be worthwhile.

A plywood back is accommodated in a rebate and fixed by screws.

DRAWERS

The nine drawers on three levels are graded in size from useful top drawers to large and deep drawers at the bottom, well proportioned and practical.

Drawer fronts are chosen so that each level of drawers are got out of one length of wood, and maintained in this position, so that the grain runs nicely through (showing some thought was taken). *Having a reasonable match of figuring for all the fronts is also essential.*

Sides and backs are of chestnut and need to finish no less than ⅜ thick for hard-working drawers in a situation like this. Drawer slips Fig. 4. hold the bottom in place (a couple of screws into the back) and also act as an extra bearing surface on the runner.

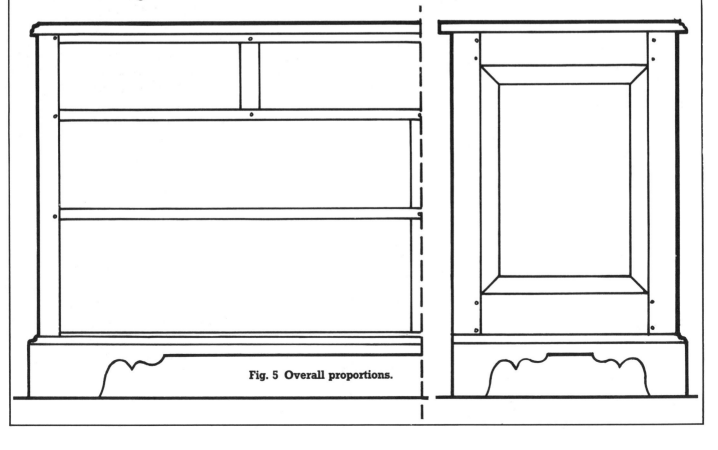

Fig. 5 Overall proportions.

Hand-cut dovetailed drawers will always be a sign of quality and fine craftsmanship; this piece will surely emphasise the dovetail. Every woodworker has his own preference regarding dovetailing. Sockets first and cut by eye has always been my approach. After assembly, the drawers are fitted and stopped in their respective compartments. Chestnut planes nicely and makes drawer fitting a pleasure.

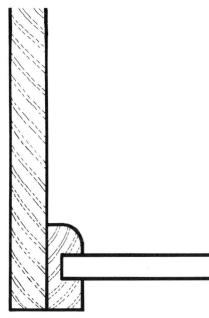

Fig. 4 Typical drawer slip arrangement.

The choice of handles can range from a variety of brass styles to turned cherry knobs. The ones on this piece are dulled brass swan neck, chosen because they enhance the colour of the wood.

POLISHING

A "pale outside" polish, hard wearing and durable, is used to finish the piece. One sealing coat brushed on and, after cutting down, further coats applied with the fad (pad). When a reasonable depth has been achieved (about three faddings) the piece is left overnight to harden and then dulled with fine wire wool and waxed.

Fig. 6 The completed project.

PART	DESCRIPTION	L	W	T	MATERIAL	QTY
1	Top	66″	21″	13/16″	Cherry	1
2	Corner posts	30⅜″	2½″	1¾″	Cherry	4
3	Top rails[1]	16¾″	2⅝″	13/16″	Cherry	2
4	Bottom rails[1]	16¾″	4¼″	13/16″	Cherry	2
5	Panels	20″	15″	⅝″	Cherry	2
6	Drawer rails[1]	63½″	2½″	13/16″	Cherry	6
7	Bottom drawer rails[1]	63½″	2½″	1⅛″	Cherry	2
8	Runners/kickers[1]	16¾″	3¼″	13/16″	Cherry	7
9	Runners/kickers[1]	16¾″	1¾″	13/16″	Cherry	8
10	Drawer divisions[2]	6⅜″	1¾″	13/16″	Cherry	2
11	Drawer divisions[2]	8¼″	1¾″	13/16″	Cherry	1
12	Drawer divisions[2]	10¼″	1¾″	13/16″	Cherry	1
13	Base	66″	5″	13/16″	Cherry	1
14	Base returns	21″	5″	13/16″	Cherry	2
15	Drawer fronts	15⅝″	5⅝″	¾″	Cherry	2
16	Drawer front	26¼″	5⅝″	¾″	Cherry	1
17	Drawer fronts	29⅝″	7½″	¾″	Cherry	2
18	Drawer fronts	29⅝″	9½″	¾″	Cherry	2
19	Drawer backs	15⅝″	4¾″	⅜″	Chestnut	2
20	Drawer back	26¼″	4¾″	⅜″	Chestnut	1
21	Drawer backs	29⅝″	6⅝″	⅜″	Chestnut	2
22	Drawer backs	29⅝″	8⅝″	⅜″	Chestnut	2
23	Drawer sides	17″	5⅝″	⅜″	Chestnut	6
24	Drawer sides	17″	7½″	⅜″	Chestnut	4
25	Drawer sides	17″	9½″	⅜″	Chestnut	4
26	Drawer bottoms	14½″	17¼″	¼″	Plywood	2
27	Drawer bottom	25⅛″	17¼″	¼″	Plywood	1
28	Drawer bottoms	28⅜″	17¼″	¼″	Plywood	2
29	Drawer bottoms	28⅜″	17¼″	¼″	Plywood	2
30	Back	62¼″	22⅝″	¼″	Plywood	1

NOTES:[1] Measurements include 1¼″ tenons.[2] Measurements include ⅜″ tenons. Cutting list does not include the odd batten, block, drawer guide, peg or drawer slips which can usually be found in the form of scraps or offcuts.

SUNDRIES: 12 suitable drawer handles or knobs, wood glue and screws.

MAKING TOOLS FOR MINIATURE TURNING

The article we promised you in the last issue. Now you can really have fun and put fine detail on some of your full-scale work.

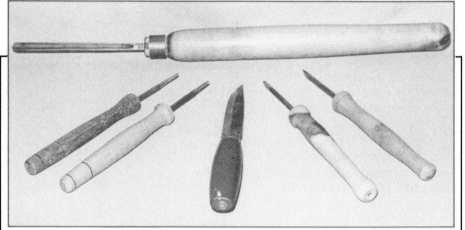

Tools used for miniature turning include ¼" gouge, sharp knife, homemade scrapers.

Making miniature wood turnings is not only easy but also a great deal of creative fun. All that is needed is a tune up on your lathe, a few standard tools, and some custom scrapers that you can easily make.

If you've already done some wood turning you more than likely have a quarter inch gouge for roughing square stock and forming the intial shape of the work. You also probably have a good quality knife with a blade three or four inches long which is used for making the final parting cut. These tools, when used with dense, close grained hardwoods, like maple, birch, or apple, will help you get a good start in turning miniatures.

TUNED-UP LATHE

Better miniature turning can be accomplished by using a tuned-up ten or twelve inch lathe rather than a miniature lathe. The larger lathe is at the right working height, and the greater weight mass absorbs vibration much better. The main thing to aim for when tuning up your lathe is to get rid of all vibration, including a thumping belt, out of round pulleys, rough bearings or shaking motor. Draw filing all nicks and bumps from your tool rest will give smooth cutting responses. Any of these problems make good woodturning a hundred times more difficult and more frustrating than it need be. In fact, miniature turning is just about impossible with a badly vibrating machine.

Stock for miniature turnings can be mounted between centres but, when tension is placed on the wood, many broken turnings will result. This can be overcome by holding stock by one end only, in a three or four-jawed chuck, a collet chuck, or a homemade chuck. (See The Practical Woodturner by F. Pain. pp 50 & 91.)

CAUTION

A great deal of caution must be used with a three or four-jawed chuck because the spinning jaws are exposed and can badly smash knuckles and tools alike. I prefer the four-jawed chuck. Squared stock can be mounted directly without having to round stock between centres first as with all other chucks.

Stock should not be longer than four inches to keep flexing to a minimum and for safety and accurate turnings. With a spindle speed of about 2000 r.p.m. stock can very quickly be roughed out, shaped with scrapers, and sanded lightly using 120–180 grid paper. Finish can be applied while the miniature is still on

Miniatures turned with above tools. ¾" button rests on table leg for size comparison.

the lathe, or the miniature can be removed with a sharp knife and finished later.

CUSTOM SCRAPERS

To make your own custom scrapers follow the directions in the diagram and pictures, keeping the following points in mind.

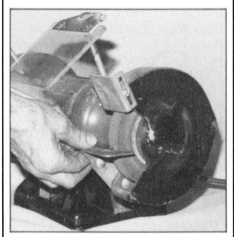

Step 1. Grind off head of concrete nail.

Step 1. Wear protective eye gear while grinding hardened masonery nails. They are brittle and may break.

Step 2. Use the fine grinding wheel of a bench grinder with the tool rest set as close as possible to the grinding wheel and tool rest.

Step 3. Dip the tool that you are grinding in water often to prevent losing the tempering in the steel.

Step 4. Use a small flat or triangular file to make the base side so that all other angles can be

Step 2. File a flat side along the total length of nail.

Step 3. Drill a hole in handle and mount nail with pointed end in handle.

positioned correctly. This base side should be about ⅛″ wide. It is also used as a stop-lock to keep the chisel from turning in the handle when it is being used.

Step 5. Make the handles five inches long out of ⅝″ or ¾″ dowels, or you can turn up fancy ones similar to the diagram. I like to make every one a little different shape or a

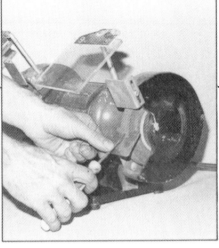

Step 4. Grind scraper to desired shape. Be sure to dip tool in water often to cool.

Step 5. Sharpen on sander/grinder.

different type of wood for easy identification when the tool is buried in a pile of shavings.

BELT SANDER

If you do not have a belt sander/grinder similar to the one in the picture, clamp a portable belt sander in a vice for final shaping.

Once you have made your scrapers and tuned up your lathe you are ready, not only to make miniatures, but put fine details on articles like drawer knobs, thimbles, chessmen, and crochet needles.

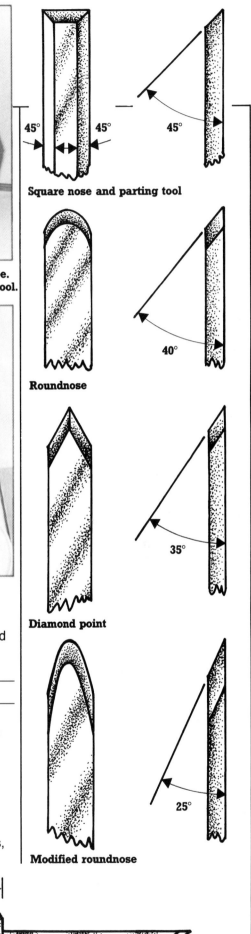

45°   45°   45°

Square nose and parting tool

40°

Roundnose

35°

Diamond point

25°

Modified roundnose

5″

¾″

Dowel or hardwood handle

Drawings not to scale

TORSION BOX COFFEE TABLE

A high quality piece of furniture of excellent design but with no traditional joints.

This design was the final solution to a commission to produce a small coffee table of "modern design". The table to be – low, square, based upon the torsion box principle; open on one side to accept record sleeves, cassette boxes, etc.; fitted with a glass top and to match teak finished furniture. With the need to match furniture of simple line and smooth veneered surfaces there was no scope for decorative joint work. The decision was therefore made to go to the other extreme and construct the table with the minimum of joints.

The torsion box top presents no problems being constructed from good quality 9mm thick multi-ply glued and screwed together. The top being decorated with teak veneer, quartered. The sides (inside and out), the bottom (inside and out) and the inside of the top of the box being covered with leather cloth. The material used was the type of leather cloth used for upholstery in the better class car trade. Thick luxurious leather, textured and of a rich chestnut colour. The top and bottom edges of the top being trimmed with mouldings of solid timber (teak), with the top mouldings rebated to accept the glass top. The base is simple box construction, again of 9mm thick plywood, dimensioned to balance the top and clad with polished copper. The polished copper reflects the floor covering and gives the illusion of a "floating" top.

METHOD

The method used was as follows:
Prepare the five pieces of plywood for the top, mark off, drill and

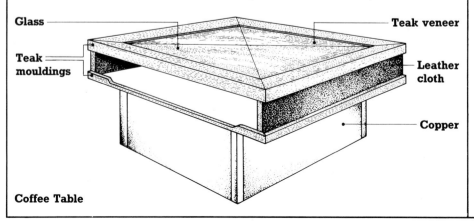

Glass

Teak mouldings

Teak veneer

Leather cloth

Copper

Coffee Table

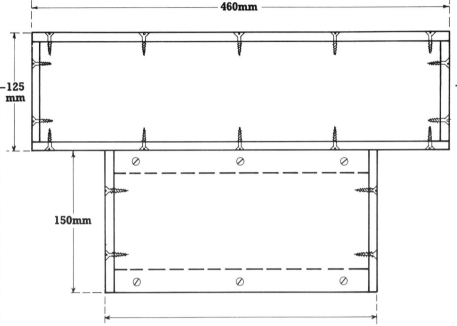

Front Elevation. Showing timber construction – less leather cloth, copper and teak mouldings.

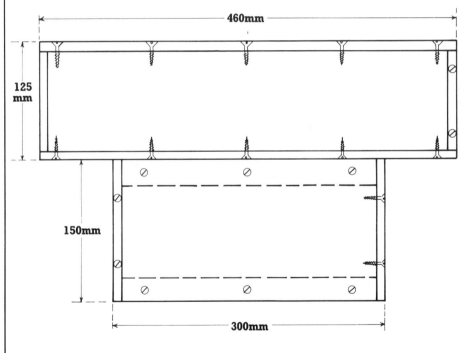

Side Elevation.

countersink for the woodscrews in all pieces. A "dry run" assembly (without glue) is advisable at this stage, a check that all dimensions are correct and square, together with holes ready to accept the screws makes assembly that much easier when all mating surfaces are wet with glue.

Before gluing up it is necessary to veneer the top. If the hot glue method is used final trimming of each section of the veneer will be made at the time of laying and the user will probably be well acquainted with the requirements of this method. A very satisfactory result can be obtained using an ordinary adhesive of the P.V.A. type but preparation of the veneer is somewhat different. The strip of veneer will need to be slightly wider than half the width of the top with four sections of veneer cut in the form of triangles with the grain running parallel to the edges of the top.

It will be seen that the length of the grain diminishes towards the point in the centre. To avoid these fragile pieces breaking away, precautions must be taken. Traditionally gummed paper tape is used (for ease of removal later). The method is to cover the cutline with a strip of tape to support and reinforce the veneer before cutting. Match the four pieces of veneer, trim as necessary for as near a perfect joint as you can get, and secure the four pieces with strips of tape.

When cramping up after gluing it is necessary to apply pressure evenly over the entire surface. A pad of newspaper and a stout cover board held down with battens and "G" cramps will give good results. Check that the veneer has not crept out of square as pressure is applied. When thoroughly dry the tape can be removed and the veneer sanded, or better, cleaned up with a cabinet scraper. The top box structure can now be glued and screwed up in

final assembly. It will be noted that as plywood is used for the base for the veneer it will not be necessary to counter veneer on the underside as would be the case if solid wood had been used.

The bottom box section is cut, marked out for drilling and countersinking for the wood screws, drilled, countersunk, glued and screwed up. To give a more substantial area in contact with the

floor and to give a means of fixing the base to the top, simple mitred frames are fitted, glued and screwed to the top and bottom of the base. The two sections can now be screwed together and dimensions checked.

MOULDINGS

The solid teak mouldings for the top are of simple section, the upper

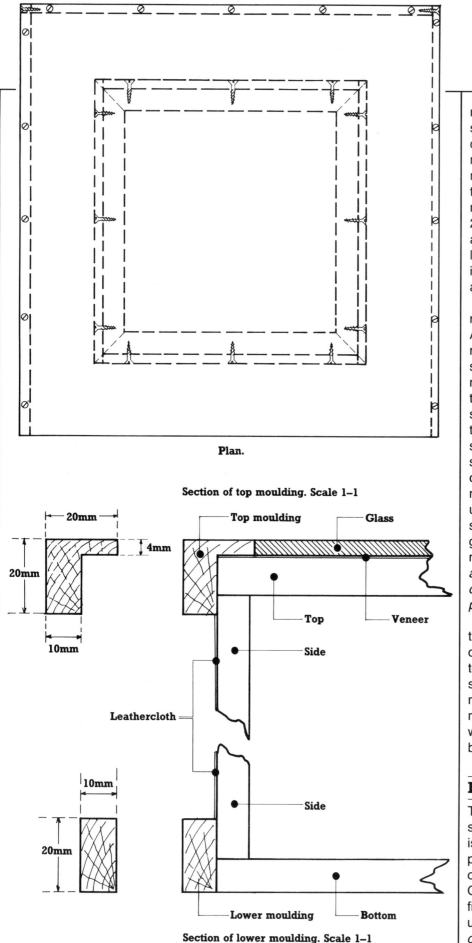

Plan.

Section of top moulding. Scale 1–1

20mm

4mm

20mm

10mm

Top moulding

Glass

Top

Veneer

Side

Leathercloth

Side

10mm

20mm

Lower moulding

Bottom

Section of lower moulding. Scale 1–1

mouldings being cut from 20mm square timber rebated as per the drawings. Framing the top with mitred corners and providing the recess for the 4mm thick glass top is the next operation. The lower mouldings being simply 20mm x 10mm rectangular section, again mitred at the corners. The lower front moulding being cut away in the centre to give uninterrupted access to the inside of the top box.

In the original table these mouldings were glued to the box with Aerolite 306 resin glue to avoid the need for pinning or screwing through show faces on the mouldings. The method used was to fit and cramp up the two opposite mouldings using sashcramps, then to fit and cramp up the two remaining mouldings of the set, adjusting until as near a perfect set of joints as possible was obtained. The original pair of mouldings was then removed, glued up, replaced and cramped up. The second pair was then removed, glued up, and replaced in like manner. *The benefit of this apparently lengthy procedure is that one is always cramping back to a positive location.*

When gluing up teak, which is a timber containing natural oils, it is desirable to wipe over the surfaces to be glued with a little methylated spirit to remove the oil. The lower mouldings were affixed in like manner. After final cleaning up, a rub with teak oil brought out all the beauty of the timber.

LEATHER CLADDING

The leather cloth cladding to the top section is not difficult to apply if care is taken with the cutting out. If possible clad the sides inside and out with one piece of material. Commence in an inside back corner fixing down with any good quality upholstery cement. *Care with this operation will add immeasurably to*

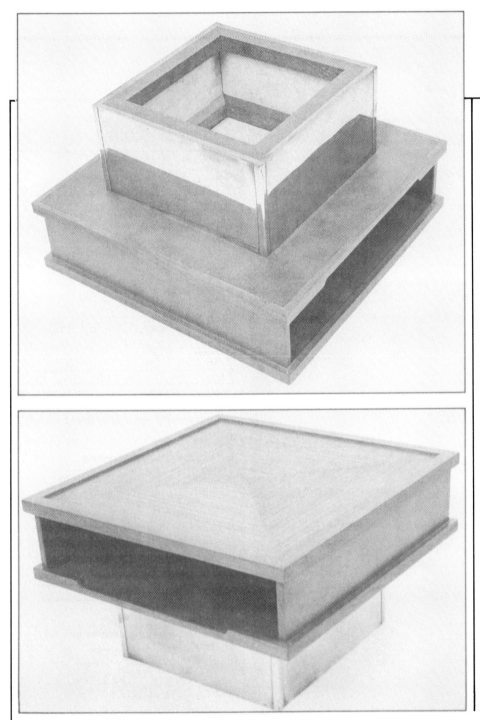

not to blemish the surfaces; scratches and bruises are almost impossible to remove and are only emphasised by the final high polish.

Obtain four pieces of copper sheet, dimensioned to suit the base, and four strips of copper 20mm wide by the depth of the base. Fold up these strips to form four equal sided angles. Folding can be done by clamping each strip between two pieces of smooth hardwood, half of the width of the strip protruding. Dress over to form the angle using a strip of softwood and light blows from a hammer. Try to turn over the entire length at once taking several blows to turn the full angle required.

The panels should be positioned, the corners covered with the angles and all secured with three small round-headed brass wood screws in each flange of the angles (a total of twenty-four screws). The copper cladding should now be polished; a polishing mop in an electric drill will rapidly bring up a superb shine. The base can now be fixed to the top section.

All that remains is to obtain a piece of 4mm glass (cut 2mm undersize to the aperture in the top moulding) with the edges polished. The glass, when placed in position, will accentuate the beauty of the quartered veneer, provide a durable top surface and complete a useful and decorative item of furniture.

the final appearance. Cut and fit the top and bottom inside cladding. Again a "dry run" to obtain exact size will make the gluing down a simpler job. A leather cloth finish to the underside of the top is not essential but does add a touch of quality to the overall article. Cut and glue as for the other pieces.

COPPER CLADDING

Cladding the base with copper is straightforward. Care must be taken

CUTTING LIST						
PART	DESCRIPTION	L	W	T	MATERIAL	QTY
1	Top section t+b	460	460	9	Plywood	2
2	Sides of top section	460	107	9	Plywood	2
3	Back of top section	442	107	9	Plywood	1
4	Sides of base section	282	150	9	Plywood	2
5	Base section frame	282	25	25	Softwood	8
6	Top moulding	1880	20	20	Teak	1
7	Bottom moulding	1880	20	10	Teak	1
8	Veneer	1120	240	—	Teak	1

SUNDRIES: Leather, copper, glue, screws, teak oil, 4mm glass cut 2mm undersize to aperture in top moulding.

WOODWORKING TIPS

Easy method for producing bowl with exact matching lid

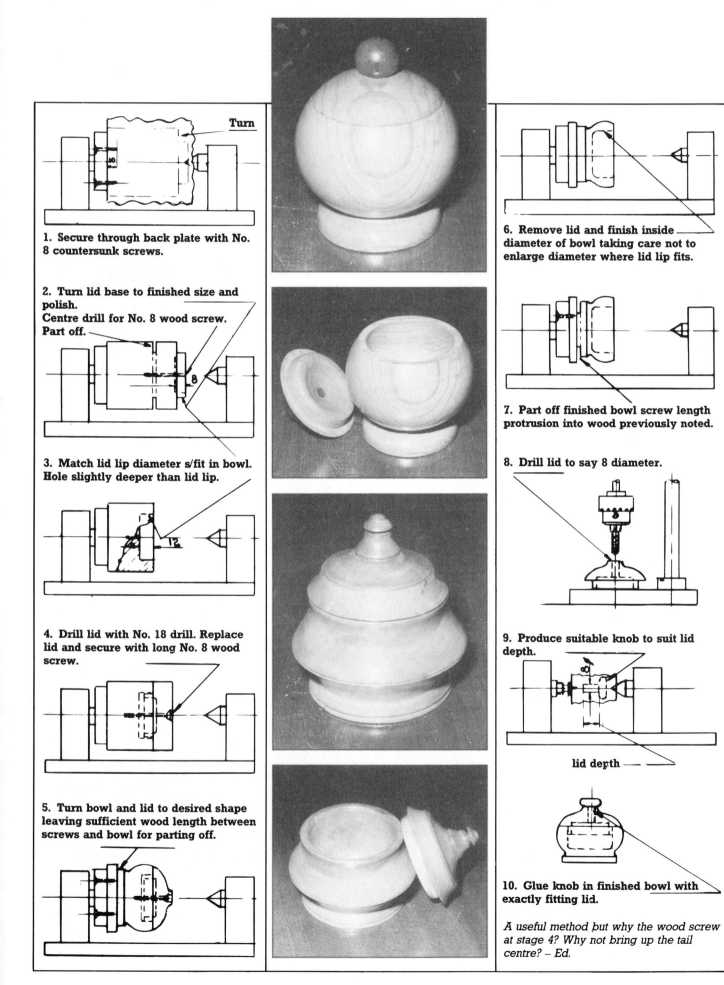

1. Secure through back plate with No. 8 countersunk screws.

2. Turn lid base to finished size and polish.
Centre drill for No. 8 wood screw.
Part off.

3. Match lid lip diameter s/fit in bowl. Hole slightly deeper than lid lip.

4. Drill lid with No. 18 drill. Replace lid and secure with long No. 8 wood screw.

5. Turn bowl and lid to desired shape leaving sufficient wood length between screws and bowl for parting off.

6. Remove lid and finish inside diameter of bowl taking care not to enlarge diameter where lid lip fits.

7. Part off finished bowl screw length protrusion into wood previously noted.

8. Drill lid to say 8 diameter.

9. Produce suitable knob to suit lid depth.

lid depth

10. Glue knob in finished bowl with exactly fitting lid.

A useful method but why the wood screw at stage 4? Why not bring up the tail centre? – Ed.

TURNING A LIDDED CONTAINER

Lidded containers, call them what you will, boxes or bowls with lids, have fascinated turners for centuries and the recipients have been equally intrigued. Obviously, before starting to turn, the size, proportion and shape will have been decided.

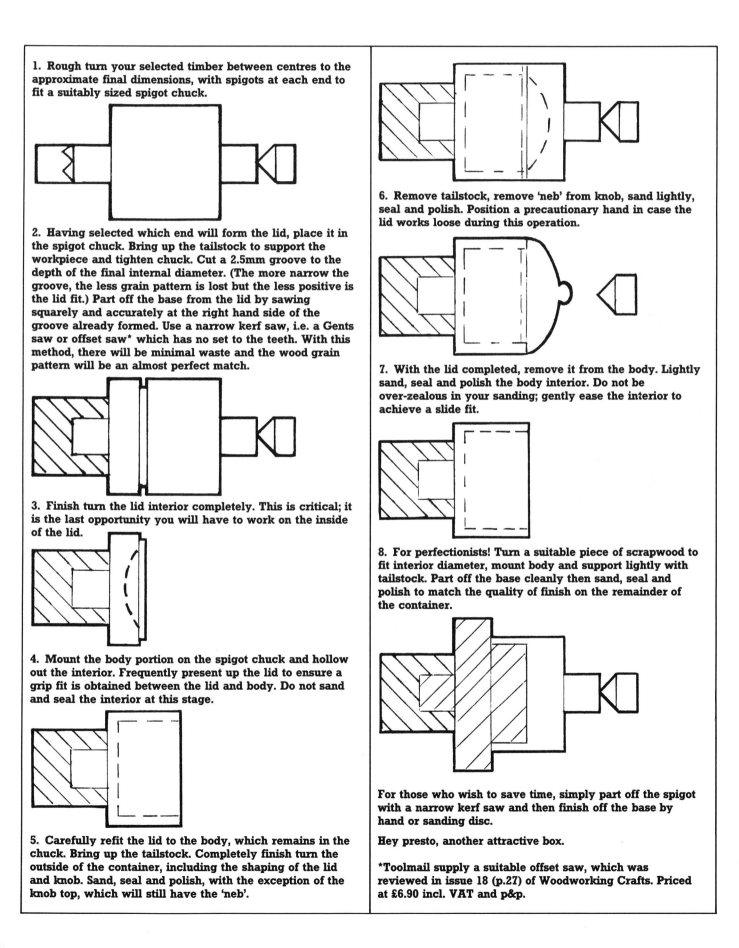

1. Rough turn your selected timber between centres to the approximate final dimensions, with spigots at each end to fit a suitably sized spigot chuck.

2. Having selected which end will form the lid, place it in the spigot chuck. Bring up the tailstock to support the workpiece and tighten chuck. Cut a 2.5mm groove to the depth of the final internal diameter. (The more narrow the groove, the less grain pattern is lost but the less positive is the lid fit.) Part off the base from the lid by sawing squarely and accurately at the right hand side of the groove already formed. Use a narrow kerf saw, i.e. a Gents saw or offset saw* which has no set to the teeth. With this method, there will be minimal waste and the wood grain pattern will be an almost perfect match.

3. Finish turn the lid interior completely. This is critical; it is the last opportunity you will have to work on the inside of the lid.

4. Mount the body portion on the spigot chuck and hollow out the interior. Frequently present up the lid to ensure a grip fit is obtained between the lid and body. Do not sand and seal the interior at this stage.

5. Carefully refit the lid to the body, which remains in the chuck. Bring up the tailstock. Completely finish turn the outside of the container, including the shaping of the lid and knob. Sand, seal and polish, with the exception of the knob top, which will still have the 'neb'.

6. Remove tailstock, remove 'neb' from knob, sand lightly, seal and polish. Position a precautionary hand in case the lid works loose during this operation.

7. With the lid completed, remove it from the body. Lightly sand, seal and polish the body interior. Do not be over-zealous in your sanding; gently ease the interior to achieve a slide fit.

8. For perfectionists! Turn a suitable piece of scrapwood to fit interior diameter, mount body and support lightly with tailstock. Part off the base cleanly then sand, seal and polish to match the quality of finish on the remainder of the container.

For those who wish to save time, simply part off the spigot with a narrow kerf saw and then finish off the base by hand or sanding disc.

Hey presto, another attractive box.

*Toolmail supply a suitable offset saw, which was reviewed in issue 18 (p.27) of Woodworking Crafts. Priced at £6.90 incl. VAT and p&p.

OCCASIONAL TABLE

DESIGN SPONSORSHIP BY RECORD MARPLES LTD

An advanced project that provides an opportunity to acquire two useful skills – those of laminating and jig making.

This table is designed as an exploration of the relationship of various curves and radiused forms. While not a job for the novice, it could be an opportunity to discover some of the principles and applications of laminating and jig making. Although the use of larger machinery may make the job a little easier and quicker, the only really essential power tool is a reasonably powerful portable router. *(This is important. – Ed.)*

I have used a combination of ash and yew to achieve a quiet contrast in materials, but this choice is largely a matter of personal taste. I would however recommend that fairly straight grained, mild timber be used for the leg laminates in particular. The lipping laminates are of course eventually glued to the top so movement there is less of a problem: if you are new to laminating, though, be fair and give yourself a chance.

THE TOP

The ground material used was 12mm plywood. This is not essential but used in preference to chipboard or MDF because of its relative lightness.

The final overall diameter of the top, including a 12mm thick lipping, is 600mm; therefore the ply diameter is 576mm. This can be marked out using a large compass or trammels and leaving a good 5mm all round. The veneers can now be prepared. In this job I have laid it straight across, though more elaborate methods are possible if desired. (On a previous similar job a geometric, matching pattern was built up dividing the round top into three wedges. This however calls for very accurate shooting of the veneers and painstaking fitting, though it shouldn't be beyond anyone with a little experience of using veneers.)

I have used bookmatched leaves, shot together while pressed between

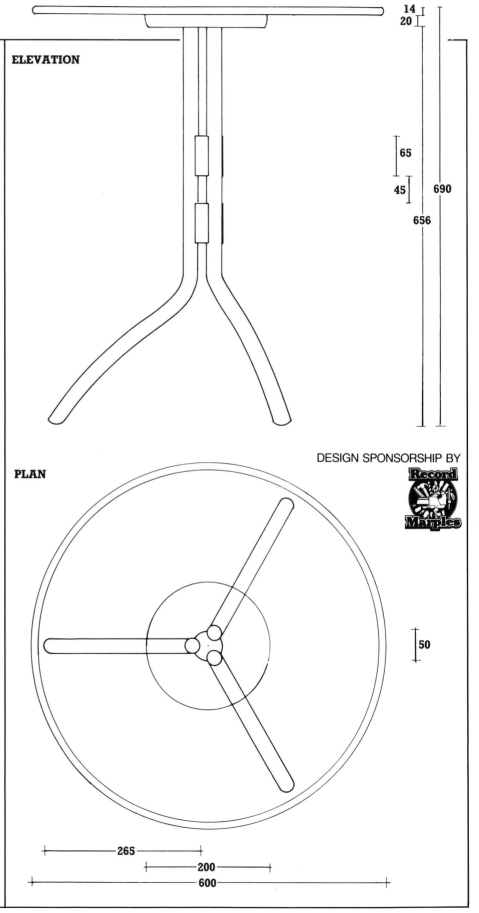

ELEVATION

14
20
65
45
690
656

DESIGN SPONSORSHIP BY

PLAN

50

265
200
600

Photo 3 Lipping bends and top panel

ply battens, then taped. If a central joint line is to coincide with the centre of the circle, rule a faint pencil line through the centre and mark it out on the edge of the ply, to assist in lining the joint up. I laid the veneer using a simple homemade press consisting of 2 × 1200 × 600 sheets of thick chipboard and a series of curved battens. Put paper or polythene sheet between the veneer and press to prevent glue seepage sticking your top to the press! *(Polythene sheet is safer since seepage of glue through paper can sometimes lock the whole thing up into a solid mass if porous veneers let overmuch glue through. – Ed.)*

The glue (Cascamite or PVA are suitable) should be spread evenly on the ground material, the first sheet of veneer applied, glue spread on the other side and veneer applied to that. Make sure veneers are correctly positioned and the grain direction of each side is the same. (If ply is used, lay across the grain of the face veneers.) Put the assembly in the press and arrange the curved battens to apply pressure evenly. It pays to have the cramps set up to correct length in advance – remember your glue is beginning to cure. When cramping, make sure pressure is applied evenly from both ends of batten so that it bears down in the centre of the caul first.

When pressing is complete, the top can be roughly cleaned up on both faces, the centre found and the final true circle routed using a trammel bar. Use the underside of the top to swing the trammel bar on,

Photo 1 Lipping bends and jig

otherwise you will have to patch the hole that the pin makes. *(Should it be desirable to mark from the face side, a small piece of thin plywood or hardboard, secured with double-sided tape, will protect the veneered face. – Ed.)*

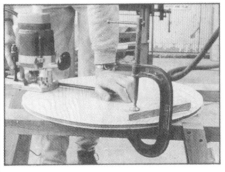

Photo 2 Trimming top panel

LIPPINGS

These are of laminated construction and applied in three sections around the table top. The laminating jig consists of a male and female former, routed using a 12.7mm cutter (the thickness of the assembled laminate). I used MDF but chipboard or good quality ply will do.

The thickness of the jig material should be at least 19mm and the veneers at least that wide to allow for trimming. The diameter of the top being 576, the inside radius of the lipping will be 288mm and this is the radius of the curve to be routed, again using the router and trammel bar. However, if thick saw cut veneers are used as individual laminates (I used 4 × 3.2mm thick), a fair degree of springback will probably take place when the assembly is removed from the jig.

This will be relatively less of a problem if thinner (and therefore a greater number of) laminates are used. A little experiment may be necessary as there are many variables – the type and quality of wood and number and thickness of the laminates. It is important that the combined thickness of the laminates equals the diameter of the cutter used in making the jig. If serious springback occurs, reduce the radius of jig curved by 10 to 15mm. (This will mean making a new jig – don't try and modify an existing one.)

It is helpful to pin or screw a baseboard to one side of the jig to keep the two sides in the same plane when cramping. Wax the jig before gluing up laminates. The veneers used to make up the laminates can, as previously mentioned, be either knife cut decorative thickness (approximately 0.6mm) bought from the merchant, or you can prepare your own, bandsawing or circular ripsawing from the solid.

If sawing from the solid, mark the wood before cutting, and keep the veneers in sequence. Avoid wild grain, knots and obvious defects. Quarter sawn stuff will be less liable to twist but is not essential in this application. Neither hand or machine planing of the sawn veneers is essential though it can be done if desired. If the veneers are planed, sand them lightly before gluing. However I glued up straight from the saw.

According to my simple arithmetic, the circumference of 600mm diameter circle, divided into three

Photo 4 Cramping lipping bends to top panel

Photo 5 Final trimming of lipping

that for the lipping. However we first of all have to make a template of the profile of the leg, out of thin ply or hardboard. The exact height (length) or curve of the leg is not critical and can be adjusted according to personal preference.

Make a drawing and transfer that information to the template material by using a grid or simply tracing it off. Saw and smooth the template using spokeshaves, plane, rasp and sanding. Lay the template on a

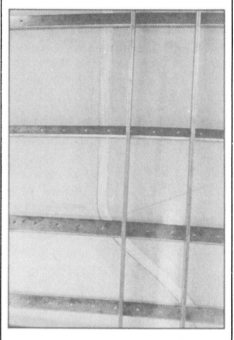

makes 628.4mm. Allow at least 60mm on the length at this stage.

Once the bends have been made they should be degreased on the inside surface to remove any wax from the jig, using meths and a light sanding. Measure the required lengths off and cut two sections to length. The butt joint at the end of each section is most easily worked with a disc sander, but can be sawn and pared.

The three sections are glued on one by one to maximise the control over the gluing process. This is of course somewhat time consuming, but using a fast acting PVA glue, not too much so. It also reduces the number of cramps needed at any one time. A web cramp was used to apply general pressure, with lipping cramps (of which I never seem to have enough) used as back up and local pressure.

Once the first lipping is on, cramp on the second section dry and fit the third and final section into the remaining space. If care is taken to be accurate here the three sections will exert sufficient end to end pressure on each other to make very neat joints. Glue on the second section with the third in place but dry. Finally glue on the third section.

The lipping can then be trimmed flush with the veneered surfaces using the router to remove most of the waste. (Simply fix a piece of chipboard or ply to the base of the router, then set the cutter depth to just above the veneer surface.) Finish the process with a finely set plane and scraper. Finally the lipping can be radiused using a rounding over cutter.

THE LEGS

Similiar principles apply to the making of the jig for the legs as to

Photos 6 and 7 Cramping of leg bends

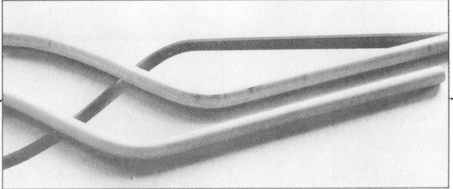

Photo 10 Legs in various stages of being rounded

further piece of ply and scribe a line 25mm from it exactly parallel to it. This will give the profile of the opposite side of the jig.

The templates can be checked for parallel by inserting 25mm spacers at several points between them. They should all be a snug fit. If not, it would be wise to line the jig with thin cork to take up any error.

Next the jig material: the final section of the leg being 25mm, this will need to be about 30mm thick. To achieve this, glue together sheets of suitable material to an appropriate thickness. (I used 2 × 15mm MDF.)

Pin the templates down in the required position, leaving plenty of material either side to distribute cramping pressure evenly. The two sides can be first sawn to within 1 or 2mm then routed in stages with a following cutter running off the template.

The whole process of making this jig can be simplified by using a 25mm cutter and a template follower. This necessitates the making of only one template and guarantees a parallel cut but a 25mm tungsten tipped cutter is a fair investment for the home workshop!

Once the jig is made, prepare the veneers. They should be approximately 30mm wide.

Make sure the combined thickness of the veneers *when cramped together* is 25mm or even a fraction more. Don't rely on arithmetical

Photo 8 Leg bends

calculation for this, as it is quite possible to compress the laminate more than one might think.

Leave plenty of extra length on the laminates (this should be catered for in the jig). Use an end stop screwed to one or both ends of one side of the jig to keep the two sides in the correct relationship to each other. Cramp on both sides of the jig to prevent the two sides from pinching in on the top edge of the laminate.

Again use a baseboard. Wax the jig and be liberal with the glue which I suggest should be cascamite because of the increased open assembly time, and its gap-filling properties. Allow the glue to cure thoroughly.

Photo 9 Routing radius onto leg bends

When the assembly is released from the jig you should have a bend with a section of approximately 30 × 25mm. This can now be trimmed to length and cleaned up straight and parallel prior to routing on a table with a 12.7 radius cutter, with a guide pin. Don't expect to achieve a perfectly round section straight from the machine. You will need to leave

a slight flat for the guide pin to bear on when making the last pass. Finish rounding the section, scraping, rasping, sanding – using any convenient means, paying special attention to the accuracy of the upright parts which are to be jointed with connectors. It would pay to make a thin ply template to check this, drilling a 25mm hole then sawing through, leaving a half round section.

Photos 11 and 12 Connector about to be routed

THE CONNECTORS

These are turned to finish at 50mm diameter. If sufficiently thick stock isn't available to do this, laminate sections together. With hindsight I think it better and quicker to turn a sufficient length for two connectors – plus a generous allowance for waste.

Photo 14 First connector slot routed

The jig for routing the half round slots consists of a box into which the 50mm turned section will fit snugly (err on the tight side). The sides are slightly higher than the turned section and should be exactly level and parallel, for the router base to run on. At one end is a fixed stop, at the other either a bolted sliding stop or a cramped stop. The sides should run on past the end stops, to prevent the router tipping at the end of the cut.

The stops need only be half the height of the turned section; a reference line is scribed across the centre of the fixed end. The end of the turned section should be trisected, and marked out with a centre square. To do this, draw a slightly smaller circle from the centre of the turned section and then, using the radius of that circle, step off six sections around its circumference with dividers. With a centre square, mark through three of these points to give you the centres of the slots.

The turned section can now be inserted into the jig, the reference line coinciding with one of those marked on the end grain and the whole cramped up securely to prevent movement while routing.

It is surprising how much the action of the cutter will attempt to turn the cylindrical part in the jig, thus ending up with a gently spiralling slot. Not the desired effect!

Photo 13

The router cutter used is a 25mm diameter, radius cutter. Set the depth of cut to 12.5mm or slightly less and rout the slot in several passes. When all three slots have been routed cut the connectors to length.

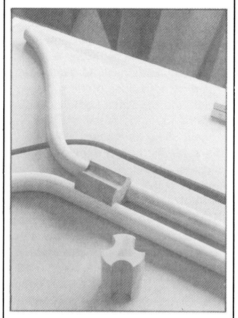

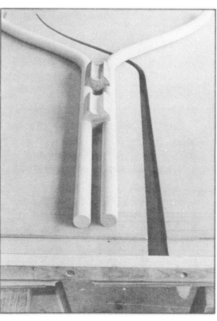

Photos 15 and 16 Connectors being fitted

Photos 17 and 18 Marking and drilling jig

Some relieving of the bottom of the slot may be necessary as, due to the way the cutter is ground, it produces a small flat at the tip. This can be dealt with by scraping and sanding using a length of dowel as a sanding block.

The legs are fixed to the connectors using two 25mm × 8 screws into each slot, counterbored and plugged. Mark out the position for drilling the counterbore and clearance holes on the leg, measuring down from the top which should have been previously trimmed to length. As an aid to accuracy, an L shaped jig can be quickly made to steady the leg during drilling, though this isn't essential. Once this is done each connector can be fitted onto the

Photo 20 Legs and connectors fixed into undertop, showing domed plugs and plug cutter

Photo 21 Underside of finished top

leg and screws pricked through to give the pilot hole drilling position.

The legs are now ready for final fitting and fixing to the connectors.

THE UNDERTOP

This consists of a disc of solid wood, into which the tops of the legs are let. The top is then fixed to it by countersunk screws.

The disc is best made from well seasoned, quartersawn stock, as even over 200mm there can be some noticeable cupping of the timber. Alternatively stained ply or MDF could be used, or ply with a veneer lipping ironed on. The stock should be prepared in the usual way and can be bandsawn and routed to a circle.

From the centre of the disc mark out in pencil a 50mm diameter circle. Trisect this circle by the same method as used in marking out the connectors. These points are then the centres for 25mm drilled holes, 8mm deep to take the legs.

The legs are fixed into the undertop by means of screws. A long grain plug is inserted close to the end of the leg to avoid relying on end grain screwing. This plug can be

worked on the inside face of the leg, not taken through, and therefore remain unseen. The plug itself is easily made with a Ridgeway plug cutter available in a variety of sizes. These, while seeming initially quite expensive, have proved a constantly useful tool in my workshop for a variety of purposes.

The plugs for the connector fixing holes can be left long and domed over to make an appropriate decorative detail. In a previous incarnation of this table, I have left

the structural elements unglued and relied on the good fit and dry fixings. Even the plugs can be left a tight friction fit straight from the cutter, and so far everything has held together well. That is not to say that glue must not be used on the connections or undertop joints. If you do decide to use it, I would again recommend a gap filling U.F. glue like Cascamite.

Polishes used will depend very much on the materials used and whether a high finish, or an especially water resistant surface is required. Oil, wax and lacquer finishes are all appropriate, though I have some reservations about the effectiveness of oil on a veneered surface which will already be well saturated with glue.

Photo 22 Completed table

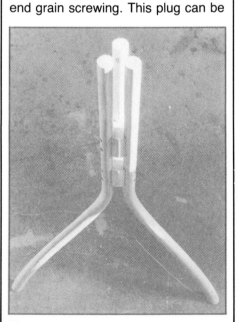

Photo 19 Legs and connectors fixed

CUTTING LIST						
PART	DESCRIPTION	L	W	T	MATERIAL	QTY
1	Leg Veneers[1]	900	30	2.5	—	10
2	Lipping Veneers[1]	700	20	3.2	—	12
3	Connectors[2]	150	55	55	—	1
4	Top	600	600	12	12mm Ply	1
5	Undertop	220	220	20	—	1

NOTES: 1. Refer to text. 2. To be turned to 50mm diameter.

SUNDRIES: Veneers for top, at least 8 sq.ft. are required. Cascamite or PVA glue for fixing veneers, screws.

DISPLAY SHELVES

This sound traditional design by an accomplished craftsman reflects considerable care in planning and techniques. Joint work is particularly neat and sensible for this piece of work.

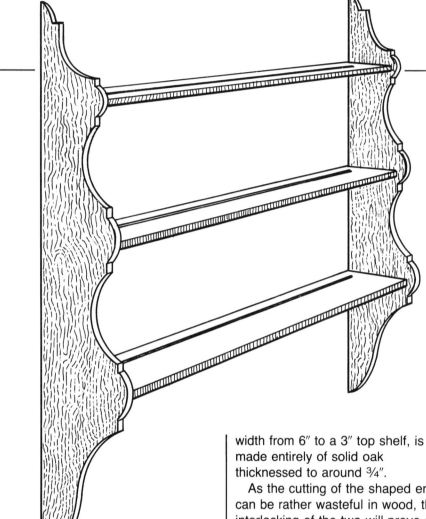

decorated with a small bead. The provision for the display of decorative plates is catered for by the machining of a 'plate groove' into the upper surfaces of the shelves. This shallow groove is run out about 2″ from each end, Fig. 2.

(How the groove is formed will depend upon the tools or machinery available. You can of course bring out your grand-daddy's moulding planes or revert to the portable router with the appropriate cutters.

Fig. 1 The outline of the shaped ends

The brief for this project was "a kitchen shelving unit to display functional pieces of kitchenware". The setting was a traditional cottage kitchen – a Welsh dresser, cottage table and sink cupboard unit, all in oak that had over a relatively short period attained a warm golden colour.

To complement the existing furniture and fittings, the piece was traditionally styled and would later be stained up to match the finish as well. The overall size of the shelves can of course be varied to suit any given situation. The ones illustrated here were 32″ × 36″ high, and proved to be of pleasing proportions.

width from 6″ to a 3″ top shelf, is made entirely of solid oak thicknessed to around ¾″.

As the cutting of the shaped ends can be rather wasteful in wood, the interlocking of the two will prove a beneficial saving. After roughing the ends out, the two can be held together by a couple of discreet panel pins for cutting to exact shape, Fig. 1. A bandsaw is the ideal tool for this type of work, but equal results can be achieved with a jigsaw or for the true hand woodworkers, the coping saw.

Moving over to the workbench, the ends still held together are cramped in the vice for final cleaning up of the shaped form. This is achieved by a combination of files, spokeshave, scraper, chisel and sandpaper. Keeping the edges square and maintaining a nice clean outline is the main priority. Before cleaning up the inside and outside faces, shelf positions are marked.

SOLID OAK

The piece, consisting of two shaped ends and three shelves, graded in

PLATE GROOVE

After sectioning and cutting the shelves to length, the front edge is

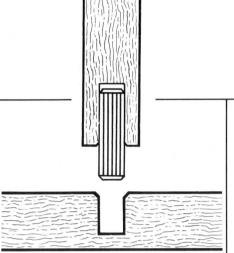

Fig. 3 Typical dowel joint details

Alternatively, use a bench circular saw or radial arm saw, with a moulding block and suitable cutters. Some radial arm saws double as routers and De Walt supply a router mounting bracket for attaching the router to the motor yoke. We are sure that you will have your own method for solving the problem. Write and tell our readers if you have a different solution.

The bead. This is formed with a corner bead cutter in the router or the appropriate cutter in a universal or combination plane.

For simplicity itself, why not use the scratch stock. This simple home-made tool will work both the bead and the plate groove! – Ed.)

DOWEL JOINT

The medium for fixing the ends and shelves together will be the dowel joint, Fig. 3. Dowels are often frowned upon because of their association with chipboard construction but, in situations like this, they are ideal for fixing two pieces of wood together.

Fig. 2 Shelf details

One of the 'secrets' to accurate dowel jointing is careful marking out and drilling. Here a centre line should be marked where the shelf meets the end and also on the end of the shelf. This gives us a definite line of reference.

The best method I have found of final marking is the old tried and trusted panel pin location of centres. Insert panel pins about half their length at the desired dowel centres in the ends of the shelf, then behead them with pincers. Careful positioning of the shelf on the end, and light pressure, will highlight the dowel centres.

A drill with a centre point is a must for accurate drilling of dowels, as is the ability to be able to drill at right angles to the work. The homemade depth stop, Fig. 4, allows maximum hole depth to be achieved on the ends without the risk of breaking through. After drilling, the holes are lightly counter-sunk to provide a lead-in and a reservoir for surplus glue.

I have for many years now used the ready-fluted and chamfered, commercially available dowels, which I find very good and convenient. If ordinary dowel is to be used, this must be fluted to allow glue to escape when cramping up. Glue under pressure, and without a convenient escape route, will cause the wood to split around the joint. This should obviously be avoided as it may cause weakening of the joint, as well as unsightly splits.

(Dowel joints. Admittedly the author's well known method of marking the centres for drilling is successful but many of our readers will have a dowelling jig or centre points for this purpose. – Ed.)

Six sash cramps were needed to cramp the assembly, care being

taken to maintain squareness and avoid twist.

MIRROR PLATES

Provision for fixing the shelves to the wall is achieved by a couple of mirror plates discreetly positioned above the top shelf. Where walls are very uneven (as is the case in many old houses), extra fixings may be necessary.

The matching of the colour of the original furniture required that the piece was given a light wash of stain. Afterwards it was sealed with best white polish and further coats built up with the fad (pad).

The final waxing gave colour that was very close to the naturally achieved finish I was copying. A spot of distressing (creating some of the everyday marks that one expects to find on furniture in use) gave the piece the used look and guaranteed that it didn't stand out in the kitchen as alien.

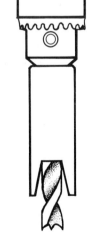

Fig. 4 Depth stop for use with electric hand held drill

CUTTING LIST						
PART	DESCRIPTION	L	W	T	MATERIAL	QTY
1	Ends	36"	6¼"	¾"	Oak	2
2	Shelf	30½"	6"	¾"	Oak	1
3	Shelf	30½"	4½"	¾"	Oak	1
4	Shelf	30½"	3"	¾"	Oak	1

SUNDRIES: 2 Brass mirror plates and screws, 16 1½" × ⅜" diameter dowels.

BUILDING A BEEHIVE

A project that could introduce you to another fascinating sideline or hobby.

One has only to examine the neat regular six-sided cells which bees draw out from wax foundation to appreciate that they are precise and accurate little insects. Their hives *have* to be made precisely and, as bees have not gone metric, all their equipment is still made in Imperial sizes and their produce, namely honey and wax, is sold in 1lb quantities.

When talking about beehives most people have in mind the "W.B.C." hives with their span roofs and double wall construction. These have several disadvantages, one of which is that the roof is liable to blow off in a high wind.

MODIFIED

The modified national hive shown in photo 1 is a more efficient hive. It has larger combs, is of single wall construction which facilitates manipulation and is not difficult to make. The hive comprises a stand, a floor with an entrance block, a brood chamber (deep box), several supers (shallow boxes) where the honey is stored, a crown board and a roof.

Western red cedar is a most suitable wood to use throughout, being resistant to rot and light in weight. This is a decided advantage when carrying supers containing a good weight of honey.

STAND

Making the stand (Fig. 1) could not be simpler, being butt-jointed, glued and nailed together. Waterproof glue is used for all joints in the hive. The stand is 3″ high and made from ¾″ thick material. The front slopes towards the entrance and forms an alighting board, the vertical face of which butts against the floor and projects 1⅛″ above the sides of the stand. Two handholds 5″ and ¾″ are cut into the lower edge of the sides and enable the hive to be moved more easily if the need arises.

FLOOR

The floor (Fig. 2) is 18⅛″ square and its sides and floorboards are all ¾″ thick. The sides are 2″ wide and, at a distance of ⅞″ from the top edge, a ¾″ wide groove is ploughed to a depth of ¼″. The floorboards are let into these grooves. A high speed router is an excellent tool for this

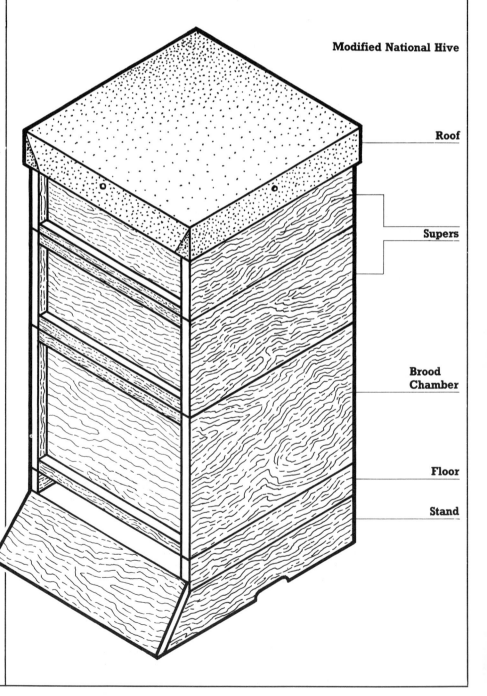

Modified National Hive

Roof

Supers

Brood Chamber

Floor

Stand

operation. A strip of wood 16⅝″ × ⅞″ × ⅞″ closes the back at the top while the front is closed at the bottom by a piece 16⅝″ × ⅞″ × ⅜″. These two closing strips are glued and nailed in position.

An entrance block (Fig. 3) 16½″ long is planed ⅞″ (bare) by ⅞″ (bare) and is placed on the floor, deeper side uppermost, when it is necessary to restrict the entrance to the hive. One of its faces is cut away 5″ × 5/16″ to enable the bees to fly in and out. So that the block cannot be accidentally pushed too far into the hive two small staples are driven into the inside faces of the side rails at a distance of ⅞″ from the front and are allowed to stand proud ¼″.

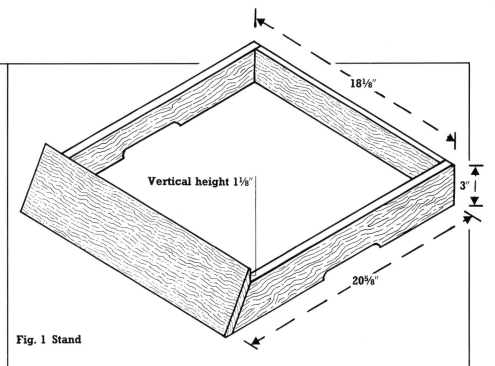

Vertical height 1⅛″

18⅛″

3″

20⅝″

Fig. 1 Stand

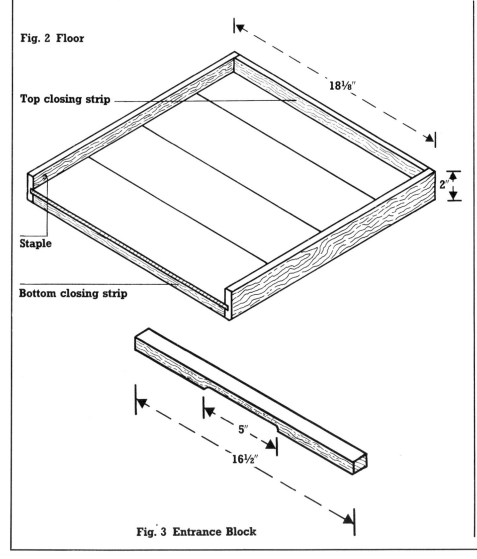

Fig. 2 Floor

Top closing strip

18⅛″

2″

Staple

Bottom closing strip

5″

16½″

Fig. 3 Entrance Block

BROOD CHAMBER

The brood chamber, where the queen lives and lays her eggs, is shown in Fig. 4. It accommodates eleven frames of wax foundation 14″ × 8½″ with two 1½″ lugs so that the top bar of the frame is 17″ long. The four walls are all ¾″ thick and the outside dimensions are 18⅛″ × 18⅛″ × 8⅞″. The end walls are 17″ × 7 15/16 and are let into grooves in the side walls.

These grooves are 1″ from each end and are ¾″ wide and 3/16″ deep. Here again the high speed router will make a quick clean and accurate job. When glueing the end walls into these grooves the top edges of the ends are set 11/16″ below the top edges of the sides.

The 1″ space between the ends of the side walls and the outer faces of the end walls is closed with two fillets 16⅝″ × 1½″ × 1″. One fillet is glued and nailed at the top and the other at the bottom. The inner face of the top fillet is rebated 11/16″ deep by ½″ wide to form a recess for the ends of the frame lugs. To provide bee-space the lower inner face of the bottom fillet is rebated ¼″ deep by ½″ wide. The top face is chamfered to throw off the rain.

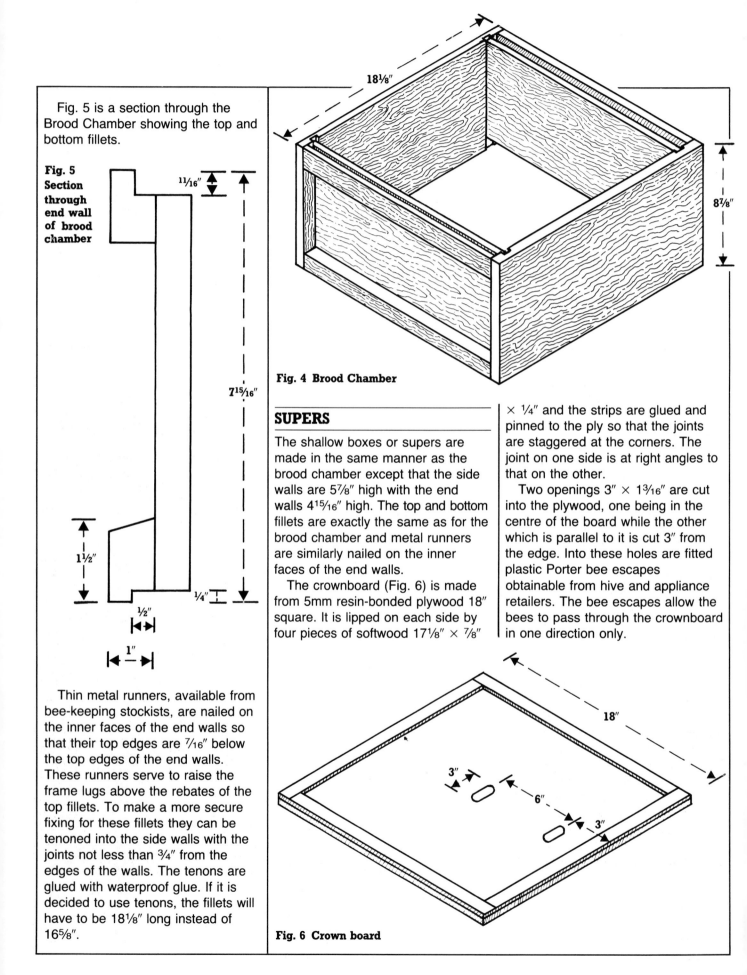

Fig. 5 is a section through the Brood Chamber showing the top and bottom fillets.

**Fig. 5
Section
through
end wall
of brood
chamber**

11/16″

7¹⁵/₁₆″

1½″

½″

¼″

1″

Fig. 4 Brood Chamber

18⅛″

8⅞″

Thin metal runners, available from bee-keeping stockists, are nailed on the inner faces of the end walls so that their top edges are 7/16″ below the top edges of the end walls. These runners serve to raise the frame lugs above the rebates of the top fillets. To make a more secure fixing for these fillets they can be tenoned into the side walls with the joints not less than ¾″ from the edges of the walls. The tenons are glued with waterproof glue. If it is decided to use tenons, the fillets will have to be 18⅛″ long instead of 16⅝″.

SUPERS

The shallow boxes or supers are made in the same manner as the brood chamber except that the side walls are 5⅞″ high with the end walls 4¹⁵/₁₆″ high. The top and bottom fillets are exactly the same as for the brood chamber and metal runners are similarly nailed on the inner faces of the end walls.

The crownboard (Fig. 6) is made from 5mm resin-bonded plywood 18″ square. It is lipped on each side by four pieces of softwood 17⅛″ × ⅞″

× ¼″ and the strips are glued and pinned to the ply so that the joints are staggered at the corners. The joint on one side is at right angles to that on the other.

Two openings 3″ × 1³/₁₆″ are cut into the plywood, one being in the centre of the board while the other which is parallel to it is cut 3″ from the edge. Into these holes are fitted plastic Porter bee escapes obtainable from hive and appliance retailers. The bee escapes allow the bees to pass through the crownboard in one direction only.

18″

3″

6″

3″

Fig. 6 Crown board

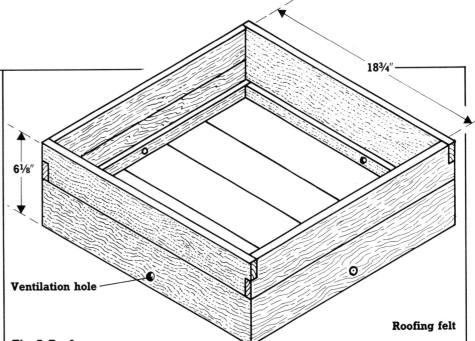

Ventilation hole

Roofing felt

Fig. 7 Roof

ROOF

Making the roof (Fig. 7) can be quite a simple job with the sides butted, glued and nailed together. It makes a better job if the corners are box-jointed, glued and nailed in both directions. The *inside* measurements are 18¾″ × 18¾″ × 5¾″. The roof boards are ⅜″ thick and the sides are ½″ thick.

Four wooden strips 18″ × 1¼″ × ¾″ are nailed round the top of the roof inside to give 1¼″ headspace above the crownboard. Bored centrally through these strips are four ventilation holes ¾″ diameter. Perforated zinc is used to back these holes, permitting ventilation but preventing the ingress of unwanted intruders.

To ensure the roof is completely waterproof it can be covered with sheet zinc. Commercial hive makers usually use zinc but I have covered my hives with green mineral felt and this has proved most satisfactory. It is recommended that the felt be extended down the sides for at least 1½″ and be well secured with galvanised felt nails.

Wooden frames to hold the wax foundation can be made but in view of their low cost it is probably better to buy them and assemble them as required.

Hives made from Western Red Cedar do not need treating with preservative but softwood hives do. It is better to avoid paint which does not allow the wood to "breathe" and may cause the inside of the hive to sweat. Preservatives containing insecticides must not be used for, like woodworm killers, they are fatal to bees. Green Cuprinol is safe to bees and provides adequate protection.

Information regarding your nearest beekeeping equipment stockist can be obtained from your local Beekeeping Association whose address should be available at the reference library.

CUTTING LIST						
PART	DESCRIPTION	L	W	T	MATERIAL	QTY
STAND						
1	Alighting Board	18⅛″	5″	¾″	Western Red Cedar	1
2	Side pieces	20⅜″	3″	¾″	″	2
3	Back	16⅝″	3″	¾″	″	1
FLOOR						
4	Side pieces	18⅛″	2″	¾″	″	2
5	Back Closer	16⅝″	⅞″	⅞″	″	1
6	Front Closer	16⅝″	⅞″	⅜″	″	1
7	Floor Boards¹	17⅛″	18⅛″	¾″	″	
ENTRANCE BLOCK						
8	Entrance Block	16½″	⅞″ bare	⅞″ bare	″	1
BROOD CHAMBER						
9	Side Walls	18⅛″	8⅞″	¾″	″	2
10	End Walls	17″	7¹⁵⁄₁₆″	¾″	″	2
11	Fillets²	16⅝″	1½″	1″	″	4
HONEY SUPER						
12	Side Walls	18⅛″	5⅞″	¾″	″	2
13	End Walls	17″	4¹⁵⁄₁₆″	¾″	″	2
14	Fillets²	16⅝″	1½″	1″	″	4
15	Crown Board	18″	18″	5mm	Resin Bonded Ply	1
16	Lippings	17⅛″	⅞″	¼″	Western Red Cedar	8
ROOF						
17	Sides	19¾″	5¾″	½″	″	4
18	Strips	18″	1¼″	¾″	″	4
19	Roof Boards³	19¾″	19¾″	⅜″		

NOTES: 1. Sufficient number of pieces to make up a width of 18⅛″. 2. 18⅛″ if tenoned. 3. Sufficient number of pieces to make up a width of 19¾″.

SUNDRIES: Waterproof glue, nails, green mineral felt, galvanised felt nails, perforated zinc, green Cuprinol (if hive not made from Western Red Cedar). Metal runners, wooden frames and wax foundation can be obtained from the local Beekeepers Association.

TWO SIMPLE MILKING STOOLS

*These little and large stools may prove the answer sometime to a
similar present problem you may have.*

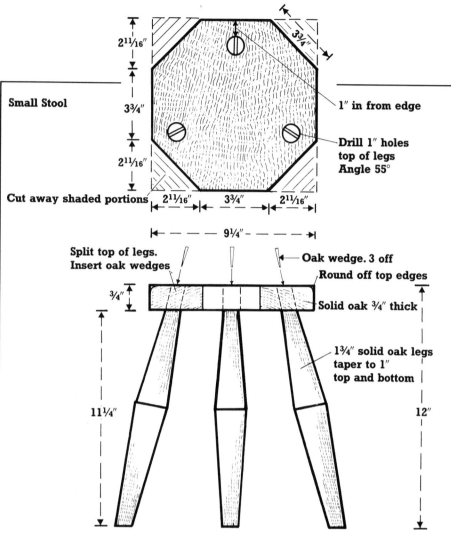

Small Stool

2¹¹/₁₆″

3¾″

3¾″

1″ in from edge

Drill 1″ holes
top of legs
Angle 55°

2¹¹/₁₆″

Cut away shaded portions

2¹¹/₁₆″ 3¾″ 2¹¹/₁₆″

9¼″

Split top of legs.
Insert oak wedges

Oak wedge. 3 off

Round off top edges

¾″

Solid oak ¾″ thick

1¾″ solid oak legs
taper to 1″
top and bottom

11¼″

12″

The piece of oak was just the right thickness, and was as hard as iron. It would only need a good waxing once it was assembled, and would not take long to make. I knew it was just the thing for our friends, and would be handed down to future generations. Of course, the idea could be adapted for a variety of finishes. Plain pine, waxed, or matching stools in deal could be brightly lacquered and stencilled for a nursery . . . a set could be made with long legs for bar stools, or matching ones of equal size could stand each side of a fireplace . . . little patchwork cushions could be tied on with tapes to make suitable kitchen or dining stools, or just one could be a useful stand in a small bathroom or bedroom . . .

SEAT

Cut out two squares of wood 10¾″ × 10¾″ × ¾″ and 9¼″ × 9¼″ × ¾″, and mark out as given in the diagrams and cutting list. It is a good idea to make a cardboard template, both for accuracy and also to keep for future reference.

Mark the angles and cut away the surplus wood, shaded in the diagram, keeping all the corners sharp.

Mark the holes for the legs, as indicated, and drill a 1″ hole at an angle of 55°. There will now be three holes in each seat. The legs will be hammered into these holes, and finished with a wedge in the split top, in the traditional way.

With a light plane, round off the edges of the seat, curving them round, but keeping the bottom edge straight. Then finish off with coarse, then medium, then fine glasspaper, until it is all absolutely smooth.

LEGS

I had a 6′ length of old oak which matched the tops perfectly, and I

One of our friends was getting married shortly. They both love old wood and antiques, and would be living in an old farmhouse they had bought, sadly in need of restoration. The question was, what to give them for a wedding present? Obviously it would have to be something hand-made, but time was running short, and still no ideas had come to mind. It would have to be something small and simple, and yet something they would both like.

I got out a piece of old oak I had by me – I had last used it to make two plinths for a yachting trophy which took the form of a large and small engraved goblet. I had made them hexagonal in shape. I had quite enjoyed that . . . what about something octagonal this time . . . A large and a small one . . . I thought about the old farmhouse where the present was to go . . . in the kitchen? . . . I had it, a milking stool! A large one to sit on, and a smaller one to stand a large jug of dried flowers on, or display a copper kettle!

CUTTING LIST – SMALL STOOL						
PART	DESCRIPTION	L	W	T	MATERIAL	QTY
1	Top	9¼″	9¼″	¾″	Oak	1
2	Legs	12″	1¾″	1¾″	Oak	3
3	Wedges	1½″	1″	⁵/₁₆″		3

NOTE: [Traditionally stools were made of oak, ash, elm or pine. Contrasting timbers could be used for the legs, stretchers and wedges. – Ed.]
SUNDRIES: Coarse, medium and fine glasspaper. Steel wool. Wood glue (Evostick Resin W.)

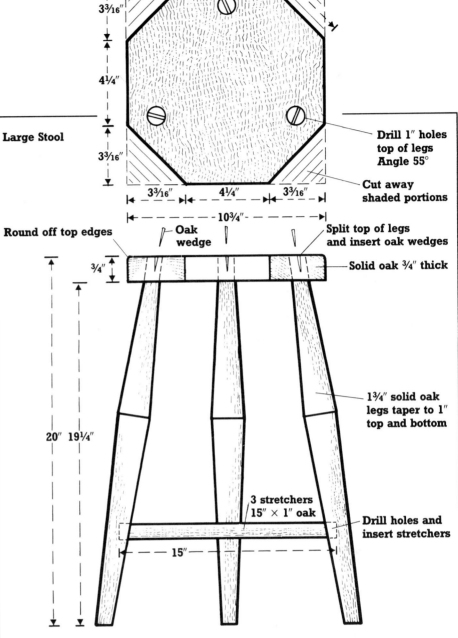

Large Stool

1″ in from edge

3³⁄₁₆″

4¼″

3³⁄₁₆″

3³⁄₁₆″ 4¼″ 3³⁄₁₆″

10¾″

Drill 1″ holes
top of legs
Angle 55°

Cut away
shaded portions

Round off top edges

Oak
wedge

Split top of legs
and insert oak wedges

Solid oak ¾″ thick

¾″

20″ 19¼″

1¾″ solid oak
legs taper to 1″
top and bottom

3 stretchers
15″ × 1″ oak

Drill holes and
insert stretchers

15″

was able to get all the legs out of that. If you have to buy wood, get a 3′ length 1¾″ square, which you can cut into three 12″ lengths for the small stool, and a 5′ length 1¾″ square to be cut into three legs each 20″ long for the large stool. In addition you will need three pieces for the stretchers, each measuring 15″ long by 1″ square.

TO ASSEMBLE LEGS AND STRETCHER

Cut out pieces for legs and stretcher as given in the diagrams and cutting list. You will see they measure 1¾″ in the centre and taper out to 1″ at each end. Cut three legs for the stool 12″ long (no stretcher) and three legs 20″ long for the tall stool. Plane away the surplus wood, keeping the centre measurement 1¾″ and tapering to 1″. With a chisel or saw, split the centre of each top of leg carefully for about 1″ down the centre. This is to take a wedge later on. Finish to a smooth surface.

STRETCHER

Only the large stool needs a stretcher. When you have made the three legs, drill a 1″ hole into each side leg ½″ in depth and 8″ up from the base. Do another hole similar on each other inner side. This is for the stretcher. Now take your three pieces, 15″ long × 1″ square, and round them off with a plane and sand and finish as usual. Glue and clamp these rounded stretcher pieces into the drilled holes on the inside legs and allow to dry and harden.

TO ASSEMBLE LARGE STOOL

Knock the legs, plus stretcher, through the holes drilled at an angle of 55° in the seat. Insert a small wedge into each top of leg and

hammer down to make a tight fit. You can use a bit of glue if you like. Trim any surplus wood away, and rub smooth.

TO ASSEMBLE THE SMALL STOOL

Knock the legs through the holes in exactly the same way, and finish with a small wedge to keep the whole leg firmly in position. Trim and finish in the same way.

FINISHING

Give a good rub over with glasspaper until everything is smooth and there are no rough bits anywhere. Stain with golden oak stain and when thoroughly dry, overnight if possible, rub over and hand wax. If you are using different woods, undercoat and enamel, or stain and apply polyurethane, or whatever finish you prefer.

CUTTING LIST – LARGE STOOL						
PART	DESCRIPTION	L	W	T	MATERIAL	QTY
1	Top	10¾″	10¾″	¾″	Oak	1
2	Legs	19¾″	1¾″	1¾″		3
3	Stretchers	15″	1″	1″		3
4	Wedges	1½″	1″	⁵⁄₁₆″		3

VACUUM CLAMPING

A much underrated means of clamping the workpiece

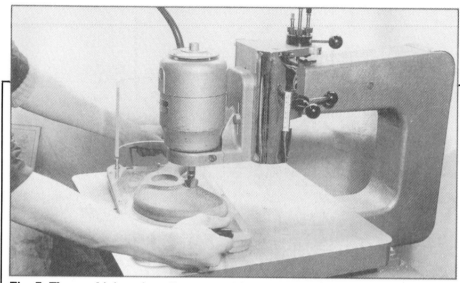

Fig. A The machining of small trays on this overhead router was assisted by using vacuum for clamping the workpiece onto the workframe. In operation, the guide pin on the router table engages the template mounted on the base of the workframe.

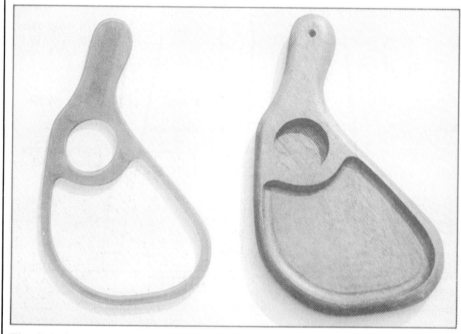

Fig. C Left Illustration – Template (item 8 in Fig. B). Right Illustration – Workpiece (item 1 in Fig. B).

The vacuum system of clamping is rather neglected, possibly because it is not a mechanical device, and therefore suspect. However, the small pump shown in Fig. G is approximately 1ft long and has a vacuum displacement of 17 psi. A vacuum chuck area of say 1ft × 1ft will hold a workpiece down surprisingly firmly. It could not easily be prised off without considerable effort. Certainly, it would not normally be dislodged when machining, if the vacuum chuck had been constructed on the basic lines recommended.

VACUUM CHUCK CONSTRUCTION

A typical vacuum chuck construction for producing a small hand tray is now described. It also provides an excellent example of the template system, ideally adapted for batch production.

The end product is a hand tray, which is machined on an overhead router (see Fig. A). One template performed the four tasks: Namely, the perimeter cutting, the edge moulding, the centre cutting, and the central moulding.

The four cutters used for this work are described at Fig. D. A number of these trays were produced in the way described. The workpieces were first rough cut on a bandsaw, before machining.

I will show how vacuum can be applied in fixed head routing applications.

There are certain shortcomings with the conventional system for clamping of the workpiece. Often toggle clamps hinder the operator's movement and vision. It becomes necessary to move the clamps to a new position when profiling. Furthermore, it is most inconvenient at times to screw or pin the workpiece on the template frame.

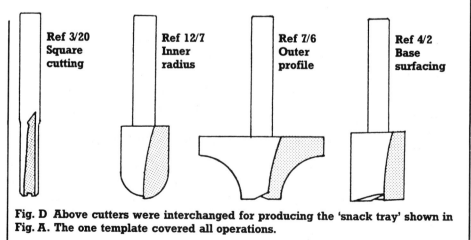

Ref 3/20
Square
cutting

Ref 12/7
Inner
radius

Ref 7/6
Outer
profile

Ref 4/2
Base
surfacing

Fig. D Above cutters were interchanged for producing the 'snack tray' shown in Fig. A. The one template covered all operations.

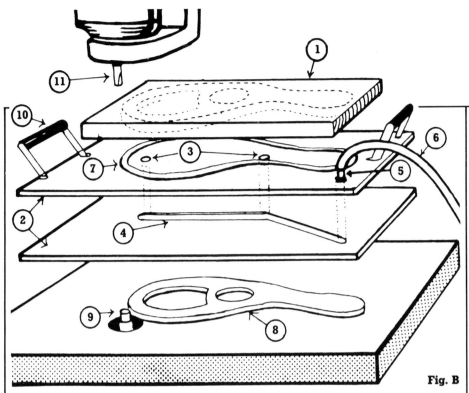

Fig. B

commercial vacuum extractor.

For long runs, say ten minutes or more under vacuum, a vacuum pump is preferable, as a dust extractor will be inclined to overheat when ventilation is totally inhibited.

BASIC VACUUM CONSIDERATIONS

There are certain rules, to which one must adhere, when making a vacuum chuck, and visual sketches describe them more effectively.

The larger the exposed area to vacuum the more efficient will be the holding power.

The three diagrams H, H1 and H2, illustrate this point clearly. They are symbolic sketches only.

SEALANT MATERIAL FOR VACUUM

This is offered in narrow strip form (see Figs. I and J) or in sheet form for cutting with a sharp knife.

LISTED PROCEDURES FOR BUILDING A VACUUM CHUCK

1. Workpiece.
2. Work frames are glued or fixed together with double-sided tape.
3. Two ¼″ diameter holes drilled in top frame to line up with –
4. Channel routed out in bottom work frame to link up with –
5. Hose connector (threaded ⅛ bsp ¼ bsp into top half of work frame).
6. Plastic vacuum tube leading to pump.
7. Neoprene lip seal with self-adhesive backing is cut to length.
8. Template glued with double-sided adhesive to underside of work frame.
9. Guide pin must line up with cutter, and should not project more than thickness of template.

PROFILING USING ROUTER MOUNTED FROM BELOW

For profile cutting and edging small components on a table router, the use of vacuum to hold down the workpiece is an attractive proposition.

The template itself can be converted into a vacuum chuck, by applying self-stick neoprene sheeting on the underface. See Fig. I.

The chuck/template, which is a replica of the end product, should be made of a relatively hard matter, e.g. Acrylic, PVC or Tufnol. Vacuum is obtained from a vacuum pump or a

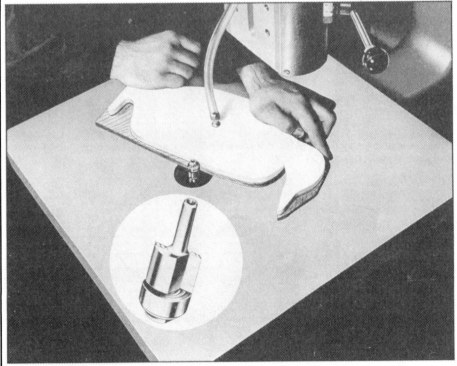

Fig. E Profiling a 'penguin' plaque using a vacuum chuck which acts as a template. The edge trimming is carried out with a self-guide 90° T.C. Cutter. (Type 46/2 in Trend range.)

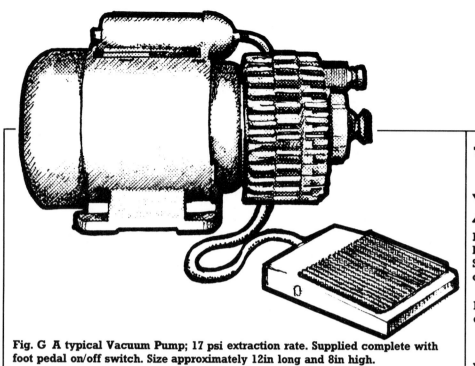

Fig. G A typical Vacuum Pump; 17 psi extraction rate. Supplied complete with foot pedal on/off switch. Size approximately 12in long and 8in high.

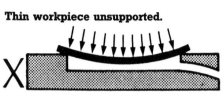

Thin workpiece unsupported.

Fig. H WRONG. Thin material has bowed with the vacuum. Small pads are needed to support central area.

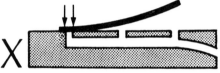

Poor vacuum feed to workpiece, no effective seal.

Fig. H1 WRONG. Support pads are too large reducing vacuum area to unacceptable limits.

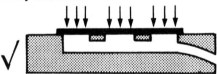

Good vacuum with large chuck area and centre supports if material thin and likely to buckle.

Fig. H2 RIGHT. Large vacuum area with small pads.

The self-adhesive backed neoprene should be 1.5-2.5mm thick. It must be the closed cell variety. If thicker material was used, vibration could arise and a poor finished edge result.

The neoprene strip is normally 16mm wide and can be cut easily into lengths, with reliable joints made by overlapping and then cutting both layers with 'razor' knife. The vented hole (3-8mm diameter) can be anywhere within the chuck area.

Small cut strips may be needed to provide support pads, to prevent workpiece from bowing.

In an overhead router, the neoprene in sheet form, can be applied in a quite ingenious manner by using the router to profile cut the shape. Assuming the template has been affixed to the chuck base, the procedure is as follows. Remove adhesive backing, and apply a sheet of neoprene across the proposed chuck area. Now make a profile cut,

with cutter depth set to penetrate neoprene plus approximately 1mm. Following the template path, the neoprene 'chuck' is obtained in a matter of seconds. The waste material can be peeled off quite easily, if this is done within a few hours of applying the material.

Fig. J

Fig. I Neoprene strip with self stick backing 2mm thick. Supplied in sheet form or in 16mm wide rolls.

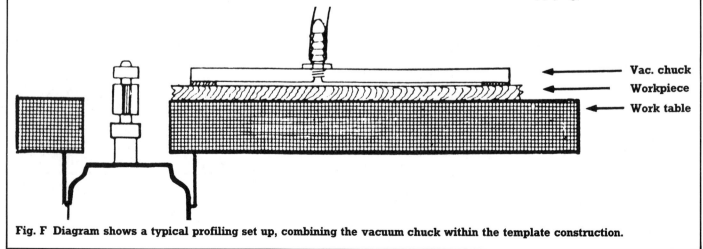

Vac. chuck
Workpiece
Work table

Fig. F Diagram shows a typical profiling set up, combining the vacuum chuck within the template construction.

GLASS TOP TABLE WITH MAGAZINE RACK

A general design for a modern coffee table of traditional construction. The design lends itself to the inclusion of any personal embellishments you may favour.

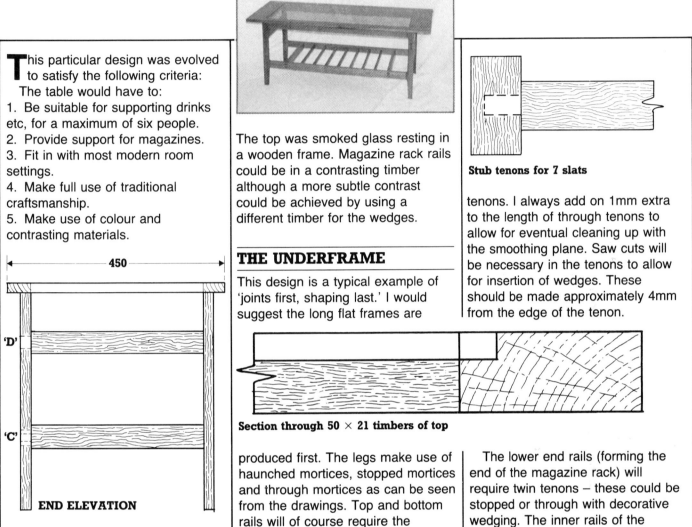

This particular design was evolved to satisfy the following criteria:
The table would have to:
1. Be suitable for supporting drinks etc, for a maximum of six people.
2. Provide support for magazines.
3. Fit in with most modern room settings.
4. Make full use of traditional craftsmanship.
5. Make use of colour and contrasting materials.

END ELEVATION

The prototype was produced in elm as a rich brown colour was required. However, most common hardwoods, with reasonably attractive grain figure, could be used.

The top was smoked glass resting in a wooden frame. Magazine rack rails could be in a contrasting timber although a more subtle contrast could be achieved by using a different timber for the wedges.

THE UNDERFRAME

This design is a typical example of 'joints first, shaping last.' I would suggest the long flat frames are

Section through 50 × 21 timbers of top

produced first. The legs make use of haunched mortices, stopped mortices and through mortices as can be seen from the drawings. Top and bottom rails will of course require the corresponding tenons for the leg mortices.

Upper end rails should next be produced using tenons of sufficient length to allow for the through

Stub tenons for 7 slats

tenons. I always add on 1mm extra to the length of through tenons to allow for eventual cleaning up with the smoothing plane. Saw cuts will be necessary in the tenons to allow for insertion of wedges. These should be made approximately 4mm from the edge of the tenon.

The lower end rails (forming the end of the magazine rack) will require twin tenons – these could be stopped or through with decorative wedging. The inner rails of the magazine rack simply make use of stopped mortice and tenons; these rails can either be fitted in the position A or B.

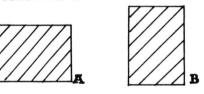

With all joints individually fitted, it is probably a good idea to try the entire underframe together to check that nothing is obviously wrong. Remember CHECK TWICE, CUT ONCE.

LEGS

The sculptured form of the legs can next be marked out in pencil, the waste being removed by either a fine bandsaw or coping saw. Cleaning up

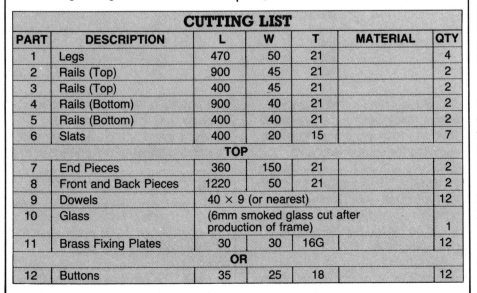

PART	DESCRIPTION	L	W	T	MATERIAL	QTY
CUTTING LIST						
1	Legs	470	50	21		4
2	Rails (Top)	900	45	21		2
3	Rails (Top)	400	45	21		2
4	Rails (Bottom)	900	40	21		2
5	Rails (Bottom)	400	40	21		2
6	Slats	400	20	15		7
TOP						
7	End Pieces	360	150	21		2
8	Front and Back Pieces	1220	50	21		2
9	Dowels	40 × 9 (or nearest)				12
10	Glass	(6mm smoked glass cut after production of frame)				1
11	Brass Fixing Plates	30	30	16G		12
OR						
12	Buttons	35	25	18		12

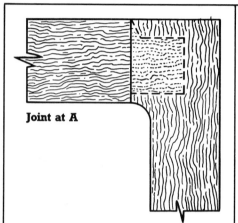

Joint at A

of the shaping can be done with files, spokeshaves or gouges if preferred.

Before gluing-up, all inside surfaces need finishing with the smoothing plane, F2 and flour grade glasspaper. It is a good idea to polish all areas which cannot easily be cleaned up after gluing before any glue is applied. I like the finish obtained from two or three coats of matt polyurethane varnish lightly rubbed down with flour paper between coats. A final waxing can very much enhance the timber.

On completion of the polishing of all inner parts, cramp up dry the two long frames, then if all is well, glue together with PVA adhesive. When dry, clean up and polish inside surfaces of frames as noted above. The next stage requires considerable care and ample time. Try all parts together in the front and back frames

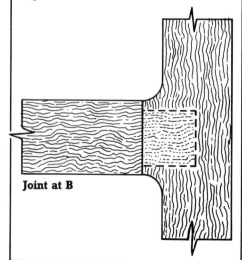

Joint at B

and get *all* cramps and cramping blocks ready *before* applying glue. Glue all joints and cramp together, checking for squareness and diagonals and twist. Adjust cramps if necessary. Insert wedges for each joint *together* – not hammering one right in because the second saw cut would be closed up. Take care to glue wedges in.

After drying, clean up all outer surfaces, remove any sharp corners

and polish. Take extra care when working over the wedged joints because these can either help make or ruin the effect of the underframe.

TOP

The top is simply fastened together with dowels, but if you really want to try your skill, long and short shouldered mortice and tenons could be used. The rebates would best be

FRON

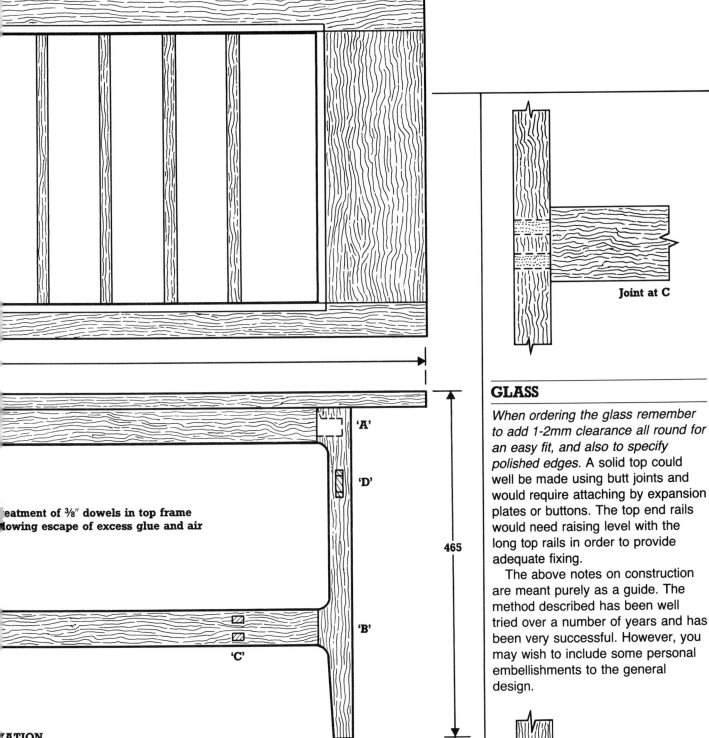

Joint at C

reatment of ⅜″ dowels in top frame
lowing escape of excess glue and air

465

'A'

'D'

'B'

'C'

GLASS

When ordering the glass remember to add 1-2mm clearance all round for an easy fit, and also to specify polished edges. A solid top could well be made using butt joints and would require attaching by expansion plates or buttons. The top end rails would need raising level with the long top rails in order to provide adequate fixing.

The above notes on construction are meant purely as a guide. The method described has been well tried over a number of years and has been very successful. However, you may wish to include some personal embellishments to the general design.

Wedged joint at D

'ATION

made with a power router but if this is unavailable, chisels and a shoulder plane would work perfectly well. When checking the depth of the rebates, remember to allow for the thickness of the strip of felt which will be glued in the rebate to help cushion the glass. Cramp up dry and check. Remember to make a saw cut along the length of each dowel to allow escape of air and surplus glue.

Clean up and polish inside edges as noted above and glue together. Plane all remaining surfaces clean and flat before sanding and polishing. Glue narrow strips of felt in rebates using a minimum of glue to retain softness of the felt.

The top can be attached to the underframe by brass plates, pocket screwed or counter-bored to the long top rails. Brass plates would be neater as they would not be visible through the glass top.

CORNER SHELVES

An eminently suitable project for an aspiring craftsman to practice high quality workmanship.

The design is, as quoted, for shelves to be close fitted into a corner. There appears to be no strong reason why the design could not just as well look right if fitted away from a corner. The generously wide diminishing chamfers worked on the underside of each shelf are made to be seen mostly below from a sitting position. The 'sculptured' Henry Moore influence shapes worked into the vertical distance pieces pose a test of skill and balanced eye judgement enough to allow the maker a fair assessment of his own capabilities. The original article was made in Afromosia which responded well in every respect. However, any one of the fine grained hardwoods almost could give similar results.

CUTTING LIST

Make a Cutting List for Item 1 the three shelves; Item 2. Add together end to end the upright end piece and the two distance pieces. Have all pieces machined to ¾″ thickness. Any machine planer marks on the broad surfaces should be removed now.

Begin joint making by squaring up one end of each shelf and the two ends of the upright piece. Common dovetails are used for the top and bottom joints with the two half tails cut to show a mitre at the front (see drawing). The middle shelf to be mortise and tenon with haunch notched back and front to hide the housing.

SHELVES

Cut off and square up the two distance pieces. Use a cutting gauge to mark the shoulder lines of the housed dovetail joints. Shape the dovetails. Hold together tight the top and middle shelves – and later the middle and bottom shelves while the dovetail housings positions are located. Carry these the calculated distance across the width with a try-square and marking knife. Gauge the depth of the housing on the back edges and gauge the housing stop 6¾″ from the back edge. Cut and fit the joints.

Erect the shelves with dry joints. When all parts are seen to be assembling satisfactorily proceed to mark out, cut and finish the shelf end

shapes. Gauge and cut the sinkings for the wall fixing plates.

The sculptured distance pieces are best first drawn on tracing or drawing paper and transferred to the wood afterwards. Blacking the lines on the

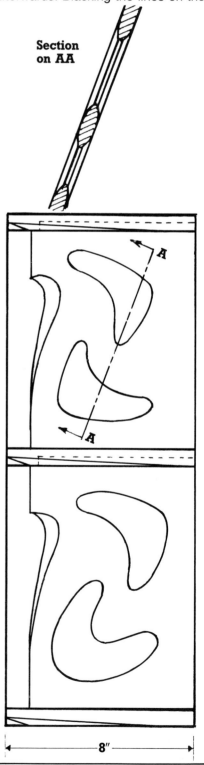

Section on AA

8″

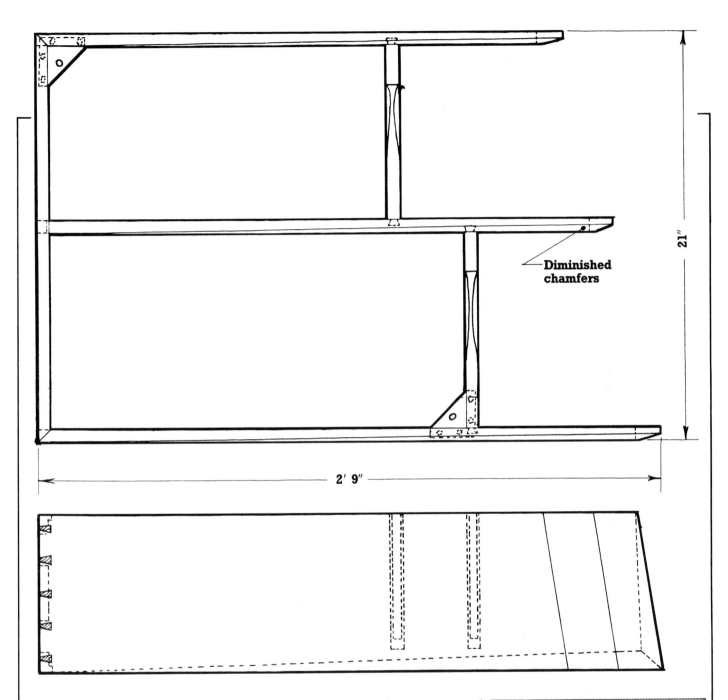

Diminished chamfers

21"

2' 9"

back of the tracing paper will allow the outline to be transferred on to the wood. Carbon paper between the drawing paper and the wood will allow the shapes to be copied through.

The piercing will need a fret-type saw (it is difficult with coping or bow saw) to remove the bulk of the waste. The rest is a matter of experiment with many shaping tools but mainly using the wide firmer chisel bevel-side down should enable the worker to bring each chamfered shape to a stage where coarse to fine glasspaper may be used on a suitable former to arrive at a smooth-to-the-touch finish.

Pencil in the diminishing chamfers on the undersides of the shelves and work these, if possible, to a finish with a sharp plane.

Well fitted dovetail joints should need no cramping when glued up. Wedges, fitted horizontally, may be used on the middle shelf tenons. Check for squareness before leaving.

After cleaning off excess glue and protruding wedges finish the surface with a dull gloss for preference. A high gloss might be unwise where many different angles of surfaces toward the light are busy reflecting light rays.

CUTTING LIST
Steel measuring tape
Steel rule
Large try-square
Small try-square
Marking gauge
Marking knife
Handsaw, crosscut
Tenon saw
Coping saw
Jack plane
Smoothing plane
Router plane
Spokeshaves, round and flat
Firmer chisels, 1″, ½″
B.E. chisels, ¾″, ¼″
Cabinet scraper
Dovetail gauge

A CONTEMPORARY ROCKING CHAIR

A superb piece of furniture which can be produced without the use of expensive machinery.

This chair is a contemporary interpretation of a traditional style made in the traditional way. As such, while it holds elements of the past, it embraces the present and is in no way a 'reproduction' (how I hate that word!) piece of furniture. It is, I believe, an honest 1980's style and will, I hope, go on into the future, cherished in ownership and passed on, with love, into the care of others – a true heirloom.

I designed the chair for an American lady, wife of the English publisher of my book, 'Making Family Heirlooms' (David & Charles). The chair is English Windsor in concept but its simple lines and plain turnings reflect my interest in American Shaker styles while its shape and dimensions owe much to the study of anthropometrics.

ELM/ASH

The seat is a solid piece of English elm into which the legs are socketed in the true Windsor chair method of construction. All other components are in ash which I cut and cleft from a Lake District coppice. Legs and cross stretchers are plain turned, without ornamentation, with plain substantial rockers to complement them. The main back stiles are continuous with the curved arms, being bent to that shape and inserted into the shaped comb so that this continuity is retained across the back of the chair. The forward ends of the curved arms are supported on plain turned arm stumps securely socketed into the seat; intermediate arm supports are omitted without loss of strength. The seven back sticks taper in their length and are curved to follow the contours of the sitter's back.

The ash for legs, stretchers and back sticks was cleft and not sawn in order to retain the maximum strength and natural resilience of the wood. Traditionally, this is how the old chair

'bodgers' began their work and the proof of their good sense is to be seen in the highly priced examples of their work to be found in almost every antique shop today.

Round components were rough shaped with a draw knife and then turned to the sizes shown in Diagram 1. I used the rotary planes or rounders which I always use in this work but they could have been turned conventionally on a lathe. The long back sticks – not so easy to turn between lathe centres – could be shaped with a spokeshave and (plenty of) glasspaper. All other components were sawn.

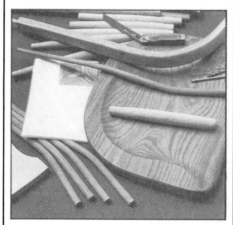

Photo. 1 The design stage – parts in preparation

Sawn material can of course be used for everything if cleft material is unobtainable. But straight grained stuff is essential if a strong, resilient chair is to be achieved. And where a suitable elm board wide enough to yield a seat is not available then one will have to be built up by edge-jointing narrower pieces. If dowels are used for this keep them low down to avoid revealing them when the seat is hollowed.

Diagram 1

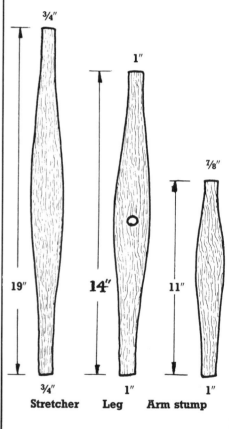

| Stretcher | Leg | Arm stump |

SEAT

The seat is cut to shape and hollowed or saddled as shown in Diagram 2.

(Traditionally, this was done by means of an adze. The author however used an inshave – a kind of curved drawknife. This, he tells us, requires practice to use effectively but he gets a good finish from it, requiring very little glasspaper at the

Photo. 2 Fitting legs temporarily

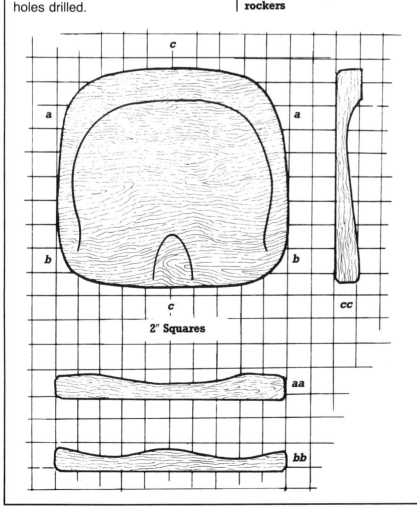

end. *"I much prefer to cut wood,"* he says, *"rather than abrade it."*

*Another method is the use of gouge and mallet, finishing off with curved scrapers and glasspaper. Working **across** the grain with the gouge will produce good results before final finishing. This will be a time-consuming operation but well worth the effort.*

Power tools can also be considered but constant checks for depth will be required. – Ed.)

The underside is marked out and drilled for leg sockets as shown in the same diagram. Use Forstener bits to give flat bottomed, parallel sided holes. Legs are then temporarily fitted to enable measurements to be taken for true lengths of stretchers. These are cut to size and their respective socket holes drilled.

Next, the rockers are made (Diagram 5); bandsaw to shape and finish with a spokeshave. Legs and stretchers are again temporarily fitted

Photo. 3 Checking the fit of the rockers

and the rockers offered up and marked out for drilling. When these are drilled, check that they fit, then dismantle the complete underframing of the chair and put aside; it is easier to do the rest of the work with the seat resting flat on the bench surface.

The upper surface of the seat is marked out and drilled for arm stumps and back sticks. Arm stump sockets go right through the seat so that they can be wedged in for added security (See Diagram 3). *Note that the drilling angle for the back sticks is forward and not backward as would seem more correct in a chair back.* This forward angle is correct, however, and is due to the lumbar curve of the back sticks described later.

In making the two continuous arms a combined technique of steam

2" Squares

Sight lines for drilling

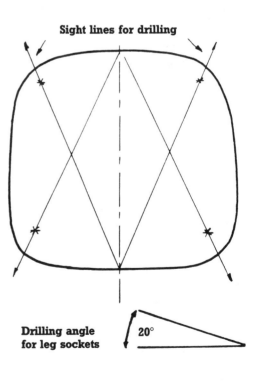

Drilling angle for leg sockets 20°

Diagram 2 Seat cut out and shaped to pattern and profiles given here. Underside marked out and drilled as above

bending and laminating was used. It would be possible to make the bend in solid, steam bent, ash, or, alternatively, to use constructional veneers and do a normal laminate job.

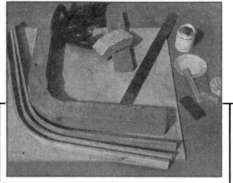

Photo. 5 Ready for gluing-up

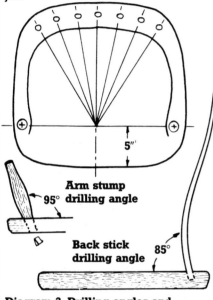

Diagram 3 Drilling angles and alignments for back sticks and arm stumps

Arm stump 95° drilling angle

Back stick drilling angle 85°

5"

FORMER

Whatever method is used a former must be made and this is shown in Diagram 4 and in the photographs. It is made from 2" thick softwood

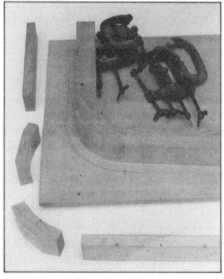

Photo. 4 Bending former ready for use

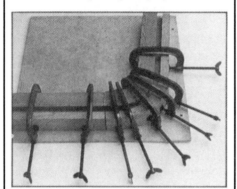

Photo. 6 Laminated bend under pressure in former

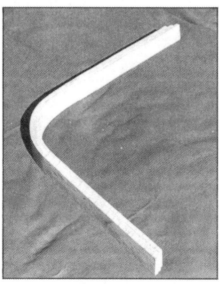

Photo. 7 Completed arm/back stile

Photo. 8 Draw knife used to shape arm/back stile

screwed and glued to a piece of ¾" block board. Note that as in all work of this kind, account must be taken of the difference between the inside radius and the outside radius of the curved portion of the former, which in this case is 1½".

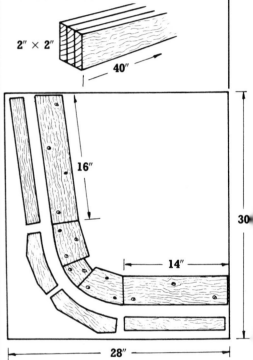

2" × 2"   40"

16"

14"

28"

30

Diagram 4 Continuous arms and back stiles cut and bent on former as here

For the method used, a piece of straight grained ash is sawn into three ½" thick strips and the separate pieces marked together as cut for grain matching. These are steamed for approximately thirty minutes then quickly bent onto the prepared former and held there under pressure for several days until set. (The time will vary according to environmental conditions.) Then the pieces are removed from the former, glued together with a waterproof adhesive (Cascamite), replaced in the former and left under pressure for a further twenty-four hours. The result is a curved component, rectangular in section, which can be shaped with a drawknife and spokeshave to the desired profile;

Diagram 5 Back sticks bent on former as shown below

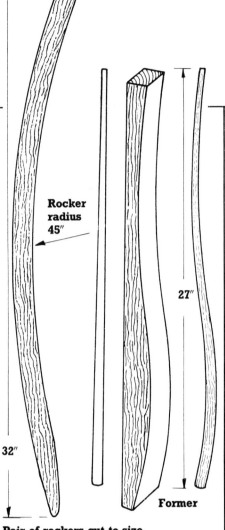

Rocker radius 45"

32"

27"

Former

Pair of rockers cut to size and radius as shown above

the top section should finish at 1¼" square.

COMB

Next, the comb or cresting rail is cut to shape. This not only has a slight curve along its length but also thickens at its ends and tapers across its width, being thicker along its bottom edge. The sections given in Diagram 6 will help in understanding this but, providing the ends of the comb match-up with the uprising back stiles, the exact profile can be your own interpretation. The final shaping where these two components join is carried out *after* they have been assembled and glued-up.

The lower edge of the comb has nine holes drilled in it to

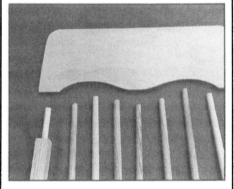

Photo. 9 Back stile and sticks ready for jointing into comb

accommodate the two back stile joints and the seven back sticks. All are ½" in diameter. For an odd number of sticks, simply mark the centre of the comb and space out the stick positions equally to each side. The back stiles are dowel jointed, the dowels inserted into the

end of the stile and left extra long for deep entry into the comb. This helps to strengthen the short grain in the area of the joint and ensures that the dowel passes through into an area of greater strength. *The shoulders of these joints should be a close fit – any gap here will not only spoil the chair's appearance but it will also affect the strength of the joint.*

BACK STICKS

The seven tapered back sticks require shaping to the lumbar curve, a shape determined largely by the curve of the human spine and the hollow in the back formed at what is known as the lumbar region. This varies individually but a compromise figure of 9" above the seat for the centre of this shallow curve is acceptable. A simple former for bending these is required (Diagram 5) and about thirty minutes in the steamer is needed. Finished stick lengths vary in accordance with the lower contours of the shaped comb.

When the sticks are made, set up the back assembly, i.e. arm/stiles, comb and back sticks, put the arm stumps in position on the seat, bring the arms down on to them and mark in the position of their sockets on the underside of the arm. Drill these with a Forstener bit.

A   B

AA   BB

A   B

2" Squares

Diagram 6

Enlarged detail of back sticks and stile dowel joint into comb

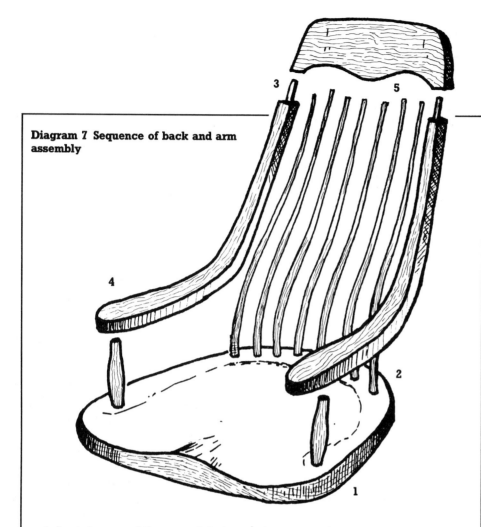

Diagram 7 Sequence of back and arm assembly

Wipe off all surplus glue and remember to protect the wood against the hard faces of the cramps. Do not overtighten the two back cramps as there is a great deal of springiness in the construction which works against the cramping action.

When the glue is set the cramps are removed and the area around the comb and back stile joints is smoothed into a continuous shape. Then, after the rockers have been fitted, the whole chair is sanded down and made ready for polishing. The chair described was required to match existing furniture and so it was first stained then sealed with two coats of sanding sealer, each rubbed down with fine grade garnet paper and finally wax polished. Omission of the stain will give a very pleasing natural wood finish.

Diagram 8 Cramping method and detail of pegged joint

A final dry run of the completed components is now made and when all is satisfactory legs and stretchers are glued into their respective sockets. Rockers are best left until later. Then the back assembly is begun (Diagram 7). First, arm stumps are glued and wedged into the seat – make sure wedges are across grain of seat to avoid splitting – and back sticks are glued into their respective socket holes. The two back stile dowels are then inserted into the comb and the arms brought down onto the arm stumps while the top ends of back sticks are manipulated into their socket holes simultaneously.

CRAMPING

Sash cramps are used to keep these joints under pressure until set (see Diagram 8). Check that the shoulders of the back stiles and the comb are in close contact and that the arm stumps have entered the arm sockets to their full depth. As an extra security measure this joint may be pegged as shown in the diagram.

Photo. 10 Completed comb detail. Shows continuous line with back stile and carved initials.

CUTTING LIST						
PART	DESCRIPTION	L	W	T	MATERIAL	QTY
1	Seat	20″	20″	2″	Elm	1
2	Legs	15″	1¾″	1¾″	Ash	4
3	Stretchers	20″	1½″	1½″	Ash	2
4	Rockers	33″	5″	1½″	Ash	2
5	Arm/back stiles	40″	2″	2″	Ash	2
6	Arm stumps	12″	1½″	1½″	Ash	2
7	Back sticks	28″	⅞″	⅞″	Ash	7
8	Comb	18″	6″	2″	Ash	1

DOVETAILING THE CORNERS OF A SPLAY-SIDED BOX

A project to whet the appetite of anyone wishing to extend his skills by practicing craftsmanship at a high level.

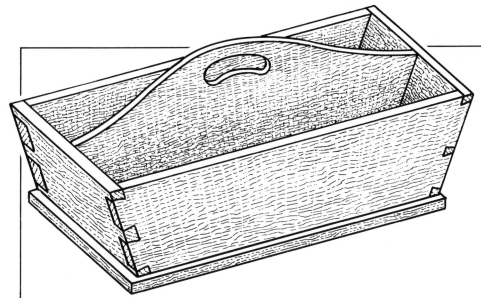

Fig. 1 Knife box with all four sides splayed and corners dovetailed

Making a box in which all four sides are splayed requires some geometrical knowledge in setting out. Further complications arise where the box corners are dovetailed.

The diagram in Fig. 1 shows a knife box in which all four sides are splayed outwards. The corner joints cannot be marked out with a try square in the usual manner and the top and bottom edges of the sides are also not square. Instead of using a try square a sliding bevel is required but before we can set the bevel it is first necessary to ascertain the various angles involved.

Consideration has also to be given to the method of construction. The simplest method is to butt joint the corners, nailing and glueing as required. A neater appearance is gained by mitreing the corners and securing with glue and nails as in the butt joint. The strongest and most workmanlike job is to dovetail the corners with through dovetails.

BEVEL ANGLES

Whatever the method of jointing, the first stage is to ascertain the bevel angles and Fig. 2 shows how this is done. A large piece of paper is pinned to the drawing board and a line DE is drawn. If no drawing board

is available a sheet of plywood will suffice. Start by drawing an end view of the side as shown in the top right hand corner of the diagram. Make the drawing full size and at the required angle of slope.

Moving on to the main diagram the various steps are as follows. The line AB which represents the width of the side of the box is drawn. The

distance along AC is the amount of splay required. A is drawn on the line DE and using A as centre and the compasses set to the length AB, the arc BF is drawn. The line AF is drawn at right angles to DE so as to cut the arc. The distance AF is accordingly the width of the box side when laid down flat. The thickness of the edge of the wood, AH, is set out above the line KL but parallel to it and forms the horizontal line MN. A line is projected from point B to J and points AJ are joined. The angle KJA is the face bevel.

The line PG is drawn and G is projected to O while P is projected to R. JO are joined and so are JR. The angle KJR will be the butt bevel and at the same time will be the dovetail bevel. The angle KJO will be the mitre bevel.

It is perhaps worth mentioning that the length of the sides of the box will need to be greater if they are to be through-dovetailed than if they were to be butted and pinned because

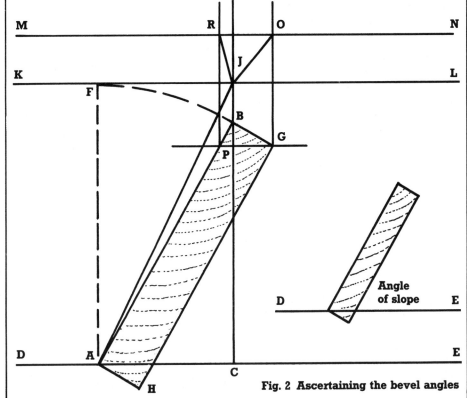

Fig. 2 Ascertaining the bevel angles

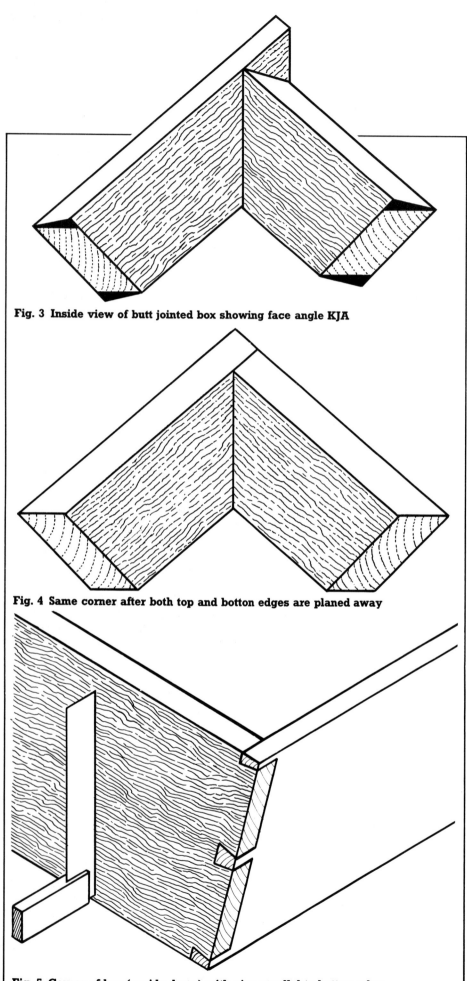

Fig. 3 Inside view of butt jointed box showing face angle KJA

Fig. 4 Same corner after both top and botton edges are planed away

Fig. 5 Corner of box (upside down) with pins parallel to bottom edge

there must be enough wood to follow through to form the dovetail pins or tails as the case may be.

BUTT JOINTED

Fig. 3 is an inside view of a butt jointed box with the face angle KJA marked on it. In this diagram the edges of the wood have been left at right angles to the face side but have been blacked out to show where the edges will be planed away. The same corner is shown in Fig. 4 after both top and bottom edges have been planed away. The bottom edge has to be planed to enable the baseboard to fit properly.

When dovetailing the corners, the pins are cut parallel to the bottom edge of the box. The direction of the grain makes for a stronger pin. Fig. 5 shows a corner of a box which has been turned upside down where the pins are parallel to the edge. A try square has been drawn standing alongside the box to show the amount by which the sides of the box slope.

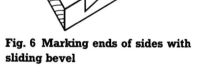

Fig. 6 Marking ends of sides with sliding bevel

The angle KJA is transferred to the sliding bevel which is then used to mark the ends of the sides (Fig. 6). The bevel is then set to the butt

Fig. 8 Setting out centres of tails with sliding bevel

bevel KJR and the top and bottom edges of each side are marked with this angle. These lines are now joined up across the inner faces of each side and the ends are sawn and planed to these lines.

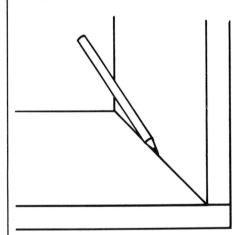

Fig. 7 Thickness of wood marked out on ends

DOVETAILS

The first stage in setting out the dovetails is to mark the thickness of the wood on the ends of each piece (Fig. 7). The centres of the tails are set out parallel to the edges with the sliding bevel, as shown in Fig. 8, and then each tail is set out from its centre line. The side is gripped in the vice with one set of tail slopes vertical while these slopes are sawn with a dovetail saw. The side is then sloped in the vice in the opposite

direction to enable the other dovetail cuts to be made.

The work is now released from the vice and the waste between the tails chiselled away. The pins are then marked from the tails with the point of the dovetail saw (Fig. 9) and lines are drawn down parallel to the edges. The side is then held vertically in the vice and, with the dovetail saw on the waste side of the line, the pins are sawn down to the shoulder lines.

Next the waste between the pins is cut away and the top and bottom edges bevelled to the angle KJR in readiness for assembly. Before this can be done however there is just the matter of cutting the stopped housing (Fig. 10) whereby the centre division is secured to the two ends.

Finally, a suitably shaped hand hole is cut into this centre piece.

(Anyone tackling this project for the first time would be well advised to read through the explanation several times and do all the setting out on paper before touching the wood. Care, and constant reference back to the instructions, should guarantee a satisfactory outcome.

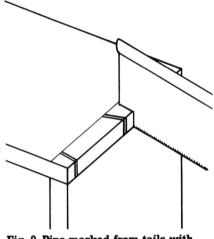

Fig. 9 Pins marked from tails with point of dovetail saw

Two boxes constructed in this manner and placed one on top of the other make a beautifully proportioned Sarcophagus-shaped box which lends itself to all manner of uses. Suitably veneered or inlaid, it would be well on the way to becoming a classic. – Ed.)

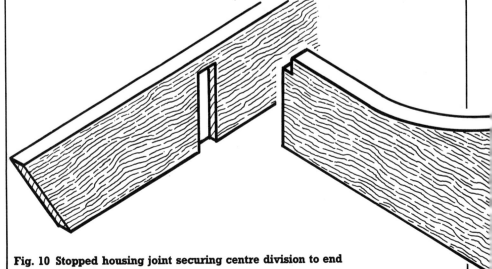

Fig. 10 Stopped housing joint securing centre division to end

BALL AND CUP TOY

You have played with one in the past, now is your chance to pass on the pleasure to a young relative or friend.

The Ball and Cup must surely be one of the oldest toys in the world. Certainly it goes back to Elizabethan times, if not beyond. (See Photo 1.)

I have seen some, beautifully turned from ivory and bone, which were so delicate looking that I wonder how much they were actually played with and how much simply admired.

The first I had, a very rudimentary affair, was made for me by my father during the war. The ball must have been all of a maiming 2″ in diameter and I remember it made a very good weapon.

When playing with it on my own I soon learned to duck and side step. Quick footwork was definitely preferable to headaches.

The balls which I make are from ⁷⁄₈″ diameter dowel and I suggest nothing more than 1″ is used.

METHOD

I start the job by drilling a hole in the end of the piece of 1½″ square timber. Usually I use beech as it is suitable for such work and not as expensive as some timbers.

The lathe can be used for this job. (See photo 2.)

For the sake of concentricity the hole should be no more than ¹⁄₃₂″ larger than the diameter of the driving centre which is to be used. It should also be about ⅛″ longer than the parallel section of the centre, as the sides and bottom of the hole is used as a location for the driving centre. (See fig. 1.)

I use a tool rest as a depth gauge to control this last dimension.

If a flatbit, or similar tool, is used to produce the hole the lathe should be switched off prior to removing the wood from the bit. I usually drill at 1,000 r.p.m.

Various methods can be used to effect the drive. A counterbore tool with the central boss removed,

Photo. 1 Testing the project

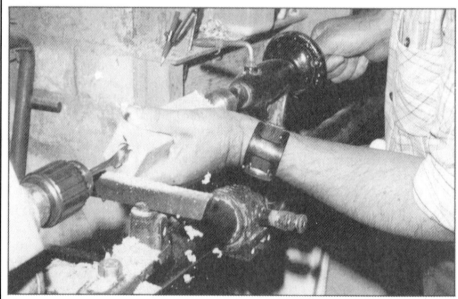
Photo. 2 Drilling on the lathe

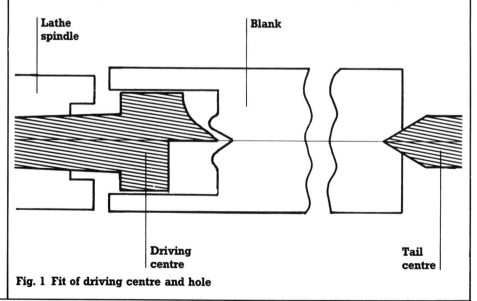

Lathe spindle — Blank — Driving centre — Tail centre

Fig. 1 Fit of driving centre and hole

or even a wooden bung, fitted to a woodscrew chuck and the end turned to suit the drilled hole, should do the job. I usually use a four-prong driving centre.

The hole depth should be recorded prior to loading the unturned blank onto the lathe. This is to ensure the hole will not be cut into when turning the outside shape. It could be a frightening experience, especially when the hole is full of driving teeth.

SPEED

The rectangle is now turned to a cylinder. I use a speed of 1,500 r.p.m. but this is not a hard and fast rule. Turning down to a cylinder can be done with almost any gouge but some work better than others. I usually use a square-ended roughing gouge, with the last cut made by using the 'wing' of the tool, taking a shearing cut to obtain a smooth surface. (See photo 3.)

Next I mark on the outer surface where the bottom of the hole comes and then use spindle gouge, parting tool and skew chisel to produce the shape of the cup and the handle. I deliberately vary the shape of the handles within each batch so that each toy can be easily identified by its owner and disputes about ownership avoided.

It is important, however, to have some sort of cove in the design, usually just under the neck, to take the nylon.

The final turning operation is to take a light cut off the cup end with a skew chisel so as to remove the sawn face and leave the end smooth. (See photo 4.)

If the hole is drilled too deep to start with then part of the lathe spindle might restrict the access of the skew. Alternatively, if the hole is not deep enough, the long point of the skew may contact the driving centre, which would not do either of them a power of good.

Photo. 3 Shearing cut with roughing gouge

Photo. 4 Light cut with single-sided skew

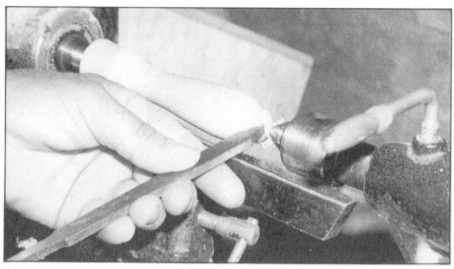
Photo. 5 Taking care not to lose the honed cutting edge

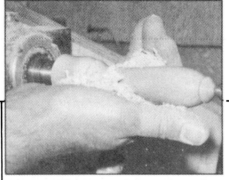

Photo. 6 Woodturners' secret ingredient

You will notice I have had to remove the thread protector from the spindle of the lathe whilst working between centres on this job so that the required clearance can be achieved.

Care should also be taken at the tail centre end so as to avoid running a tool into the revolving centre. (See photo 5.) I find it preferable to leave a small collar of unturned wood at the tailstock end rather than have the cutting edge of a tool destroyed during metal to metal contact. With practice the collar can be kept to a minimum. It is soon removed with a sharp knife, or even just sanded off, when the job is off the lathe.

SEALER

Next I give the job a coat of sanding sealer, whilst the lathe is not running, and then switch on and wipe with a cloth to produce a dry, sealed surface which can be rubbed with 0000 grade steel wood and finally burnished with shavings, still with the lathe running. (See photo 6.)

The steel wool can be loaded with a soft paste wax, if preferred, prior to burnishing with shavings or polishing with a clean cloth.

A quick word on cloths. I have found that calico is best for lathe work as some of the man-made fibres react to various polishes and the friction of the rotating wood. This can end up as an 'orrible gooey mess. Also, calico is softer, lint-free and cheaper than many other types of materials.

I now check for any rough areas which the sanding sealer may have shown up and which the steel wool did not deal with. If I find any, they receive individual attention from the waxed wool, whilst the lathe is stationary, and are then blended in with the lathe running again.

The job is now taken from the lathe and the top face, cup and tail centre 'Vee' hole are sanded, sealed, wiped dry and finally rubbed with steel wool and wax. The cup hole may need more attention from the abrasive paper, after the sanding sealer and before the wax, depending on how sharp the drill was.

BALL

Now we come to the ball. Some time ago I was asked at a demonstration if it was easy to turn an egg. I said that I would rather turn eggs than balls as eggs can be many different shapes but a ball is a ball. If an egg goes wrong it is still an egg, but with a different mother. If a ball goes wrong it was designed by a committee.

I prefer to hold the timber in a handy collet chuck but any device which allows access at the tailstock end will do.

As I said earlier, I use 7/8″ diameter Ramin dowel for the balls, as this material will go into the chuck without much preparation work having to be done to it. A four inch length usually gives me four balls, each about ¾″ diameter.

The first job, after loading the blank into the chuck, is to drill a two diameter hole about one inch into the free end of the blank. This can be done in two stages but I have a screw shaped bit which does an adequate job in one operation. (See photo 7.)

Generally I prefer to drill holes first and then locate from them so they are concentric to the outer diameter of whatever it is I am turning.

The smaller of the two diameters should be a little larger than the cord

Photo. 7 Drilling the dowel

Photo. 8 Roughed out and ready for final shaping

to be used. The larger diameter should then accommodate the knot without too much trouble.

Having drilled the blank, I support it with the tailcentre and true up with a roughing gouge. Next comes the actual shaping of the ball. I start at the tailcentre side of the ball and, with the parting tool, I get close to the final shape of the ball in four or five cuts.

Next I produce both the other side of the ball and the rear face of the next ball, so that I am gradually working down to a small neck which will join the two partly turned balls together. (See photo 8.)

The tailcentre is now taken away and the final shaping done with the parting tool as far as possible, without actually parting off. At this stage it is a good idea to ensure the ball will actually fit inside the cup.

About ⅛″ clearance is an acceptable dimension. Any more and the ball will look lost. Any less and the maker will be accused of cheating.

I now finish the ball by sanding, sealing, wiping and burnishing with shavings. I do not use steel wool here as the wool could get caught in the narrow neck between the two balls and cause a finger stretching 'nasty'. (I wonder, was E.T. a woodturner?)

Finally, I part off using a single sided small skew chisel. I find I can get greater access when working in restricted areas with this tool, which is only ½″ wide. (See photo 9.)

I now finish off the area which has just been parted off and then assemble the toy. I feel that some 15″ to 18″ of cord is about right for the length but ideas differ and some customers prefer a maximum of 12″.

KNOT

The knot which secures the ball to the cord is quite important. It should be small enough to fit into the hole in

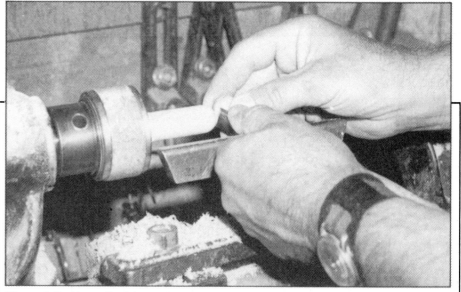

Photo. 9 Parting off with small skew

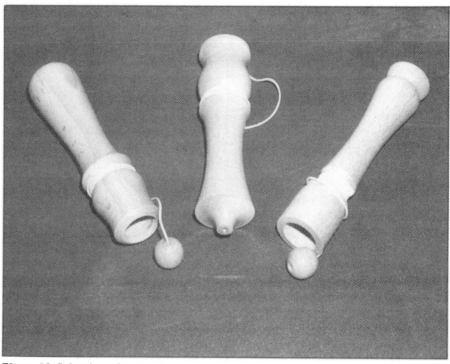

Photo. 10 Selection of patterns

the ball, without affecting the fit of the ball in the cup, and yet it must also secure the ball.

Whilst writing this article, I have deliberately avoided going into too much detail regarding actual turning techniques with the tools as

experienced turners have their own methods anyway and the novice turner could do little better than to be guided by one of the many books on turning written for them. The relevant parts of the book could then be applied to this project.

CUTTING LIST						
PART	DESCRIPTION	L	W	T	MATERIAL	QTY
1	Cup	6″	1½″	1½″	Hardwood	1
2	Ball	3″	1″	1″	Hardwood	1

NOTE: As the job is made from offcuts, the timber type and size can vary to suit the available material.
SUNDRIES: 1 piece of nylon, or similar cord, approximately 18″ long.

THE BULL'S-EYE WINDOW

An interesting project that should prove tempting to many of you – even if it means knocking a hole in a wall!

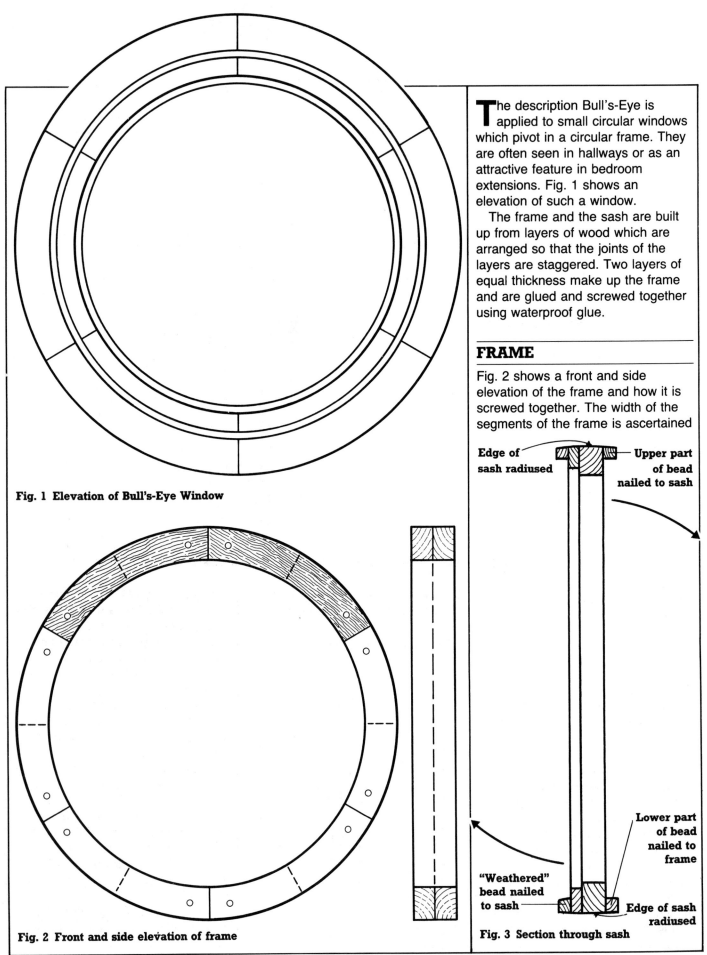

Fig. 1 Elevation of Bull's-Eye Window

Fig. 2 Front and side elevation of frame

The description Bull's-Eye is applied to small circular windows which pivot in a circular frame. They are often seen in hallways or as an attractive feature in bedroom extensions. Fig. 1 shows an elevation of such a window.

The frame and the sash are built up from layers of wood which are arranged so that the joints of the layers are staggered. Two layers of equal thickness make up the frame and are glued and screwed together using waterproof glue.

FRAME

Fig. 2 shows a front and side elevation of the frame and how it is screwed together. The width of the segments of the frame is ascertained

Edge of sash radiused

Upper part of bead nailed to sash

Lower part of bead nailed to frame

"Weathered" bead nailed to sash

Edge of sash radiused

Fig. 3 Section through sash

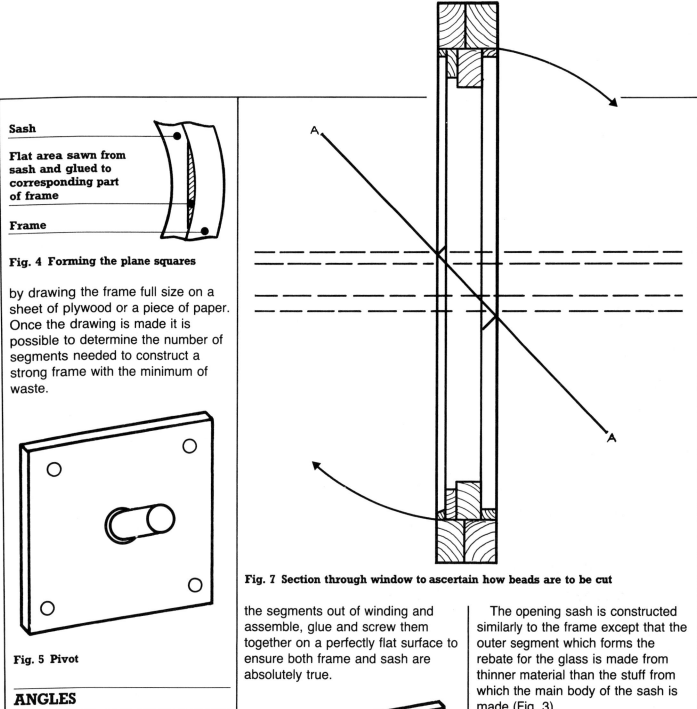

Sash

Flat area sawn from
sash and glued to
corresponding part
of frame

Frame

Fig. 4 Forming the plane squares

by drawing the frame full size on a
sheet of plywood or a piece of paper.
Once the drawing is made it is
possible to determine the number of
segments needed to construct a
strong frame with the minimum of
waste.

Fig. 5 Pivot

ANGLES

The drawing will also show the
angles at which the joints must be
cut. In the window being described
there are six segments in each layer
so that the total number of segments
in the frame is twelve and there will
also be twelve segments in the sash.
Sawing the curved segments is
simplified if a bandsaw is available; if
not a bowsaw can be used. When
the frame is assembled it can be
trued up with a spokeshave but a
better result will be obtained by using
a plunge router and a trammel bar.

It is of course essential to plane all

Fig. 7 Section through window to ascertain how beads are to be cut

the segments out of winding and
assemble, glue and screw them
together on a perfectly flat surface to
ensure both frame and sash are
absolutely true.

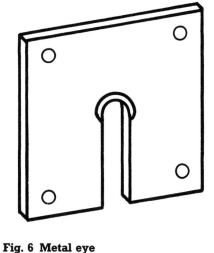

Fig. 6 Metal eye

The opening sash is constructed
similarly to the frame except that the
outer segment which forms the
rebate for the glass is made from
thinner material than the stuff from
which the main body of the sash is
made (Fig. 3).

To enable the window to pivot
freely it is necessary to have plane
surfaces on the frame at the centre
which are equal to the thickness of
the frame. Consequently these plane
surfaces are square. The sash must
have corresponding plane squares
worked on it. The easiest method of
achieving this is to saw off from the
sash and beads pieces of the
required size. Using waterproof glue,
the sawn off pieces are glued to the
frame (Fig. 4).

For work that is exposed to the
weather it is best if plane surfaces

are left on the frame as it is shaped. This will obviate the danger of there being any small glued arcs which might break off.

PIVOT

The pivot (Fig. 5) is screwed to the frame exactly in the centre of the square and the fixing plate is let in slightly below the surface of the timber. The metal eye (Fig. 6) which rotates on the pivot is let into and screwed to the square of the sash. A groove to allow the sash to be slid onto the pivots is cut in the eye and is concealed by the beads when the window is shut.

BEADS

To ensure the window is draught and weatherproof, beads are fitted, parts of which are fitted to the frame and parts of which are fitted to the sash. As the sash opens inwards at the top, the bead at the top is nailed to the inside and the bead at the bottom is nailed to the outside of the sash. The bead is nailed to the outside at the top and the inside at the bottom of the frame.

To determine where these beads are to be cut and the angles at their ends a full size drawing as in Fig. 7 should be made. The dotted lines show the open sash in the horizontal position. Through the pivot a line AA is drawn and at right angles to this line at the points of intersection the beads are cut.

The lower portion of the outer bead should be 'weathered', i.e. it has a downward slope on its top edge to throw off rainwater.

To ensure the window will pivot freely in its frame there must be about 1/8" clearance all round between the sash and frame. This will also enable the edges to be painted without causing the sash to bind. Easy pivoting will be further facilitated if the top and bottom edges of the sash are radiused as in Fig. 3.

THE YORKSHIRE LIGHT

Apart from its weatherproof and security features, this country window is useful where a window is required which, when open, will not impede passage inside or outside the house.

Fig. 1 Elevation of Yorkshire Light

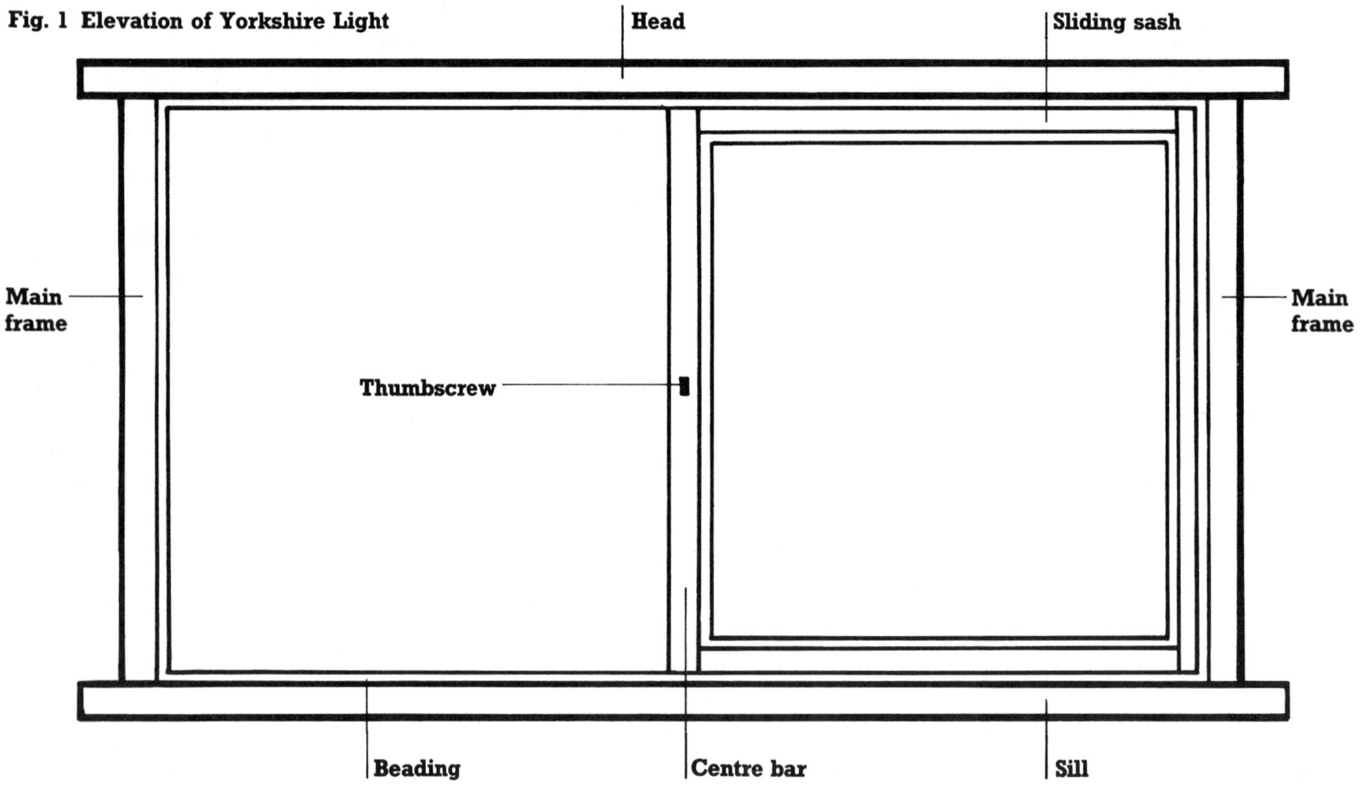

Head · Sliding sash · Main frame · Main frame · Thumbscrew · Beading · Centre bar · Sill

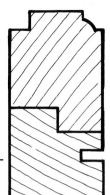

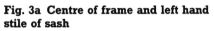

Fig. 3a Centre of frame and left hand stile of sash

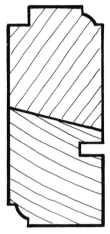

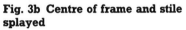

Fig. 3b Centre of frame and stile splayed

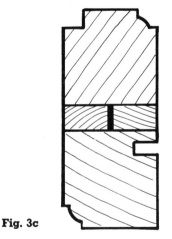

Fig. 3c

This type of window is frequently found in the bedrooms of Dales cottages and comprises a wooden frame secured into the brick or stonework. One half of the window is glazed and the other half is a horizontally sliding sash running on a metal bar let into the sill. A big advantage of this window, particularly in the wilder parts of the country, is that it is completely weatherproof and when secured with a thumbscrew through the meeting stiles, is very difficult to force from the outside. Fig. 1 shows the front elevation of a Yorkshire Light.

The head and sill of the main frame both run through and the stiles are tenoned into them. The sill is preferably made from hardwood although the other members of the window are usually of softwood. The head and stiles are rebated for the sash to slide in and the sill is ploughed to accommodate the metal runner.

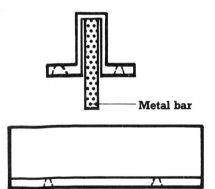

Fig. 2 Elevations of metal shoe

SLIDING SASH

The sliding sash is made from 2″ × 2″ (50 × 50mm) material. The stiles run through and the rails are haunch mortise and tenoned into them and scribed to fit the moulding. The sash must be true and out of winding to enable it to slide easily. To assist it to slide smoothly, metal shoes (Fig. 2) are let into the bottom rail which is also ploughed to take the metal runner. The shoes slide on

the top edge of this runner which is not only conducive to smooth running but also saves wear and tear of the sill and the lower edge of the sash. In addition the metal runner acts as a water bar.

It is usual to plough a putty groove in the left hand stile of the sash

instead of working a rebate as this simplifies glazing. If the upright bar in the centre of the frame and the left hand side of the sliding sash are made as in Fig. 3a or splayed as in 3b they will need to be planed from 2″ × 2½″ (50 × 62mm) stuff. If 2″ × 2″ (50 × 50mm) is used then beads will have to be nailed on as in 3c.

MAIN FRAME

The main frame is made from 5″ × 2″ (125 × 25mm) material with the hardwood sill of 7″ × 2½″ (180 × 62mm). A drip groove is ploughed in the underside of the sill. This frame is mortised and tenoned and the shoulders are scribed to the moulding. The upright bar is stub tenoned and scribed. The joints and wedges can be coated with a waterpoof glue immediately prior to assembly.

Beads, mitred at the corners, are nailed to the inner faces of the main frame so as to retain the sash.

When closed the sash is securely fastened by a thumbscrew and front plate (Fig. 4). This passes through the centre of the left hand stile of the sash and screws into a plate and nut let into the fixed upright bar.

SECTION LIST	
Lengths depend on size of window	
Head and main frame	5″ × 2″
Sill	7″ × 2½″
Sliding sash	2″ × 2″
Centre bar of frame	2½″ × 2″
Left hand side of sash	2½″ × 2″

SUNDRIES: sufficient beading to retain sash is nailed to inner faces of main frame.

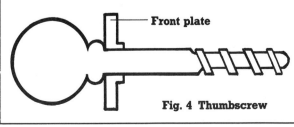

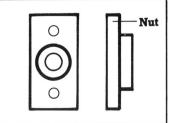

Fig. 4 Thumbscrew

WOODWORKING TIPS

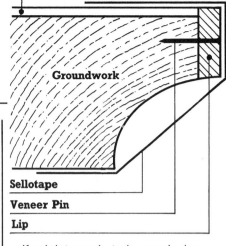

Veneer

Groundwork

Sellotape

Veneer Pin

Lip

TIPS ON LIPPING

Whenever groundwork is veneered it is necessary to protect exposed edges. Edge veneering is rarely satisfactory. Lipping – the cladding of a thin robust strip of like quality wood to the groundwork edge – is the best method, but this can be troublesome where the groundwork has a sharp curved or small circular profile. If the lipping is too thick it is difficult to bend even with heat and moisture and the ends tend to spring away. If too thin, it is liable to split or snag.

I have found that about 2mm is the best lip thickness. It is generally accepted that the best way to plane to this size from a minimal sawn strip is to clamp the lip at the end behind the direction of planing. Cut the lip with a cutting gauge (don't use a saw) a fraction wider than the edge to which it is to be applied. Trim the edges by gripping the plane upside down in the vice, presenting the lip to the plane as one would normally offer plane to wood.

If a joint needs to be made (e.g. on a circular table top) cut the joining ends at an angle of not less than 45°. It looks better and puts less strain on the butt, which is the most difficult part to fix. Drill the lip at about 2″ intervals with a ¹⁄₃₂″ drill and as close as ¼″ to the ends. A good substitute drill is a fine sewing needle with the sharp end ground spear shape.

Use impact glue giving two coats to the groundwork edge since part of this must be end grain. Starting at the middle of the lip, pin to the groundwork edge with ½″ veneer pins (NOT panel pins). Drive these home flush but do not punch below flush. The pin heads are slightly conical and hold sufficiently through

¹⁄₃₂″ holes. Punching might split the lip. The pin heads are barely noticeable when the work is cleaned up. A purist could dab a spot of colour on them before polishing if he wished.

Put a piece of sellotape across the lip where nailed, pulling down both ends hard on to both sides of groundwork. Repeat the taping at 1″ intervals as the remaining pins are hammered home left and right to meet (on circular work) at the butt joint. Put two or three layers of sellotape over butt joints. Leave for two or three days before removing tape. Do not drag the tape from one end to the other. Cut across the width and peel off to top and bottom of groundwork. Adhesion of lip to groundwork should be perfectly sound.

Appearance is improved if the lower half of the groundwork is fielded away. If machine aid is not available it is not difficult to cut with gouge and circular Surform.

R. C. Sterry

"SCALE AND POLISH" WITH A DIFFERENCE

Fellow Woodcarvers: Next time a dreaded visit to the Dentist arises ask after acquiring any redundant "scrapers" and "scalers". I am sure they would be gratefully donated if available.

A particularly useful item is the PROF. G. F. SHEPHERD scaler shown diagramatically in Fig. 1. I hope the sketch is sufficiently self-explanatory, but it is essentially a stainless steel tool of octagonal cross-section carrying a shallow spooned blade at one end (A), and a hook at the other (B). When worn,

the blade and hook become thin and brittle, but by careful grinding, re-shaping, and honing, a most useful carving tool can be fashioned. There is no need for me to list the uses for such a tool. Fellow woodcarvers will very soon discover a host of applications.

Dr Clive Harland

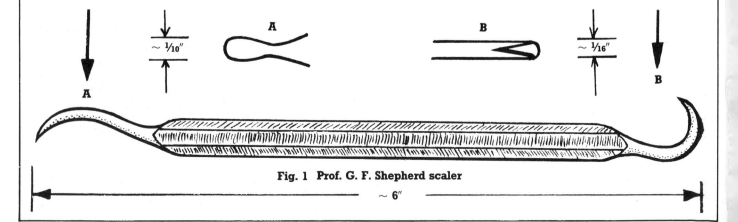

Fig. 1 Prof. G. F. Shepherd scaler

~ 6″